Rob Lilwall

Cycling Home From Siberia

First published in Great Britain in 2009 by Hodder & Stoughton
An Hachette UK company

3

A CIP catalogue record for this title is available from the British Library

ISBN 978 0340 979815

Typeset in Monotype Sabon
by Palimpsest Book Production Limited, Grangemouth, Stirlingshire.

Printed and bound by Clays Ltd, St Ives plc

Hodder & Stoughton policy is to use papers that are natural, renewable and recyclable products and made from wood grown in sustainable forests. The logging and manufacturing processes are expected to conform to the environmental regulations of the country of origin.

Hodder & Stoughton Ltd
338 Euston Road
London NW1 3BH

www.hodder.co.uk

Cycling Home From Siberia

'A journey of amazing guts and stamina.'

COLIN THUBRON

Contents

This is my dilemma . . . I am dust and ashes, frail and wayward, a set of predetermined behavioural responses . . . riddled with fears, beset with needs . . . the quintessence of dust and unto dust I shall return . . . but there is something else in me . . . dust I may be, but troubled dust, dust that dreams

RICHARD HOLLOWAY

Our moral nature is such that we cannot be idle and at ease

LEO TOLSTOY

For Christine

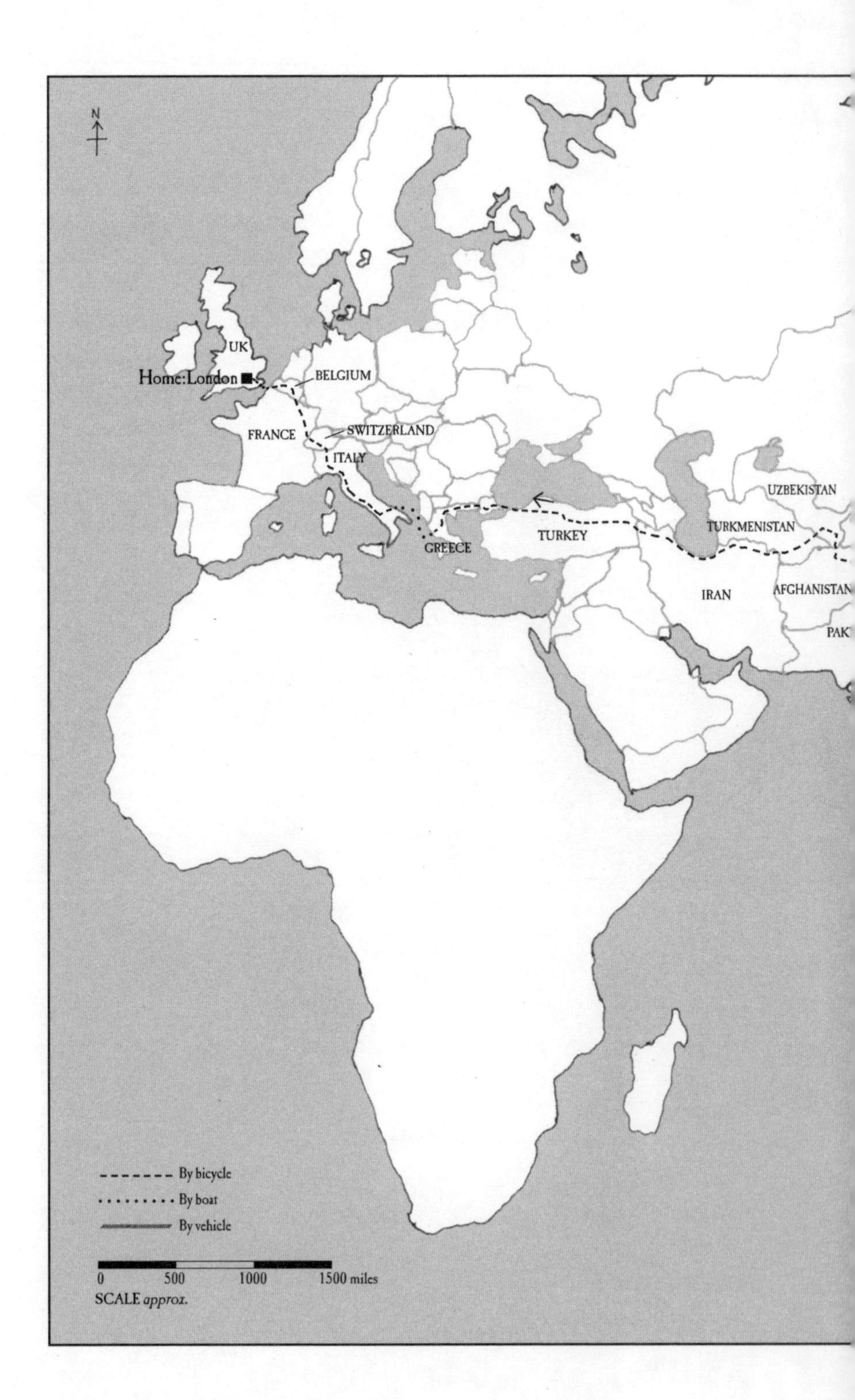
N
UK
Home: London
BELGIUM
FRANCE
SWITZERLAND
ITALY
GREECE
TURKEY
UZBEKISTAN
TURKMENISTAN
IRAN
AFGHANISTAN
PAK
By bicycle
By boat
By vehicle
0
500
1000
1500 miles
SCALE approx.

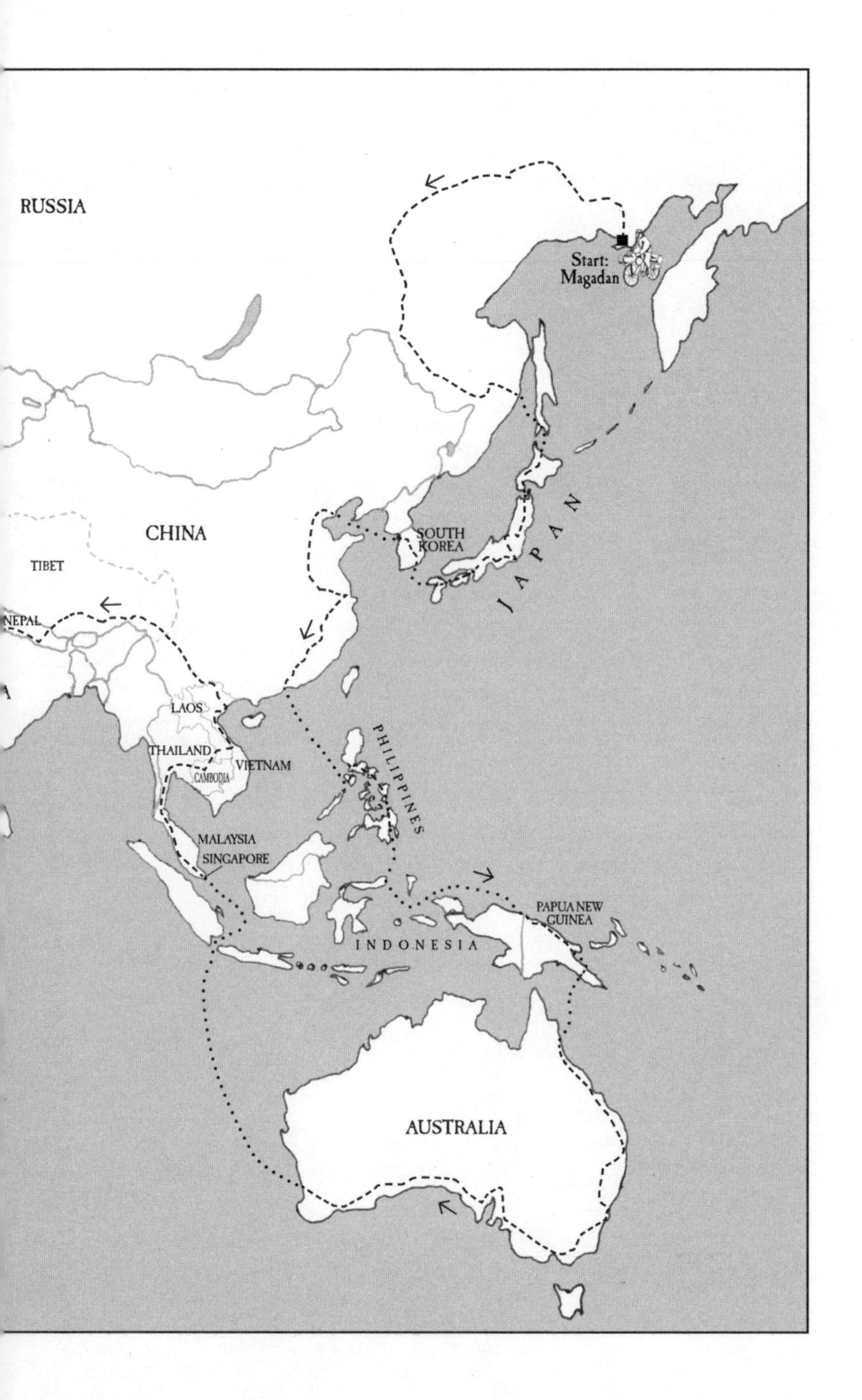

RUSSIA
Start:
Magadan
CHINA
TIBET
NEPAL
SOUTH
KOREA
JAPAN
LAOS
THAILAND
VIETNAM
CAMBODIA
PHILIPPINES
MALAYSIA
SINGAPORE
PAPUA NEW
GUINEA
INDONESIA
AUSTRALIA

Part One

England–Siberia

September 2004

I
Over Mordor

Siberia . . . impends through the darkness as the ultimate unearthly abroad. The place from which you will not return

COLIN THUBRON

We had been flying east all night and I awoke to notice that it was already daylight outside the plane. Looking out of the window onto the empty landscape below, the dark shades of brown and green reassured me that, although it was mid-September, it had not yet started snowing in Siberia. I could see no sign of human life and the view rolled away in an otherworldly blend of mountains, streams and forests to an endless horizon. I shook my head and it brought to mind Tolkien's gloom-filled Mordor.

My neighbour woke up and smiled at me sleepily.

'Good morning, Robert!' he said, pronouncing my name in a slow, Russian accent.

Sergei was a Muscovite salesman of my age who was flying to the outer limits of civilisation in order to sell safety clothing to the local mining industries. We had met the night before when we boarded the plane in Moscow. His English was almost as poor as my Russian, but with the help of a dictionary I had managed to explain to him that I was flying to the far-eastern Siberian city of Magadan with only a one-way ticket because it was my intention to return home to England by bicycle.

'But, Robert,' he had reasoned with me, 'there is no road from Magadan; you cannot ride a bicycle.'

I explained that I had reason to believe that there was a road, though not many people used it these days.

'Alone?' he asked, pointing at me.

'No, I will be riding with a friend.'

'One?'

'Yes, just one friend,' I nodded, hoping that my friend, Al, would arrive, as planned, in three days' time.

Sergei still looked unconvinced and pointed outside:

'*Holodna, Zeema?*'

Holodna was a word that I would grow accustomed to hearing over the next few months. It meant simply 'cold'. *Zeema* meant 'winter'. I had to agree with Sergei that, although the weather did not look too bad right now, the infamous weather of Siberia would not stay away for much longer. The road that we would have to follow, the only road that existed, would take us past the coldest inhabited place in the world.

I tried to bolster my case by explaining to Sergei with hand gestures towards my arms and legs that I had lots of very warm clothes, though I left out the fact that, because the trip was self-funded and without sponsorship, I was on a tight budget. Most of my clothes and equipment had been bought at slashed prices on eBay. In reality, I was not at all sure if they would be up to the job. This was especially the case for my enormous Royal Mail over-trousers which I had bought for £10. They were several sizes too big and probably more suitable for the mid-morning drizzle of London than the long, hard winter of Siberia.

Of even greater concern was the tent. It had been given to us by a kind lady who had taken an interest in the expedition after seeing our website, though we had never actually met her. We had not yet tried putting it up, but it was free, so it seemed like the ideal option at the time. Furthermore, we would have neither a satellite phone nor a global positioning system (GPS) and, in fact, no back-up whatsoever. I also did not admit to Sergei that the coldest temperature I had experienced prior to this was during a camping weekend in Scotland, nor that my main fitness training had been in the form of badminton matches against a colleague after work. Because I was not entirely sure why we were setting off at the start of winter (other than it was when we were ready to start), I just told Sergei that the winter would be an exciting and beautiful time of year to see Siberia.

'How long?' he gestured a bicycling motion.

'One year,' I said confidently. In fact, though I did not know it at the time, the ride would take several times longer than this and for the vast majority of it I would be on my own.

We dropped below the cloud level and, as the land rose to meet us, the broad, dark shapes converged as distinct mountains. They were shrouded in sparse, green forest. I felt a twinge of claustrophobia as we landed on the runway.

Inside the small, grey, terminal building the young lady at the immigration counter stamped me through, but did not return my smile. I collected my bicycle and bags and loaded them onto a 1970s-style bus outside. The gruff driver revved the engine, lit a cigarette and drove out onto the road. I was excited that I would soon be arriving in the city from where I would begin riding, but I was also daunted. Magadan did not have a good reputation with the Russians. Half a century beforehand they had nicknamed it 'The Gateway to Hell'.

2
How will I die?

If you were to die right now, how would you feel about your life?
BRAD PITT, *Fight Club*

Magadan is situated on a small neck of land which stretches feebly southwards into the Sea of Okhotsk from the colossal landmass of far-eastern Siberia. Making use of this natural harbour, the city was built as a port to enable access to the hinterlands. The bus wound down the valley towards it, amid an expanse of gently sloping, uninhabited hillsides. I could see that some of the pine trees had already dropped their needles in anticipation of winter. We emerged out of the valley, and I saw an old power station standing against the bare hills. With its two giant, smoking chimneys, it reminded me of a disgruntled old man. Entering the city, we drove past lines of rectangular, mass-produced, Soviet-style flats. Before we pulled into the bus station, I caught sight of a stagnant display of half-sized MiG fighter planes stuck on shafts. It felt as if I had suddenly fallen back through time into the dark world of Cold War rivalries.

I climbed off the bus and looked up to see a huge, half-built, Orthodox cathedral towering over me. Apart from the gold-plated domes, the remainder of the building was covered in scaffolding and was unfinished. I crammed the bike and all my gear into the back of a taxi which drove me to the newly built Roman Catholic church where I had been invited via email to stay. Father Mike, an American monk and the leader of the community, met me in the church kitchen where he was preparing lunch. He wore blue jeans and had a friendly beard and twinkling eyes. He soon overturned my notion that monks were gloomy or dull. He offered me a bowl of freshly boiled dumplings and immediately started to joke about the great likelihood I faced of being eaten by a bear during my first week on the road. I smiled back at him and, between mouthfuls of food, tried to make myself sound as though I knew what I was doing.

After lunch and having unpacked my bags by emptying them all over the floor of my room, I headed out to explore. The streets were ghostly and people walked past me with downcast faces, their blank looks buried in the uneven pavement. I walked past lines of jaded buildings. Piles of rubble lay heaped on street corners. An old woman hovered by a skip, retrieving old furniture the moment anything was put in. Through the entrance to one block I noticed adolescents sitting in the stairwell with bottles of vodka. It felt as if this city had been tossed, half-made, into a new world, as the ideology of communism collapsed and the gates of capitalism were opened up.

Life, Father Mike had told me, was hard for the people of Magadan. There had been much hope and expectation that things would improve after communism crumbled away in 1991 but, in reality, for many, life had grown worse. At least under party rule most people had a regular income, an annual holiday by the Black Sea and a cheap, if unsexy, car. Nowadays, with capitalism, there was no certainty and not much hope. More than ever, in their inner despair, the Russians of Magadan were turning to vodka. Father Mike even knew of some nine-year-olds who were regular drinkers. He also spoke of widespread problems with corruption and the local mafia stifling any attempt at entrepreneurship.

'Last year there were two brothers who set up a café,' he said. 'They refused to pay protection money to the mafia. Not long after, their café was burned down and one of the brothers was murdered. With that kind of thing going on, nobody is going to start a new business'.

Later a Russian would explain to me that 'in the West you are all trying to keep up with the Joneses. In Russia, we are trying to keep the Joneses down underneath us'.

*

I had been relieved to pass through immigration at the airport without any trouble, because I was entering the country with a bicycle and full winter gear, on the dubious pretext of being on a 'business trip'. Al and I had been forced to apply for business visas because tourist visas were valid for only one month and we would need at least three months to cycle to Japan. To obtain our business visas we had therefore invented a company: 'The English Wildman Wafflings'. We had written a letter, complete with a letterhead, which declared Al the president and me the vice-president. We had said that we needed to visit Russia to further Anglo–Russian business relations. We had been delighted when the embassy in London accepted our application and gave us a three-month visa.

But I had not yet beaten the system entirely. Even in the nineteenth century, Russia was well known for its plan-thwarting bureaucracy and under the Soviets things got even worse. Although communism was now gone, the old rules still lurked behind. The rule that affected me was the one that said that, now that I was in Russia, I had to 'register' in each town where I stayed. In order to register, I would have to visit the 'Office of Visas and Registration' to receive the appropriate extra stamp in my passport. However, as Al noted later, this was not as easy as it sounded: 'The Office of Visas and Registration hides in an unmarked office, unadvertised on a random street . . . [it] opens late, seldom and closes ten minutes before it opens, except on weekdays and days beginning with 'S' when it does not open at all.'

When I found the office at long last, my first visit ended before it had begun as the unenthusiastic, uniformed woman told me they were closing and I must come back the next day. I did so, but this time, due to my weak Russian, she told me to come back with someone who could interpret. I returned with Father Dave, one of the monks. Together, we discovered that I would have to go to the bank to pay a very small fee (of about £1) and bring back the receipt. I did this, but was then sent on another errand to the bank, after which the office had closed, so I had to come back the next day. In the end it took eleven trips to the office to receive the stamp on my visa which registered me legally in the country but, they added, this stamp would only be valid for my first ten days, after which I would have to register again. I decided from that point on to exploit a loophole in the law which said you need only register in a town if you stayed for more than three nights. As I would always move on after a night or two, I did not bother registering again for the remainder of my cycling 'business trip' through the motherland.

Apart from the old, dying structures, there were also signs of infringements from more upbeat sides of the world, indicating that at least some people had wealth: an internet café in a residential back street; a cluster of digital camera stores; a sports shop with a life-size poster of David Beckham proclaiming 'impossible is nothing'. My countryman's declaration was an encouraging thought for me to hold onto. Al would not arrive for another three days and in the meantime there was no shortage of pessimism about our prospects of survival. Everyone I met seemed to have a different theory about the precise manner in which we would die.

Some people, like the taxi-driver who had delivered me to the church, warned me that cold weather would freeze us to death. Others, such as Father Mike, cautioned that blizzards would trap us in our tent until we starved (this was his second idea, made on the assumption that we somehow survived the bears). Another man informed me that it would actually be the wolves, not the bears, that would have us for dinner. But 'No,' said an elderly nun, 'it is the *people* out there in the wilderness that you should really look out for . . . out there it's the wild, wild East. Don't trust anyone.' The occasional self-proclaimed expert would even tell me quite bluntly that the road connecting Magadan to the rest of Russia simply did not exist any more. This I knew to be untrue as Ewan McGregor and Charley Boorman had motorcycled it the previous summer on their high-profile 'Long Way Round' Expedition, but I did not know whether the road would be passable in winter. It seemed extraordinary, in any case, that no one really knew whether the only road that linked them to the world actually existed or not. Their whole life could have been like *The Truman Show*, apparently without them really caring.

One of the most surreal doses of pessimism came the evening a journalist from the local radio station came to the church to interview me. However, in the interview, rather than bigging me up, as might have been expected on an English station, he seemed determined to persuade me not to go.

'What clothes have you got?'

I explained, as I had done to many people by this stage: 'Lots of warm ones.'

'Your bike will not work in the cold.' A statement, not a question.

'I hope it will.'

'Where will you sleep?' In a disbelieving and mournful tone.

When I explained we had a tent and warm sleeping bags, he responded with a kind of exasperated huff and shrug of the shoulders, as if tired of wasting his breath in trying to talk me out of this suicidal idea. Father Janis, the American Jesuit who was translating for me, was by this point in hysterics. I could not help but join him in a splutter of laughter and even the bemused, pale-faced interviewer managed a ghost of a smile on his thin lips as he shook his head at me with uncomprehending eyes. The question seemed to be settled in most people's minds – if we insisted on setting off into Siberia on our winter bicycle ride, we would certainly die. The only thing they could not make up their minds about was how.

That night as I wrote my diary my mood began to plummet. I wrote out the odds of what I thought would happen:

25% we make it easily
25% we make it with a huge struggle
25% we have to turn back
25% we get into real trouble.

I wrote 'get into real trouble' because I could not bring myself to write 'die'.

With images of snarling fangs and frostbitten toes bouncing around my mind, I pondered some survival strategies as I wandered around the city the next day. To deal with the bears and wolves, I sheepishly entered a hunting shop and enquired about buying a gun. I was relieved when I was told that I would need a permit, as I had no idea how to use a gun. I looked for some warmer items of clothing. In the market I spent £30 on a huge fur hat, which boosted my morale considerably, especially as I felt confident that it would be bigger than Al's Alaskan fur hat, which he had boasted about in an email. My most uplifting purchase of all, though, was made when I strolled into a hardware shop and announced in my best, most manly Russian accent to the young lady behind the counter, 'I will take the biggest axe you've got, please.'

3
The Road of Bones

There is pain that is perceived and there is pain that is endured and they are two different worlds, inhabited by creatures of two different races. We cannot choose which one we belong to

JOHN LE CARRÉ

In the evenings, with clothing, books and camping equipment scattered across my room in the church basement, I spread out my map. I looked once more at the route we were planning to take.

There was only one road that connected Magadan with the rest of the world, so at least there was no dilemma about that. However, this road did not lead south in the direction of Japan, but rather north through the Kolyma River Basin for a thousand miles, before turning west to the city of Yakutsk and then south to the Trans-Siberian railway. Finally, it stretched east to bring us back to the sea where we could hop, by ferry, to Japan. In effect, we would be cycling 3,500 miles around three sides of a square through a Siberian winter in order to end up no closer to home than we started. Furthermore, we would have fewer than 80 days to do it in. Perhaps the worried looks of the Russians who thought we were stupid, mad or suicidal were justified?

After Japan, our plans were vague. Our only fixed idea was that we would eventually cycle home via the most interesting and plausibly non-lethal route we could think of. For now, though, all my attention was on Siberia. Not only were the distances huge and the conditions perilous, but a further burden to my troubled mind was the tangible sense of past horror that dwelt around the mere mention of both our starting city and the road along which we would be riding. This was a part of the world where, in living memory, humanity's worst nightmares had been real life for millions of men and women.

Even before the communist era, Siberia had a considerable history as the place where dissidents and criminals were sent. With Lenin's Brave New Empire, the Siberian work camps, the Gulags, were enlarged. Under Stalin, the steady flow of prisoners increased to a torrent. In the 1930s, 'Article 58' of the constitution prescribed that any sort of 'counter-revolutionary activities' demanded severe punishment, though the behaviours falling under this definition were horrifically broad. Hard-labour sentences were given not only for open criticism of the government, but also for even making a joke about it. Records show that men were sent to the camps for being late for work and women were sentenced for picking up grains from an already harvested field. The whole country became covered with a dark shadow of mutual suspicion, fear and complicity. Neighbours and family members accused each other. As was Stalin's habit, the administrators of the system were also periodically liquidated themselves.*

The camps were spread across the whole of Siberia and the conditions were atrocious. But it was the Gulags in the hinterland of Magadan that were the most feared. Until the twentieth century, Magadan had been a small fishing-village outpost, but with the discovery of inland uranium, nickel and gold deposits, and now the availability of workers, it developed rapidly into a large port. Cargo ships fed the growing town with thousands of prisoners. In the worst places, life expectancy was less than a month and every kilogram of gold mined was said to cost a life. There was a saying that 'if you are sent to Magadan, you will never come home'. Father Janis told me that the name Magadan now holds similar connotations

*It has been difficult for historians to estimate how many people were sent to the Gulags. According to Anne Applebaum, in her Pulitzer Prize-winning book *Gulag*, at its height there were probably seven million people in the camps, about 10 per cent of whom died each year. Estimates of overall deaths mostly range between 10 and 60 million.

for Russians to those Auschwitz has for Europeans and Americans. The prisoners had also built the road we would be riding along, dying in droves as they did so. The bodies of the dead were incorporated into the road itself, and for this reason it is still referred to today as 'the Road of Bones'.

One day Father Dave walked with me to the top of a hill on the outskirts of the city to see a monument called the 'Mask of Sorrow'. It was a multifaceted statue, recently erected, which looked down, grieving over the land as a memorial to the horrors. It was in the shape of a head, though was missing one eye, as if it could not bear to look any more. There were smaller statues fixed against it, including a kneeling, weeping child with her head in her hands. Thubron said of Magadan that 'you lost your own eyes here and start to imagine through those of the dead'.

As thoughts of the millions of dead tore through my mind, the question of death loomed larger. If innocent people had died in such great numbers in these very valleys, why did I have any reason to think that we would be so special as to survive? As we rode through the frozen landscape over the coming months, an image would sometimes flash through my mind of a degraded, innocent prisoner wheeling a barrow of slag through the ice.

His eyes are glazed and all hope is gone. He is barely a man now. He is a shell of bones and flesh, more ghost than human. As I watch, he falls by the roadside and does not get up again. He is ignored by the other phantom prisoners who trudge past him.

And a new and significant thought came to me. It was the realisation, for the first time in my life, of my own mortality. I grasped that, one day, I too would die. If I had been born in that unfortunate era, in that contorted civilisation, if I had been a victim of Stalin's ungodly purges, I would not have been so special as to have survived. I too would have fallen and not got up again. Dead, unnoticed and unremembered.

4
The fateful quantitative biology lecture

When I consider what tremendous consequences come
from little things, I am tempted to think that there
are no little things

BRUCE BARTON

Edinburgh, January 1997 (eight years earlier)

It all started in a lecture hall in Scotland. The hall that morning was full of first-year biology students who slumped and slouched in their seats. Some leant their heads on their desks and appeared to be asleep. Some were taking notes, though without energy. The lecturer droned on and the clock hand was ticking at a pace of unnatural tedium.

I was sitting a few rows from the back and thinking hard about a particular dilemma: should I ask him or not?

'Well, why not?' I decided.

I tore a fresh sheet from my pad and wrote a question on it:

'*Hi Al,*

Do you want to come and cycle across the Karakoram Highway this summer?

Rob'

In the row in front of me, asleep or awake I could not tell, slouched my old school friend, Al Humphreys. He was skinny and pale with straw-coloured hair. Later in life, people would describe him as a grown-up, intelligent version of Ron Weasley from the Harry Potter books.

I tapped him on the shoulder and passed the note.

He took it, stretched back in his seat and tried to decipher my scrawl. I was wondering what he would say. For the past four months, ever since I had spotted the alluring red line that symbolised a road through the mountains, I had been obsessed with the idea of going on a cycling adventure among the legendary peaks that divide Pakistan from China. Al scratched his head, wrote something on the paper and passed it back. It felt like a moment of destiny.

'Where is that?'

I scribbled a reply. He took the note back, read it and then sat still. I feared he was falling asleep again. But no, he scratched his head once more and wrote something else down. No doubt this would be an eloquent couplet of acceptance, or a rueful line of refusal, or perhaps even a reasoned request to think more upon the implications of such an offer.

He passed the note back. I unfolded it and held my breath while I read.

'OK.'

The dice had been rolled.

A small town in Oxfordshire, November 2003 (Eleven months earlier)

Six years later, and I walked out of my classroom, across the corridor and into the computer room. It had been another typical up-and-down day in my life as a secondary-school geography teacher. Another day of trying to persuade Dale and Andrew, both aged 15, to ignore their pulsating hormones long enough to draw a diagram of the Aswan Dam. I had been working there for almost two years and although I felt I was still far from having full control of my classes, the job did tick many important boxes for me. It was frequently challenging, rarely boring, often fulfilling and, of course, there were great, long holidays in which to chase adventures.

Twice, since I started teaching, I had used these holidays to go to meet Al. He had caught the adventuring-bug in a big way after our bike ride through Pakistan and so upon leaving university he decided to do something far more relaxing than teaching: to cycle around the world.

The first time I went to meet him was in Ethiopia as he rode down through Africa. It was six months after he had set off and I was doing my teacher training in Oxford. I arrived with a brand new bike for Al as his frame had snapped. Together we rode across the Ethiopian highlands and swam in Lake Tana, the source of the Blue Nile.

A year later, he had made it to Cape Town, crossed the Atlantic by boat to South America and cycled up as far as the Bolivian Andes, where I joined him in La Paz. We rode to Lima before I flew back to England, leaving Al on his own to ride north. As his ultimate aim was to pedal 'the full length of the world's three great land-masses', he had only North America and Asia left.

Ever since that first ride we had taken together in Pakistan, Al had been setting himself greater and greater challenges. This round-the-world-by-bike trip was certainly his greatest so far. At times he thought that the ride, or the road, would break him. Although it sounded tough, I envied him in many ways. He was having an amazing adventure, meeting extraordinary people, pushing himself beyond the limits of what he thought possible. He was proving wrong the sceptics who had told him he could not do it. He was doing something that scared him nearly every day and it made him feel alive.

In England, while feeling happily stretched and reasonably contented, I seemed to have opted, without making a conscious choice, for a conventional life. I was not sure why. Perhaps it was because I had always felt unconventional and so wanted to try to prove that I could be conventional after all. I did not really think of going exploring any more, though I vaguely recalled that I had once dreamed of cycling the breadth of Asia.

Frustrated by the unwillingness of my pupils to behave, I was beginning to think that maybe I should move to a new school. With a fresh start, maybe I could do better. Perhaps, I pondered, I should go and work at an International School in some more exotic corner of the world. I had mentioned these thoughts to a few friends and also in an email to Al who had now reached the Caribbean coast in Colombia.

So, on this typical November afternoon of my second year as a geography teacher in Oxfordshire, I sat down at a computer, breathed a sigh of relief that the day was over once more and logged into my email account.

From: Alastair Humphreys roundtheworldbybike@hotmail.com
Sent: 12 November 2003 16:13:22
To: Rob Lilwall roblilwall@hotmail.com

Aha! Changing schools, eh? It was then that I leaped on the opportunity to test him . . .

How about this:

I have been giving this some serious thought since you flew home [from Peru] and I have been scheming all sorts of devious ways to persuade you to . . . ride with me back home from Asia!

I have realised that the only real downer to my trip is just the sheer dullness of my own company and that really if it is not just going to become a stubborn purgatory penance of epic proportions then I really need to find someone to ride with. This is what I thought:

That if you wanted to do it I could rearrange/compromise so that we could make it across Asia in one teaching year (Sept to Aug). This would mean you could quit your noble yet hideously under-rewarded job, heroically cycle the world's most exciting continent, apply for a job in a non-grim country and get back home, not only in time for obligatory tea and medals, but also in time for your new job. Therefore you would only miss a year of teaching. I know that International Schools would have the good sense to appreciate the benefits of the ride and life could trundle on. [We] could give talks in schools all over Asia. In Ecuador and in Colombia I have been offered jobs: surely riding to a school is better than emailing them your CV!

And finally I would like to convince you with an apt quote from the Bible . . .

Unfortunately I can't think of one, but I will lower myself to Eminem instead:

'Look, if you had just one opportunity, just one shot, to seize everything you ever wanted, would you take the chance . . .?'

You have spoken about this ride long before I ever thought of mine.

> I am sure you know there is never a time more likely for you to do it and if you don't do it soon you know that you probably never will . . .
>
> Give it some thought,
>
> al

And that is how I ended up in Siberia at the onset of winter with a heavily laden bicycle instead of a plane ticket to get me home again. We had chosen to start up here on the north-eastern edge of nowhere, rather than at one of the more 'classic' starting points of Asia, such as Shanghai or Tokyo, just because we thought this looked a bit more epic and ridiculous and, for any aspiring, self-respecting, English explorer, 'epic-ness' and 'ridiculous-ness' were both essential requirements.

On my fourth day in Russia, Al arrived. He was fresh from a glorious summer's ride through Alaska, from where he had hitched a boat ride to Japan and then flown up to Magadan. As he strolled out of the airport wheeling his bike, I could see that this was a different Al from the one I had last seen. His hair was shoulder-length, his face was healthily weather-beaten, and his head was held high. He even looked taller than before and exuded a calm, can-do vibe, earned through his previous three years of facing deep fears and coming out the other side intact. He smiled when he saw me waiting. We exchanged an awkward, manly hug in recognition of the adventure we were about to share, and climbed onto the bus.

As we wound down the valleys back towards Magadan, I explained the many reasons why I expected that we would soon be dead. Al's attitude was unshaken: 'It can't be that bad – if Ewan McGregor has done it in summer, then of course we can do it in winter.'

With Al's arrival, I wrote in my diary with a new sense of optimism: 'I feel I will live to see 2005.'

Part Two

Siberia–Japan

September–December 2004

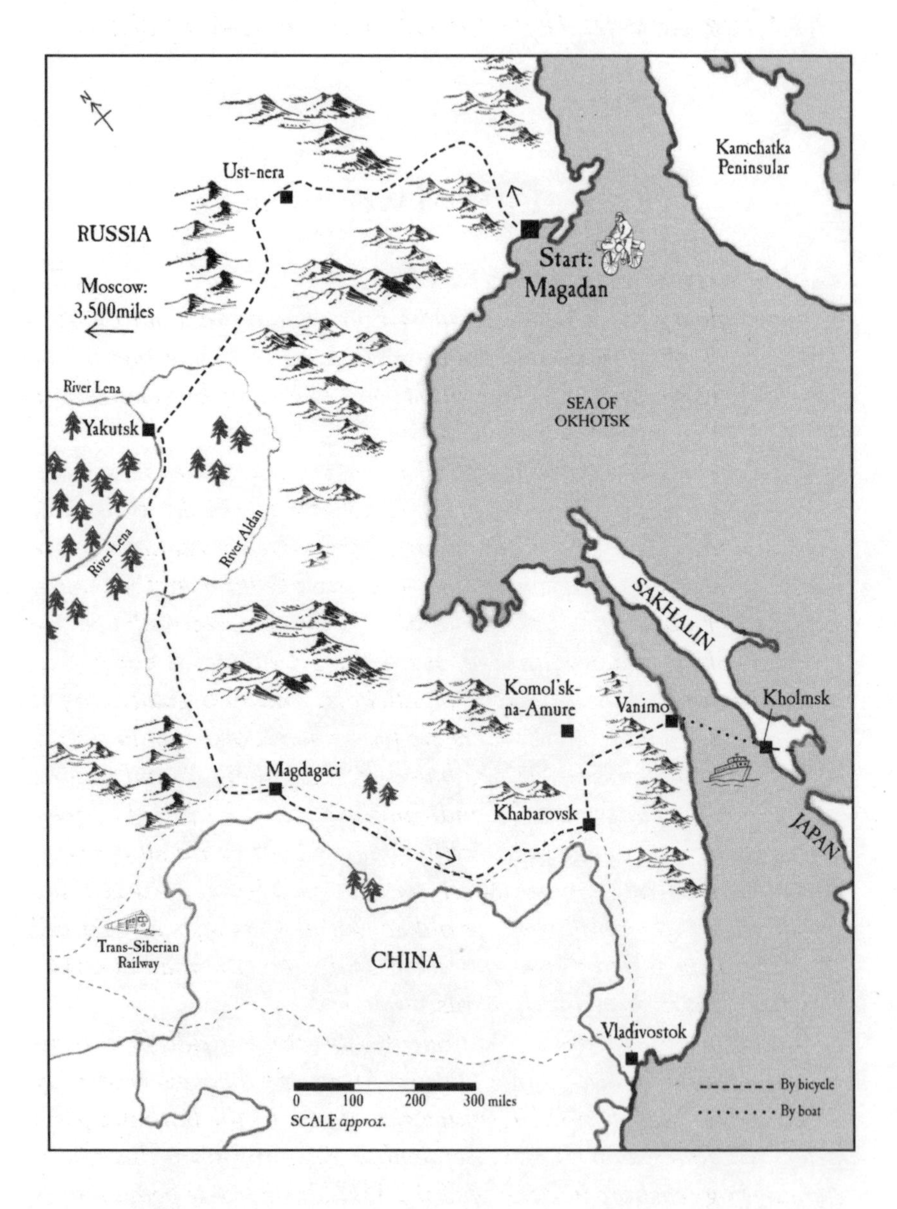
Ust-nera
RUSSIA
Moscow:
3,500miles
Start:
Magadan
Kamchatka
Peninsular
River Lena
Yakutsk
SEA OF
OKHOTSK
River Lena
River Aldan
SAKHALIN
Komol'sk-
na-Amure
Vanimo
Kholmsk
Magdagaci
Khabarovsk
JAPAN
Trans-Siberian
Railway
CHINA
Vladivostok
0 100 200 300 miles
SCALE approx.
By bicycle
By boat

5
One day in the life of a Siberian cyclist

Distance to home = 35,178 miles

24–27 SEPTEMBER 2004

'I know plenty of old cyclists and I know plenty of bold cyclists, but I don't know any old, bold cyclists.' Father Mike bursts out laughing again. We giggle nervously and wheel our bicycles out of the church courtyard and onto the road.

My bike is ten years old and her name is Alanis. She is a simple, steel-framed mountain bike, with sturdy racks on the front and back. I had come up with the unfortunate name of Alanis because I had been listening to an Alanis Morisette album at the time I bought her and wanted to name her after a woman with lots of attitude. She is laden with four overflowing panniers, a bar bag (a small bag that clips on to the handlebars) and two giant, stuffed canoe bags. Two of the panniers are full of food, one contains tools and one holds books. The bar bag contains valuables and a map. The canoe bags hold clothes and camping gear. I have tied a spare tyre and the axe on top of everything at the back. With all the gear, she weighs 60 kg – the heaviest she has ever been. Al and I say goodbye to Father Mike and, as old Soviet minibuses speed past full of staring, mystified passengers, we wobble onto the road and take our first tentative pedals towards home.

We follow a circuitous route out of the city. We ride first up to the statue of Lenin for some photos. Al had his hair cut yesterday so he looks tougher now. Then we ride down to the harbour, for a brief, symbolic swim. It is 24 September 2004 and from this silent, glimmering seashore under a blue sky, I will have to use pedal power to get me all the way back to London. The air is cool, but not cold, and the weather is not so different from an English autumn. We ride under the half-finished domes of the Orthodox cathedral, past the shop where I failed to buy a gun and past the contorted Mask of Sorrow, which looks down on us with sadness. It seems to be saying to us, 'Don't go. Haven't enough perished in these lands already?' Approaching the edge-of-town checkpoint, a young soldier conveniently turns and looks into the empty hills, pretending not to notice us. He is clearly in no mood for looking at our paperwork today and we are happy to ride swiftly past.

My legs begin to find a rhythm. They roll up and down on the pedals and heave the chain smoothly around the freshly oiled cogs. This in turn spins the back wheel and I am propelled forwards. I push my worries aside and start to enjoy the fact that we are on our way at last. We crest a small hill and wind through the sea of peaks. All around us, the terrain is painted in shades of dark greys and browns. The effort of pedalling begins to use up my adrenaline and I feel profoundly grateful to be where I am right now, daring to go where the narwhal dreams.

Al rides on ahead of me all afternoon. An hour before dark he waits for me to catch up and we agree to camp early that night. It has been a short day's riding, but at least we are under way.

It will be a journey of another 1,121 days and more than 35,000 miles until I finish.

The next morning is our first full day on the road and it begins with our waking to the faint sound of my watch alarm. Next, while I attempt to find my socks, Al climbs out of the tent and lights the stove. By the time I have my socks on, Al has passed me a cup of sugary black tea and is cooking up a breakfast of high-carb porridge. As I step out into the bright, fresh morning (which feels especially fresh compared to our tent), Al finishes his breakfast, packs the tent and all his belongings neatly into his panniers and settles down to read another chapter of Solzhenitsyn. I eat breakfast, put on my cycling clothes and expend a huge effort attempting to cram everything into my panniers. An hour later, I am finally ready. Al stands up and stretches, and together we wheel the bikes onto the road.

I climb onto Alanis and slowly judder into forward motion. The bike stabilises and the land begins to move beneath me. The russet forest drifts past, blank-faced and unimpressed, while up above, on the higher hills, a sprinkling of snow reminds me that more ominous weather cannot hold back for much longer.

Time passes slowly and every couple of hours we stop for a sandwich and a cup of tea from the Thermos® flask. We peruse the map and discuss how far we might go today or perhaps try to articulate the peculiar reflections that have been bouncing around our respective heads as we rode. My thoughts of the day, like my dreams of the night, have been filled with frozen rivers that may or may not hold our weight; grizzly bears hungry for dinner; empty, forgotten valleys haunted by emaciated ghosts; packs of ravenous, merciless wolves. I have also been thinking of my parents and the emotional farewell at Heathrow Airport barely a week ago. I remember walking through passport control, looking back over my shoulder at them – my mum, with watery eyes staring after me, and my dad, standing loyally at her side, as always. Was that concern I could see on his face? It was rare for him to show his worries.

Al tells me, in his usual humorous, open and yet somehow guarded manner, that he is pleased to be on the final leg of his round-the-world-by-bike expedition. He cannot believe that he might be home in little more than a year. He says he wants to make Asia his grand finale and he is excited that we have the opportunity to take on a Siberian winter. He has no idea about what he might do when he makes it home. When he started his journey three years ago, he had to split up with his long-term girlfriend, Sarah. He wonders whether they might get back together.

And then we are off again, riding side by side and continuing our conversation for a while before drifting apart once more. The forest slips past and we meander through hills. The wheels keep on turning and, as time ticks by, so does the distance. We pass occasional small settlements: rough, ugly blocks of flats rising from the wilderness. Some towns have been entirely abandoned, due to the seismic shifts in the economy when communism collapsed. The entire employment structure of the country had changed almost overnight. Power stations were turned off and people lost their jobs, especially out here in the hinterland, and now these empty ghost towns stand forlorn and pitiful by the roadside. Many of the flats still have furniture inside and paintings hanging on the walls, and some buildings have mysteriously lost a whole wall, as if it has been torn off.

In mid-afternoon the asphalt peters out into an unpaved but bulldozed road. We will not enjoy riding on tarmac again for almost three thousand miles. This is the first of many things that I have always taken for granted before. Cars and trucks pass us sporadically in both directions, hooting their horns, but already we have grown used to the stares of their drivers.

As darkness approaches we start scanning for suitable camping spots. Ideally these should be easily accessible, flat and clear of vegetation and rocks, while also hidden from the road. In our earlier days of adventuring together, Al and I together learned the art of wild camping and relished the absurdity of sleeping in abnormal places. Once, years ago, we had been walking without a map through Spain and managed to lose our tent poles. We spent the following night sleeping inside a pile of unused sewage pipes on a building site. The next day we were delighted by the dumbfounded looks on the builders' faces as they turned up at work to find us climbing out of their pipes, brushing ourselves down and giving them a cheerful 'Buenas dias', *before walking back out into the midsummer morning. In Siberia, though, with so much empty wilderness, it is not hard to find a suitable place to camp.*

Wheeling the bikes behind a small cluster of trees, we pitch our tent for the second time. While Al chops down a tree and attempts to start a fire, I rummage through my panniers looking for things I need for the evening. Despite my painstaking packing and repacking that morning, I have still not established a good system for remembering where I have put everything. On a regular basis over the coming weeks, I will be at a loss to find what I need – my toothbrush, my gloves, my spare batteries. Already, after just one full day of journeying, it is evident that I am slowing down our progress on many fronts. With his three years of experience, Al is supremely efficient at packing and unpacking his gear and is a lot fitter and faster at cycling than me. I am not unfit, but in the flurry of getting everything ready before the ride, I reasoned that I would get fit properly once we started riding. My inefficiency and slowness, on a normal adventure, would not matter. However, as we ride into Siberia we are both increasingly aware that this time we have two vital factors to race against: the encroaching winter and our downward-ticking Russian visas.

Al's attempts to light a fire do not go well tonight in spite of a generous pile of firelighters. The wood will only reluctantly splutter before smouldering out again. Plan B is to cook with the stove.

We have an MSR stove, which runs on almost any fuel you can think of, but we will be using petrol as it is the easiest to buy. To make the stove work we first need to pressurise the petrol by using a pump attached to a specially designed fuel bottle. It further adds to our inauspicious start when, tonight, the stove pump does not hold pressure. Luckily we have a spare to use, but hope we can fix the other one tomorrow. We are all too aware that our stove will be our lifeline when it gets colder, because it will be our only means of melting snow and making water. After a dinner of spaghetti and tinned beef, we squeeze into the tent. It is still cramped and stuffy inside even though we have left most of our panniers on our unlocked bikes outside. Thieves out in this wilderness seem extremely unlikely. Lying in our sleeping bags, we write our diaries and read for a while. And then, exhausted from the day, we sleep.

On our second full day, habits are gradually falling into place. My packing and unpacking is a little smoother and my riding a little faster. 'If this nice weather holds up,' I persuade myself, 'we might just be okay.' My speedometer is not working, so I sometimes call out to Al to ask how far we have gone. The miles pass slowly, but the road winds onwards and we follow it.

On the afternoon of our third day, despite my prayers that it will remain dry, the grey clouds unfold and it begins to rain with depressing, cold, English-style drizzle. Steadily our clothes, bodies and panniers become damp. We set up camp more rapidly tonight and cook dinner in the porch of our tent before sleeping.

*

The following morning when we wake and look outside, the dark, wet scenery has completely vanished.

Overnight the world has turned white. It is our fourth day on the road and winter has arrived already.

6
Learning not to fall

Distance to home = 34,651 miles

It's the job that never gets started that takes longest to finish
SAMWISE GAMGEE

As the days passed, we grew used to riding onwards through the twisting, snowy valleys. The flat, glaring whiteness of snow draped over everything like a cloth, shrouding the pine trees, smothering the hills and burying the empty beer cans by the side of the road. Although my fitness was improving, our pace was still slow. In addition, the traffic had compacted the snow on the road, meaning that in places it was as slippery as an ice rink. While climbing a long gentle hill, thick with trees on both sides of the road, I took my first tumble. Falling off a bike on ice feels similar to a fierce, side-on rugby tackle. One moment you are riding along merrily and the next, you find your back wheel flipping out from under you and you crash down onto the hard ground. Your bike lands with a clatter beside you. Almost every day over the next two months, one of us would take a fall. Apart from going more slowly when we spotted a shiny patch of road, there was nothing we could do about it.*

Sometimes we listened to our minidisk players while we cycled. As well as music, I tried to listen to a *Teach Yourself Russian* minidisk for half an hour each day. I had volunteered to be the expedition's Russian speaker, while Al had promised to learn some Japanese and take over linguistic duties when we arrived in Japan. When we stopped in the populated towns to buy more supplies, I practised

*The nearest shop where we could have bought special 'spiked' winter tyres was probably in Alaska.

Russian phrases on the local people, who stared at me with a mixture of bemusement and concern. In Atka, another town full of charmless concrete blocks, a round-faced female journalist flagged us down and invited us into the local radio station for an interview. There were three statues of Stalin on the office bookshelf and as she began asking us questions, Al said, 'This is your job' and pushed me in front of the microphone. I could not understand her questions and I presume from her facial expression that she could not understand my answers. The interview ended inauspiciously when both Al and I fell into a fit of giggles and I lost control of bodily functions and let out a fart.

Sometimes we also encountered Russians on the road itself. Most days, a car would skid to a halt on the ice ahead of us and its inhabitants would jump out and amble over to say a brazen hello. After asking us where we were from, what the hell we thought we were doing and didn't we know that it was *holodna*, they would invariably turn to rummaging around in their car before triumphantly producing a bottle of rum, whisky or (most frequently) vodka and encouraging us to have a drink to warm up.

The signal the Russians used to show that it was time to share a 'little' drink (which they referred to as an innocent-sounding *choo-choo*), was to grimace demonically and then, with glazed, lusting eyes, use one finger to flick their necks. Later on in Siberia, when we found ourselves invited into people's houses for the night, we always dreaded the moment when the neck-flicking routine began. It would usually mean that our kind host, who had seemed so pleasant and intelligent up to that point, would now turn into a drooling bore, growing increasingly persistent in his attempts to get us to have yet another *choo-choo* with him. Life expectancy for Russian men in 2004 was 59. I suppose the vodka might have had something to do with that.

7
The Turnoff of Doom

Distance to home = 34,463 miles

I will go anywhere so long as it is forward

DAVID LIVINGSTONE

We pressed on for ten days without a break, two small specks of colour in a black-and-white land.

When we emerged from the tent each morning, we would see that the needle on the thermometer attached to my handlebars had crept further down the scale. By the tenth day, the temperature had reached –8°C, the coldest I had ever experienced. In England, I had always found even –2° felt very cold. We had now started using our stove to melt snow for water and we were learning to squat behind road-side trees at increasingly rapid speeds when nature called. We were also riding faster and I could feel my fitness increasing. However, the knowledge that the temperatures were going to get much colder haunted my thoughts constantly.

Furthermore, we were nearing a significant junction, which we had spotted on the map. In my mind, I had labelled it the 'Turnoff of Doom', because here we faced a tantalising choice between taking the 'summer road' or the 'winter road'. The 'summer road' was the shorter of the two, but was passable only in the warmer months, before snow blocked it. On this road there were several unbridged rivers which, although partially frozen, we would have to wade across. We had been told there was only one proper settlement on it, the village of Oymyakon. In 1919 it had been in the record books for recording –71.2°C, the coldest temperature ever for a permanent settlement.

The 'winter road', meanwhile, was double the distance of the summer road, but had a better surface and more settlements. Moreover, the unbridged rivers on this stretch of road would be sufficiently frozen to cross once the temperature had been below –30°C for at least a week. Our dilemma was that it was now early October, a time when conditions would be suitable on neither the summer nor the winter road. Because of our fast-expiring visas, we did not have time to wait around.

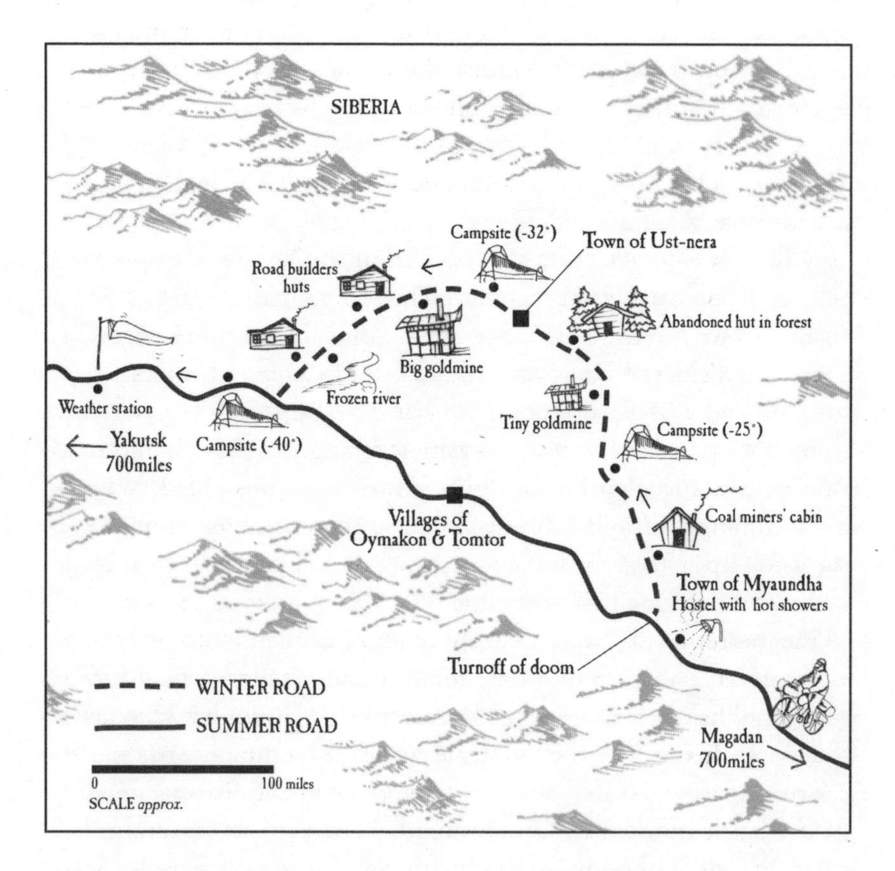

The day before we reached the turnoff, we entered a broad, snowy valley, flanked on all sides by rising mountains. As dusk arrived, we arrived in a little town called Myaundha. Another ugly power station sat on the edge of the town, and we coasted beneath its fat pipes, which were raised above ground because of the permafrost. These pipes fed the entire town with hot water, but we could see they were leaking in many places. Steam shot out into the frosty air and quickly formed huge hanging icicles. The amount of energy lost in the running of this system must have been staggering.

We had not slept inside since we set off, but in this town two elderly ladies ushered us off the street and into the local hostel, where they shouted at the receptionist until we were offered a free bed for the night.

Our rooms were dank and dirty with peeling wallpaper and there were two iron-frame beds against the radiator. But we were very grateful to be out of the cold and for the chance to take a hot shower. Apart from one occasion four mornings earlier when I had plunged myself into an icy stream because I felt so grimy, I had not washed since we left Magadan.

In the previous town we had stocked up on supplies, in preparation for the empty road ahead (whichever one we took). Our panniers now bulged with 60 Snickers bars, 9 kg of spaghetti and instant noodles,* 3 kg of oats, 3 kg of sugar, huge sausages, 1 kg of cheese and 11 cans of meat. We had also filled two plastic beer bottles with petrol for our stove, which Al taped to his bike frame. It was now a strain to lift the bikes onto their wheels, but at least we had enough supplies to sustain us for over a week should we become trapped in snow.

However, we had still not made our decision about the summer and the winter roads. The stakes were high. Al seemed to be taking the dilemma in his stride while for me the burden of choïce felt unbearably heavy. I could tell that my fretting irritated Al a little but, in turn, his confidence made me agonise even more. After much circular debating we decided on the summer road. It was shorter and it was clearly still too warm for the winter road's rivers to be frozen. We just hoped that there would be no more blizzards for a few days.

The next morning we waved goodbye to the frowning receptionist

*Spaghetti or instant noodles were my staples of choice on the journey because they were cheap and also the most compact for fitting in the panniers.

and pushed the bikes back outside. I prayed silently to God that he would protect us and even turn us back if we had made the wrong choice.

Once we started pedalling, I began to feel more confident. However, a mile before the Turnoff of Doom, I noticed that Al was lagging behind me. I looked back and saw he had stopped. He had climbed off and was examining his back wheel. I rode back to him. He said something was broken inside the wheel and that it was not rotating properly when he pedalled.

'I have never seen a wheel break in this way before,' he said. 'This part of the wheel is factory-sealed and it is impossible to open and fix.'

The word 'impossible', coming from Al, was not a good sign. It took several seconds for me to understand what he was suggesting: we must leave the bikes in the hostel and return to Magadan by vehicle to find a new wheel.

Thirty-six hours of hitchhiking and buses later, we were back where we had started. Although we would be able to pick the journey up from Meangee when we set off again, it felt as though all the ground we had gained over those first, difficult 12 days was now lost.

8
Prayers

Distance to home = 35,178 miles

Be still and know that I am God
PSALM 46

We arrived back in Magadan early in the morning to discover that it too was now enveloped in snow. We knocked sheepishly on the door of the church and were relieved when Father Mike opened it and said we could stay while we tried to work out a way to replace the wheel. There were no bicycle shops in town; thus our only option was to wait for a replacement wheel, which Al had asked his mother to send us from England via FedEx. We did not expect it to arrive for several days, so we busied ourselves with buying extra equipment. We were pleased to be befriended by a very likeable local cycling aficionado called Sergei to help us with this task. This Sergei was in his mid-forties and reminded us of an idealised Russian athlete. He was strong and humorous and had thick-rimmed 1980s spectacles that complemented his bushy 1980s moustache. When we first met Sergei he told us rather pessimistically that, in his opinion, we had only a 10 per cent chance of survival. When we went shopping together he insisted that we should buy ourselves a pair of *valenki*. *Valenki* are the felt boots that most Russians wore in winter and, although they cost less than £10 and appeared to be made of synthetic carpet material, they turned out to be a lot warmer than the plastic over-boots that Al had brought us from Alaska.

Although the broken wheel meant that we were losing valuable days from our visas and we both felt very disheartened, we were glad to have some compulsory days of rest. I continued to fret about what dangers lay waiting on the road ahead and one evening I left our room in the church basement and went for a wander around upstairs. I could hear dulcet chanting rising from the chapel. Looking in through the window I could see the habited figure of Father Mike kneeling, straight-backed, before the simple altar. I mused on how peculiar it had been for Al's wheel to have broken so critically just minutes before the turnoff. I wondered whether Al's broken wheel was even an answer to my prayer that God would look after us.

I'd had an awareness of God ever since I could remember and had always turned to prayer when I was afraid. As a teenager at boarding school, I used to sneak into the empty chapel at night to ask for God's help with the debilitating insecurities of adolescence, especially, in my case, a deep shyness. At university I started to go to a vibrant church, made some Christian friends and also had several intense 'spiritual' experiences, usually when I was on my own. The memory of these mysterious encounters still bewilders me. As the years passed, my faith gradually deepened, though I often faltered and failed to live up to my aspirations. I sometimes agonised with deep doubts. Sadly, there were also times when I alienated and infuriated friends with intense, insensitive attempts to share my beliefs. However, in spite of all this, my faith in the Christian God, who cared for me through all life's turmoil, and who loved the whole world, became a central and defining aspect of all my thoughts, aspirations and motives.

I had hopes that during the journey I would grow up as a person and as a Christian. In a way, I saw it as like a pilgrimage on which, through encountering real danger, severe adventure and extraordinary people, I might be stretched in good ways as I headed for home. I was also all too aware that having faith did not necessarily make me immune from harm. I had often pondered on the ill-fated journey of Captain Scott to the South Pole in 1912. Two of his companions, Bowers and Wilson, were devout Christians and yet they died in the tent with Scott. They were a mere eleven miles from a food stash which almost certainly would have saved their lives. As I imagined Al and myself trapped and dying in our own tent sometime in the months ahead, the final words that Scott wrote in his diary echoed around my head: '*These rough notes and our dead bodies must tell the tale . . . these rough notes and our dead bodies must tell the tale . . . these rough notes and our dead bodies must tell the tale . . .'* While hopefully steering clear of taking overly stupid risks, I certainly wanted to take some risks and not squander my life on what I perceived to be comfort and conventionality in England. And so, as I watched Father Mike pray, I too took my dreams and anxieties to God with both hands and asked that he would help us through.

A short while later, when Father Mike had finished praying, he came out into the corridor and we sat down on a bench and started chatting. I asked him how he came to leave Alaska and move to such a bleak and haunted place as Magadan.

'I was one of the first Americans to visit,' he said. 'When the restrictions of the Soviets were lifted in the early 1990s, Magadan was suddenly open to foreigners. Because it was so near to us, there was a natural link between Magadan and Anchorage.'

I wondered how, for Alaskans, a city several thousand miles away, across a cold sea, would still count as near.

'The first time I came was just for a brief visit, but even then I felt a deep calling to come and serve these people longer-term. Not long after, I came back. I have been here for ten years now and I want to stay until I die. I used to love climbing mountains in Alaska, but now I want to climb the even greater mountain of serving and shepherding these people.'

A tug of guilt about the self-indulgent nature of my own adventure rippled through me.

Father Mike went on to explain that in Russia the people had traditionally sought God by gathering around a saint or a 'holy man'. In order to help the people here to find God, he was trying to live the life of a holy man in their midst, so that people could gather with him as part of the church family. As he told me stories of families he knew and tried to help, I saw that this was real, practical faith at work. He was making use of a range of strategies: not only praying and singing, but also Alcoholics Anonymous, a youth group, food drops and a Russian translation of the *Alpha* course.*

*A course introducing Christianity, which is run all over the world.

When I asked how Russia had come to be an Orthodox country, Father Mike recounted the story of how in the eleventh century Vladimir of Russia had decided that it was time that he (and thus his whole kingdom) should convert to Christianity. But which of the two dominant forms of the faith should he choose: Roman Catholicism or Greek Orthodoxy? In the end, the emissary whom he had sent to do some research recommended Constantinople over Rome and so Vladimir followed his advice and chose Orthodoxy. Orthodox Christianity had been deeply embedded in Russia ever since.

I was impressed that, although Father Mike was visibly disappointed that Vladimir had not chosen Catholicism, he was still able generously to affirm many aspects of the Orthodox Church. He told me that he had quite a good relationship with some (but not all) of the Orthodox priests in the city. I was sorry to hear in contrast that members of my own tradition, Protestantism, were often less friendly.

However, it was not rivalry with other churches that was the chief problem for Father Mike, but rather the government authorities, many of whom still had an inherent bias against religion. They had tried to use an injunction against his crane to block him from building his new church. In a true demonstration of American problem-solving, he had outmanoeuvred them by instructing his builders to work through the night to finish the spire before the injunction took effect. The authorities had then attempted to deport him from the country, to which he had responded by secretly praying and fasting until the charges were mysteriously dropped. He was constantly alert to new problems, but ultimately trusted his ways to God and was thankful that at least now there was a semblance of religious freedom here.

I asked about the Gulags. Father Mike explained that, during the atheistic Soviet era, virtually the entire Orthodox priesthood had been exterminated and hundreds of thousands of religious believers had been sent to the camps. 'There's one man in our congregation who spent several years in a Gulag because of his faith.' He was silent for a moment and then he added sadly, 'When a government comes to hate the creator, it is not long before they also start to hate the creatures he created.'

9
The Winter Road

Distance to home = 34,463 miles

To the tune of 'I will survive':

At first I was afraid, I was petrified
All these Russians telling me that this was suicide
Trying to ride the Road of Bones
On a bike without a phone
And with winter coming fast
The summer months already past

So now go, bike out the door
Though I know I don't know how to ski
I know I will survive, etc.

FROM MY DIARY, 16 OCTOBER 2004

FedEx's expected arrival date for the new wheel was postponed several times and when we checked on their internet parcel-tracking site after a week of waiting, the wheel seemed to have disappeared altogether. My father, meanwhile, had been emailing us with the results of some experiments that he had been conducting in our kitchen in London. By placing pots of my bicycle oil in the freezer, to see what happened to it at a cold temperature, he had concluded that we simply needed to open the wheel and insert some cold-resistant oil into it, in order for the cogs' locking mechanism to work again. We therefore decided to take Al's wheel, which we had brought back with us on the bus, to Sergei, the cyclist, who was longing to have a go at fixing it anyway. Using an improvised tool, he easily opened the 'unopenable' factory-sealed part and carefully took all the pieces out. He put some cold-resistant oil on them and reassembled the wheel and then, to our surprise, it worked perfectly. Sergei beamed as we thanked him. He told us that, now we had the *valenki* and a wheel that worked, his odds for our survival had risen from 10 per cent all the way up to 90 per cent.

Thirty-six hours of bus rides later, we were back at the hostel. Our bikes awaited us in a bare cloakroom. Still intent on taking the summer road, we changed into our cycling gear and made ready to set off once more. As we were about to walk out of the door, two strangers entered. The first was the more striking of the two. He walked with a swagger, spoke with a bark. Wearing a long overcoat and an enormous fur hat, he reminded me of a mafia godfather out of a gangster movie. We discovered that he was actually the boss of the power station. The second man was shorter and thinner. He wore no fur hat, appeared rather nervous and it turned out was the local English teacher. Apparently, Fur Hat wanted to talk with us and he had brought the teacher along to translate. Which route, he began bluntly, were we going to take?

We said that after much deliberation we had decided to take the summer road.

'Well,' replied Fur Hat, 'if you take the summer road, you will be making a huge mistake. The winter road, although still not suitable for cars, will already be fine for bicycles. Certainly it will be better if you take my advice.'

It did not feel like advice. It felt like an order.

Al and I were tired of having to make up our minds about this fate-filled, life-and-death decision. It seemed that everybody we spoke to had a different opinion. We turned to each other with raised eyebrows and shrugged.

'Okay,', we announced to Fur Hat with a smile, 'the winter road it is!'

Winter had tightened her grip during our week away, since the temperature had now plummeted to –20°C. My body was shocked by the sudden embrace of cold as we stepped outside and started riding again. Every icy breath I took felt as though it was damaging my lungs. The sky was pale blue, the air crisp, and the land around us was still and lifeless. Only the dark columns of snow-shrouded tree trunks provided contrast to the glaring road, which meandered onwards through the whiteness. When we pedalled past the Turnoff of Doom, we barely noticed the summer road because it was covered in a fresh mantle of undisturbed snow. The ice made us ride slowly again and by mid-afternoon we had made less than 40 miles, barely half our hoped-for distance. Riding in such cold temperatures also made our energy levels drain more quickly and I rapidly tired despite our slow speed. As dusk arrived, stars started to sparkle in the darkening sky, and we muttered unenthusiastically about needing to camp.

As we scanned the roadside for a suitable spot, Al noticed some lights further up the road. There was no settlement marked on our map, but we kept riding and a few minutes later arrived at a cluster of cabins amid the snow. They were surrounded by bulldozers and smoke poured from the chimney of one of the huts. There was nobody around outside. Al dismounted from his bike, said something about his general life philosophy of always asking himself, 'What's the worst that can happen?', and then walked up to the cabin and knocked on the door with his thick gloves.

There was no answer, so Al pushed it open and poked his head inside. Over his shoulder I saw a hazy room, at the far end of which was a sea of rosy, moustache-bearing faces. They looked out at us with squints of surprise. One of the men strode up to the door, opened it wide and asked us a question in Russian which we did not understand.

There were some shouts from further inside the cabin and the man frowned, looked over his shoulder and then gruffly beckoned us to come in. Inside, ten or so men sat on two dirty beds slurping cups of tea and smoking. Beside them, on a stove, sat a huge pot of bubbling soup. They made space for us to sit down and thrust two cups of hot tea into our hands and then, while I attempted to answer their barrage of questions, Al dug out a letter which we had prepared for just such situations as these.

The letter was a message written in Russian to act as an introduction to whomever we met. It consisted of a light-hearted explanation of what we were doing (*Hello, we are two teachers from England. We are exploring the world on our bicycles and currently riding from Magadan to Vladivostok . . .*), why we were doing it (*we are helping a charity and we want to learn about the world . . .*), an apology for our inability to speak their language (*it is hard to learn all the languages of the world*) and our hope that whoever was reading it might act kindly towards us, which invariably, after reading the letter, they did. We would use the letter and its subsequent translations into other languages hundreds of times on the journey to England and we soon began to refer to it as our 'magic letter', because of its extraordinary effect on whoever read it.

We discovered that the pink-cheeked men were coalminers and, having read the letter, they began to ply us with food and tea, while telling us with a laugh that we were completely insane. They argued with each other about what advice we most needed, but the only thing they seemed to be able to agree on (apart from the fact that we were riding to our doom) was that, as far as our diet was concerned, there was only one thing that we had to remember: *sala lucha*. This meant 'fat is better', and they backed up their theory by cutting off some large slabs of lard and throwing it in the soup. They also questioned us further about why we were doing the ride. We were by now well used to being asked this question. Sometimes we gave serious answers: it was to test ourselves; to have an adventure; to live life on the edge; to learn about the world first-hand. But other times we came up with less serious ones: we were on holiday; we were training for a bicycle journey to the South Pole. In this instance we joked to the coalminers that we were both merely in search of a good wife. In my dreamier moments I wondered whether I might actually meet someone special along the way, but it seemed unlikely.

When we'd finished eating we realised that we had caught the coalminers in the middle of their tea break, because a few minutes later they dressed to go back to work. They insisted that we sleep that night in the two beds in the cabin.

As we wished them a good night's work, they asked us whether we might be interested in coming to see them do some mining.

Although all I really wanted to do was relax in the warmth, it sounded too bizarre an opportunity to pass up and so, out in the ice-bound darkness again, we climbed into the cab of a bulldozer. A cheerful young miner yelled enthusiastically at us over the roaring engine as he drove us down a dark track. Through the floodlighting we glimpsed massive machines churning and sifting rock, coal being poured into trucks and giant bulldozers thundering around. We shouted our approval to the driver and he, grinning broadly, indicated how pleased he was that the two crazy Englishmen were impressed by his career as a Siberian/winter/night-time coalminer. Back in the cabin we collapsed into sleep, relieved to have made it through our first day of 'proper' cold. The next night we would not be so fortunate.

10
Learning not to sweat at –40°

Distance to home = 34,423 miles

I laugh in the face of danger, I drop ice cubes down the vest of fear
EDMUND BLACKADDER

Stepping outside the next morning, we started pedalling straightaway to keep ourselves warm. The Road of Bones led upstream beside a half-frozen river. The ice encroached across it from the banks, but a fast-flowing channel of swarthy water in the middle showed that it would still be some time before it was ready to ride across. During our mid-morning break we had to throw away our usual daytime snack, bread, as it was now too solidly frozen to eat. Instead, we ate several bars of chocolate, which were crunchier than normal, but still edible. We also pulled out our thermos flask, which we had filled with boiling water and instant noodles using the coalminers' stove. However, the cup-lid of the thermos had now frozen solidly onto the flask. After numerous failed attempts to unscrew it, Al suggested: 'We could try peeing on it.' I was hungry, so agreed that this might be our only option. Fortunately, at that moment, the top became unstuck in my hand and we were saved from the pee treatment.

As the sun started to dip below the wintery hills, the temperature slipped down to –25°C. My feet were turning numb and I could feel a chill infiltrating my bones. There were no friendly coalminers in sight tonight, so we knew that we would have to camp. We laid the bikes down on a flat area beside the road and quickly put on our head-torches and down jackets. By the time we had pulled the tent out the night had come upon us. I had a sudden feeling that, apart from our two flittering little torches, there was no light or life for thousands of miles. We were all alone out here in the darkness.

While Al spread the tent material out, I started putting the poles together. As I reached the final segment of the first pole I grew confused because I could not make it click into place. I looked with my torch and saw that the elastic inside the poles had gone slack due to the cold and so was getting in the way. This was a serious problem because, if we could not put the poles together, we would not be able to put the tent up.*

'Al, the poles won't click together!' I exclaimed.

Al ran over to have a look.

'We will need to retie the elastic,' he said decisively. He sat down on a bag, removed his gloves despite the temperature, and began to untie the elastic at one end of the pole.

I was in no mood to take my gloves off and my sense of alarm was growing. My feet now felt as if they were blocks of ice and the numbness was beginning to advance up my legs. Thoughts about frostbitten toes flashed through my mind and, overwhelmed with panic and the desire to warm up, I abandoned Al with the poles and started to run around in circles while stamping my feet to try to get the blood flowing.

After several minutes, the feeling returned slightly, so I yelled at Al again, asking what I should do. He was still trying to fix the pole and shouted that I should start cooking dinner. I pulled out the stove. As I prepared to light it, I was dismayed to see that the pump for pressurising the fuel bottle was not holding pressure. This had happened several times before and usually meant that the leather washer inside the pump needed lubricating so, as I had often done in the past, I removed the washer and doused it with saliva. This was a stupid thing to do, because within a few

*I have since read that polar explorers know all about this problem with the elastic inside the tent poles, but I did not know this at the time. To get around this problem polar explorers often carry their poles on the back of their sleds only partially unattached, so they are much easier to click back together again.

seconds it had frozen solid. The whole situation was beginning to feel like a nightmare. I realised that my legs were numb again, so I instinctively dropped the stove in the snow and started running in circles once more.

Al finished fixing the poles and quickly erected the tent.

'Just get in the tent,' he told me sternly.

I climbed inside, sat down and groaned loudly while struggling to pull my boots off. Then I got into my sleeping bag and lay shivering. The feeling slowly returned to my legs and feet. Al came in a few minutes later and fixed the stove by putting the pump down his trousers to warm it up. He had collected a pile of snow, which he started to feed into the pot in order to cook dinner.

It had been a horrific hour and I was badly shaken. I had been almost hysterical. I had no idea what I would have done if Al had not been there. We fell into exhausted sleep trying not to think of how many more such experiences we might have to face over the coming weeks.

When we awoke the next morning, the lining of the tent and the outside of our sleeping bags were covered in ice crystals, the result of the moisture from our breath condensing and freezing. Al cooked breakfast and I put on extra clothes. We went out into the cold again. Our bike tyres crunched through the snow as we wheeled them back onto the road and I saw that the icicles on the fir trees were now encasing rather than hanging off the branches. We climbed onto the bikes and followed the frost-bound valley further into the unknown.

I was now wearing my full 'winter gear'. During the day it consisted of: three thermal vests and a fleece on top; thin tracksuit bottoms covered by the Royal Mail trousers on my legs; thin gloves covered by mittens on my hands; two pairs of socks and the *valenki* on my feet; a balaclava and woolly hat on my head; and a spare glove down my crotch to keep my private parts warm. We kept our cameras in their cases, hanging down inside our thermal vests, because the batteries would stop working if they became too cold.

For drinking water, we both wore a camelback* underneath our coats so that our body heat would stop the water inside it from freezing. We had also taped old rubber inner-tubes over our brake handles to prevent the cold metal from numbing our fingers, and tied a pair of *pogies*† over the handlebars.

Once we were moving, we pedalled hard and took only short breaks in the hope that our bodies would generate enough heat to keep us warm. However, even when I exerted myself hard, my feet continued to turn numb. I was obsessively paranoid about frostbite and so, although I knew it exasperated Al because it slowed us down, I jumped off the bike several times a day and jogged with it beside me while stamping my feet to try to make the blood flow again. Al's circulation seemed to be better and his feet remained warm. As well as wearing enough clothes and keeping moving, another key rule was to make sure we did not become too warm and start sweating. One day, trying to keep up with Al as we climbed a hill, I put in some extra effort and began to overheat. By the time we reached the top, my thermal vest was damp with perspiration. When we descended the other side, the dampness froze into a cold, uncomfortable ice-lining inside my coat, which did not disperse until the evening.

We began to have further troubles with our equipment. In particular, anything made from plastic became extremely brittle. Our dinner bowls cracked; my pedal toe-clips snapped off; and even the nozzles on both our bicycle pumps fell apart, so that the only way to inflate the inner-tubes was for one of us to hold the pump tightly against the tyre valve while the other pumped furiously. One aspect of the cold that did boost our morale was when the moisture in our breath started to condense onto our beards. We celebrated our new ice-beards by grimacing and taking photos of ourselves, hoping that

*A camelback is a small backpack containing a plastic water sack. There is a straw which comes out of the pack and over your shoulder, so that you can drink from it while you ride.
†*Pogies* are specially designed down-filled bags from Alaska, which covered our hands as we cycled.

we might look like Ranulph Fiennes, whose grimacing ice-beard photos we had always admired.

For the next three nights, we were relieved to find places to sleep indoors. The first night we were put up by a middle-aged couple who ran a tiny roadside goldmine. They had a big bulldozer, several portacabins and a huge guard dog. The second night, a passing truck driver saw us pitching the tent and jumped out to show us a little path through the forest up to an empty wooden hut. He said we could sleep in it and light the stove. The third night, we reached the final town of the winter road, Ust-nera. Here, the local English teacher, Igool, and her husband, Sergei, invited us to stay. Before we left we gave a talk to her English class about our journey, and when we departed Sergei's father gave us two freshly roasted chickens to strap on top of our panniers. They had frozen solid before we reached the edge of town.

We had another terrible night camping and then the next day the temperature slipped into the –30s. For some reason I had always imagined that –30°C would not feel very different from –20°C, but I was wrong: it felt a lot colder. The road entered a thick forest and deteriorated into little more than a jarring track of frozen mud and deep tyre ruts. We climbed off the bikes to push. There were no vehicles on the road now. 'I can't see how cars could get through this way,' I gasped to Al. Half an hour later, we heard a rumbling sound and a tank on caterpillar treads thundered out of the forest in front of us. The tank stopped and we thought it was the army. Three smiling, moustached men climbed out to say hello. They gave us a cup of tea from their thermos and told us they were road builders, making the winter road ready for cars.

As it grew dark, we had covered less than 40 miles, far below the distance we had been aiming for. But then we saw lights ahead. With rising hope, we rode through a gateway and into a huge, floodlit goldmine complex. Workers walked like phantoms between warehouses where loud machinery could be heard knocking and hammering. We were ushered into an office building and briefly interrogated by a bemused supervisor. He kindly offered us a room to sleep in. While eating a meal in the canteen, we noticed that the TV seemed to be perpetually screening Chelsea football matches. We wondered whether whoever owned the football club might also own that particular mine. In our warm room, before bed, I examined my feet and saw that my toes were bright red and several toe nails were falling off. At least I did not yet have frostbite.

For the next few days we continued through dense forestland. The air was completely still and I was grateful there was no wind. We came to a long climb and a long descent before reaching a series of unbridged rivers, between 5 and 50 metres wide. A mysterious set of car tyre tracks across the surface indicated that it would be strong enough to take our weight, but I let Al go first just in case. We pushed the bikes across and continued on a slightly smoother road and reached the point where the winter road rejoined the summer road. The forest now receded behind us and instead the horizon filled with row after row of white curvy hills, glittering in the sunshine. It was a terrifying beauty.

Al and I were talking less now, lost in our own, mumbling worlds for most of the day. Although Al could have cycled faster than me, he often rode slowly behind, so he did not have to keep waiting for me to catch up. He later reflected in his book:

Sometimes, when Rob was very far ahead, or a long distance behind, I stopped and watched him ride. It unsettled me to see that small figure creeping tiny over the vast landscape, making no impression on the huge scene; inconsequential, disconnected . . . a foreign body unknown to all it encountered

As the sun disappeared again, an icy shadow cast across the valley and the temperature dropped to –37°C. At that moment Al got a puncture. It was time to set up camp anyway so, while he desperately tried to fix the hole, I put the tent up and hacked some ice out of a frozen pond with my axe.* I used my bicycle helmet as a basket to carry the shards back to the tent. On the way I fell over and a searing pain shot up my arms. It was strange, but the cold even seemed to make the way my body responded to pain feel

*It was quicker to melt solid ice than snow for making water.

different. Al was now using the stove to warm the rubber on his tyre so he could force it back onto his wheel – the cold had made it constrict so that it would not fit on. We were both shivering as we climbed into the tent. It was my turn to cook and I lay in my sleeping bag with the stove in the porch. Our shelter was now drastically reduced because the tent window, made of plastic, had shattered and fallen out. 'Well, at least we now have a chimney for the cooking fumes to escape from,' Al said.

We both laughed through our chattering teeth. I melted the ice in a pan on the stove and as the water started boiling I poured in the instant noodles. I put the tin of beef, which was frozen solid, into the hot water to thaw so that I could get a tin opener into it. After half an hour, I had finally finished cooking, and we sat hunched in our sleeping bags scoffing the mushy mixture down. The food had little taste, and we had no time to relish the meal, because if we did not eat quickly it would freeze again. After eating I needed a pee but I did not want to go outside, so I peed into a bottle and poured it into the snow. Before I went to sleep, I donned my huge fur hat and pulled the sleeping-bag hood tightly around my face, leaving only a tiny hole through which to breathe. Then, exhausted from yet another long day, I tucked myself into a ball and fell into a fitful, trembling slumber.

The next morning, I woke before Al and cooked more noodles for breakfast. He was very pleased that I was finally managing to pull my weight since he had been doing most of the cooking so far. We climbed out of the tent and packed swiftly to stay warm. Before setting off I looked at my thermometer. It had reached the bottom of the scale. It was 28 October and the temperature was already −40°C.

11
The budgerigar and the naked weatherman

Distance to home = 34,184 miles

I alternate between thinking of the planet as home – dear and familiar stone hearth and garden – and as a hard land of exile in which we are all sojourners

ANNIE DILLARD

The next day, the road was piste-like and wound up the centre of a wide glacial valley. Al had a running nose and the dripping nasal water was freezing as it ran down his moustache. I took a photo of him but he looked more like a walrus than Ranulph Fiennes. At three that afternoon, we spotted a small complex of huts by the road which was marked on the map as a weather monitoring station. Both of us were cold and weary and our resolve to ride further quickly dissolved. We rode up to the first hut, knocked on the door and then, hearing no answer, pushed it open and ventured inside.

A combination of our desperation to find respite from the cold and the regularity with which we had so far been welcomed by the Russians meant that we were rather taken aback when the two young weathermen inside did not seem very pleased to see us. One of them, small and nerdy with wire-rimmed spectacles, looked as if he had only recently finished high school. The other, the grumpier of the two, had a more gallant complexion and his dark brown hair was a grown-out crew-cut. He was in his mid-twenties, had an intelligent, chiselled face and was also clearly the man who had the power to receive or reject us for the night.

They looked us up and down with nonchalant scowls and hardly glanced at the magic letter, which we held hopefully in their direction. They were clearly unimpressed. Al muttered to me that I had better put my linguistic expertise to good use unless I fancied spending another night in the tent at –40°C. However, my *Teach Yourself Russian* minidisks, although imprinting forever in my memory useful phrases such as '*gdye mozna koopit atkritki?*' (where can I buy a postcard?), had not yet equipped me to charm my way into a free bed in a remote Siberian weather station.

I remembered that I had recently been learning the names of animals, so decided that a good old-fashioned conversation about pets might serve to break the ice between the two cold English explorers and the two warm Russian weathermen.

'Er, excuse me,' I began with an enthusiastic smile directed at crew-cut, 'do you have a dog?'

He frowned, threw his head backwards and with a suspicious sideways glance at me replied: '*Nyet*' (no).

'Ah . . . errr . . .' I felt flustered. 'Okay, a cat then?'

'*Nyet*.'

Al rolled his eyes and nerdy weatherman puckered his white brow.

'Well . . .' I said, nodding wholeheartedly, 'my parents have a (in English as I did not know the Russian word) *budgerigar*.' I flapped my arms like a bird and tweeted.

Crew-cut looked at me as if I were insane, which wasn't far from how I was beginning to feel.

But, unwilling to admit defeat just yet, I ignored everyone's scowls, laughed politely and gesturing grandly to the sky asked: 'Do you like to be (again, in English) *weatherman*?'

Both weathermen sat looking at me blankly. Al looked at me as if I were a hopeless case. I smiled weakly. Perhaps the usual English topic of weather was a better bet.

'*Holodna*,' I said, pointing outside without conviction.

Crew-cut shrugged gruffly, clearly bored of listening to my psycho-babble, and snatched the magic letter again. This time he decided to give it a proper read and thus discover the origin of these two lunatic halfwits who had turned up smiling inanely in his weather hut.

Fortunately for us, as soon as he read it, the letter once again worked its magic. It was extraordinary how people's suspicions and lack of welcome could be completely overturned by these few lines of comprehensible explanation. Sasha (as we discovered Crew-cut to be called), proceeded to invite us to stay the night and he even said we could use his and Nerdy's (called Alexi) beds as they had to check the weather instruments throughout the night. At least, that is what I thought he said and thus what I translated for Al.

For dinner, Sasha mixed together a batch of dough and cooked us a gloriously stodgy dinner of pie-like pastries. We were extremely happy to be in the warm, and enjoyed an evening of writing our diaries (which had been hard to do in the tent, because the biro ink froze).

Before bed, we heard jingling bells and saw a reindeer-drawn sledge pull up outside the hut. It was a Yakut man. The Yakuts* are a minority Russian people group whose territory we were now beginning to enter. They arrived in Siberia thousands of years ago and because their language – an extraordinary blend of guttural sounds – has links with the Turkic tongues of Central Asia, it is thought that they might have originated from there. Until relatively recently they survived off the land without modern technology, but gradually the outside world has encroached.

This man on his sled, clad from head to toe in fur and with a weather-wrinkled face, had popped by the weather station to sell some reindeer meat. We went out to say hello. He looked unimpressed by our over-laden bikes and when we asked where he lived, he responded by pointing cryptically up into the mountains. It seemed that riding his sledge around this cold, empty land in the dark was just a normal day down at the office for him. He had not chosen to live like this in order to 'prove' himself, or 'test' himself. For him, such a tough life is normal.

That night, Al went to bed a few minutes before me and as I got ready for bed I saw that he had chosen Sasha's comfortable-looking bed on the inside wall and was already sound asleep. I climbed into Alexi's bed by the window, but before I closed my eyes, I noticed

*Sometimes known as the 'Sacha Indians'.

Sasha had come back into the room. I bade him goodnight sleepily and as he said goodnight to me I saw that he was removing his shirt. He must be getting changed to go and check the weather instruments, I thought.

Then, without putting on a new shirt, he removed his trousers.

Each to his own, I thought.

Then, to my concern, he removed his underwear so that he was stark naked. Then, much to my amusement, he climbed into the same bed as Al, snuggled up and went to sleep.

In the middle of the night, I left Al and Sasha sleeping happily together and wrapped myself up to go outside for a pee. The night sky was completely silent, strewn with stars and dominated by the perfect full moon. The white valley swept away on all sides, rising up at the edges into ridges of pale-crested mountains. I stood for a few seconds taking it all in. I could not believe that I was the only person who would see that scene at that moment; it seemed such a waste.

I awoke next morning before Al and had the chance to observe him waking. His sleepy expression turned to a look of horror as he opened his eyes to see a naked Russian weatherman nuzzling up against his shoulder. He climbed hastily over his bedfellow, put on clothes and told me to stop laughing and make ready as we really did have a long way to cycle that day.

For the whole morning, the wind was on our backs and we plunged effortlessly down the valley like a pair of windsurfers. It was so cold that the lens of my skiing goggles cracked. Ice waterfalls hung statically from the hillsides, frozen in mid-air. When night arrived we kept riding because we had seen a village 20 miles ahead on the map. While pushing our bikes up the side of a gully under the moonlight, we fell into a surreal discussion about which ten authors had influenced our lives the most and, if we were given miraculous powers, in whose style we would most want to write.

After a night sleeping in an abandoned, yet still heated, flat in the town of Rosomakha, we finally burst out of the mountains and left the harsh, sharp beauty behind us. The road became less spectacular and rolled onwards through a flat sea of stunted treetops and frozen swamps. At lunchtime, a minibus appeared and stopped. A smiling face invited us to climb inside to have some food. We were delighted when the occupants, hardy tourists who had come up from Yakutsk city, proceeded to feed us with fried chicken, chocolate and sparkling wine.

Two days later we pushed the bikes across the mile-wide, frozen Aldan River. Halfway across it, we came to an island where three Yakut men in fur hats were swigging vodka and grilling pieces of beef on a little fire. They invited us to join them for a snack. Behind them was a huge pile of frozen cow carcasses, which they told us they were taking across the river to sell. On the other side of the river we entered the heartlands of the Yakut people, whose wood cabin settlements were scattered at ever more regular intervals along the roads. Roughly every other night, with big smiles on their Asiatic faces, they welcomed us in to stay and fed us enormous meals of buns, berries and raw pony liver. Often they had relatives further up the road, so they would scribble a note for us to show in the next village and we would be invited to stay in someone's house again. Like the Caucasian Russians, they never asked us for money in return for their help and sometimes they even tried to give us money and fur clothing before we left the following day.

12
Anger rising

Distance to home = 33,332 miles

The Russians love a man who suffers
RUSSIAN SAYING

A week later, our map showed we were drawing near to Yakutsk at last. We had heard that Yakutsk was a large city and we planned to take a day off when we arrived. We were both extremely tired and looking forward to a hot shower and a chance to rest.

However, when we went down the small snowy track off the main road, which we thought would go into the city, we were actually led to the banks of the enormous, northwards-flowing River Lena, the tenth-longest river in the world. There was a line of idling trucks waiting for it to be frozen enough to cross. Yakutsk, meanwhile, lay on the opposite side, several miles away. Its silhouette was dark and ugly, and was made up mostly of a line of tall factory chimneys spewing smoke. This river was much wider than the other rivers we had crossed and its surface was a shattered confusion of ice fragments. While Al and I were discussing whether we should cross to Yakutsk, some of the tensions which had been building up between us under the stressful conditions began to surface. It turned into our first argument.

'Let's push the bikes across,' said Al.

'But the river is so wide here, it may not be frozen enough.' I was still terrified of falling through ice. I imagined it a horrible way to die.

We tried asking a truck driver, but neither of us could understand his reply.

'He's saying it's safe to cross,' said Al.

'No, he's saying it's not safe.' I was annoyed that Al was interpreting the Russian for himself. Hadn't we agreed that I was the Russian expert?

Next, to prove his point, Al stepped out onto the ice and started jumping up and down.

'Stop being so stupid,' I snapped at him. The sound of my raised voice was muffled by the snow.

He stepped back on the land and glared at me. Then he pointed to a silhouette of people walking around in the middle of the river. 'What about them?' he said coldly.

'They're just fishing through the ice,' I retorted, 'they are not walking all the way across.'

We were both tired and getting cold from standing around. Even if it was safe, it would probably take two hours to push the bikes across the bumpy surface. The sun started to set and we knew it was now too late to even try. So we abandoned our one day off and turned the bikes back towards the road. We were invited to stay with another Yakut family that night, but as I went to sleep I was still fuming that we had missed having a proper day off. I knew Al had probably been right about it being safe to cross but, in a way, I was becoming fed up with his always being right.

The next morning, as we wheeled our bikes back to the road, Al took the initiative in apologising for the argument we'd had the previous day. I said I was sorry I was being so grumpy. The conversation cleared the air between us, and we agreed that in future we should talk through the tension between us more often.

Leaving the Yakutsk turnoff behind, we followed the road south, as it rolled back into the empty forestland. There were now more trucks, as well as more regular villages and trucker cafes. When we reached a café, roughly once a day, we stopped to drink coffee and soup and eat bread to boost our morale. Al suggested we buy ice creams in the cafés, which we could keep in our panniers as snacks, confident that they would not melt. Although some nights we still camped, on others we were invited to stay with villagers and sometimes the roadside café owners invited us to sleep on the café floor.

In a slightly larger town we found an internet café and were able to send a message home. I had been unable to email for almost three weeks, and naturally my parents had been worried. I felt guilty and in future tried to warn them if I was going to be out of touch for a while. Al, meanwhile, received an email from Father Mike explaining that the FedEx wheel had arrived, what should he do with it? Al asked him to post it back to England.

But as we continued south, even though the road surface was gradually improving and there were more settlements, we were still riding much more slowly than we needed to. Our Russian visas were now going to run out in less than five weeks' time and we had still not covered even half the distance. It was my fault. No matter how hard I tried, Al was always quicker at packing and he was always able to pedal faster and harder and longer than me.

Several days after our aborted day off at Yakutsk, I woke up feeling weak and nauseous. When we started riding, my head was spinning and I thought I might vomit. I cycled ever more slowly and when we stopped in a truckers' café for lunch, I told Al that I would need a day off. A mile down a side road there was a small town called Kakicatcy with a workers' hostel. We checked into a room for the night and I felt a fever coming on as I went to bed and slept for thirteen hours.

I spent most of the following day in bed too and when I awoke in the evening, two drunk truck drivers were arguing loudly in the corridor. Our room was strewn with half unpacked panniers and Al was sitting in his bed with a map and a diary on his lap.

I sat up and said, 'I'm feeling better now. I think I'll be able to ride again tomorrow.'

'I've been studying the map,' Al said, looking up at me. 'We have almost exactly 2,000 miles left to go and 30 days remaining on our visas. This means that we are going to have to do a minimum of 67 miles a day with no days off if we're going to make it in time.' He passed the map to me. 'Rob, do you think you can do this?'

I looked at the map and saw the long road heading due south to where it met the Trans-Siberian railway and from there eastwards to the coast. Cycling 67 miles a day was quite easy on good roads, but here in Siberia our bikes were heavy, the roads were slippery, and our bodies were already completely worn out. Our average daily distance so far had often been only 50 miles after seven hours' riding through the whole of daylight. To make 67 miles we would certainly have to ride into the night.

'Yes, I am up for it,' I said, trying to sound tough and wondering whether Al was beginning to regret asking me to join him for the ride in the first place.

'Great,' said Al, but he did not sound convinced. 'You know that if we fall short of this distance on any one day, it will mean that we will have a bigger distance to do the following day. We will be even less likely to achieve that and any chance we have will just spiral away from us. We really have to make this every single day.'

Al was talking a lot of sense and I agreed that we would have to keep on riding every night until we had actually done 67 miles. To further motivate ourselves, we talked through what our options would be if we did fall further behind schedule. We already knew that it was impossible to extend our visas, and so our first option would be to catch a lift with a truck. Both of us counted this as 'cheating' and so did not want to do that. The other option was to face the consequences of arriving at the Russian border with expired visas. We had heard that this would probably involve either a severe fine or some nights in a Russian prison. Neither of these prospects appealed.

Before we slept we lightened our loads by getting rid of dead-weight. I gave away my beloved axe to some Russians we had met in the corridor. Al gave away his pair of flip-flops, which he had been carrying since Peru. We also had another conversation about the anger we were beginning to feel towards one another. I told Al how I resented his superior fitness and he explained how frustrated he was by my lack of speed.

'But I know I shouldn't expect you to be as fit as me, because I have spent three years cycling, while you have been a teacher in England,' he said.

I said I was sorry I had been slowing us down and that I had been grouchy. We agreed that it was inevitable that we would get annoyed with each other, being as fatigued as we were. Talking it through was a bit like lancing a boil. It cleared the air between us, for the time being in any case.

The next morning, we got up before dawn and I could feel butterflies in my stomach as we wheeled our bikes back onto the road.

'67 miles a day, 67 miles a day, 67 miles a day,' we chanted to ourselves as we started pedalling again.

It was time for us to race.

13
Sixty-seven miles of snow, sweat and exhaustion

Distance to home = 33,328 miles

8–18 NOVEMBER 2004

Another week later, it is mid-November, the time is three in the afternoon, and the temperature is –20°C. We are pedalling south across the unending plains of Yakutia. The trees spread away from us in all directions and the sky, grey with an oncoming blizzard, is darkening rapidly. The only sound is the wheels rasping across the compacted snow. They slide around on the road beneath me and I am gripping the handlebars tightly. I fell twice this morning and I am worried I will fall again. I breathe in cold air through my mouth, wipe frozen snot from my beard and shout over my shoulder to ask Al how far we have gone that day.

'Forty-four miles,' he shouts back.

We have been awake and pedalling since seven o'clock this morning and it will be dusk in half an hour. But we are determined not to stop. Since the day off in the hostel, we have been rising before dawn every morning and cycling hard through all of daylight and for several hours into the night. Riding in the dark on these icy, bumpy roads is horribly unpleasant and agonisingly slow. We barely move above walking pace. When we finally get to bed, whether in the tent or on a café floor, we sleep for less than six hours a night. Life has become a haze of snow, sweat and exhaustion.

I scarcely have strength to write my diary, but, a few nights ago, I simply scribbled:

> *The last few days are rather a blur – setting off at 7 a.m. (dark), cycling until 10 p.m. (dark). We are struggling to get enough sleep as so many hours cycling. Al carrying much more weight*

> *than me and yet I am still usually slower – I don't have the strength . . . some days cycling in blizzards, scrappy roads. Desperately trying to keep up with Al. Tired. Gasping. Pressing on. No energy. Break. Mars (bar). Cold. Off we go again. Café – relief, warmth, food, tasty coffee. We must keep going. Back into the cold – pedalling again. Sun setting. Getting dark. Still 30 miles to go. Into the night. Okay at first. Getting tired. Getting very tired. Cold. Mars. Where's this town? We must stay on schedule. 28 days of this. Can we keep it up? I'm so weak. We've stayed 1 night tent – okay. 1 night on floor of café. 1 night in hotel courtesy of Sheriff – who also fed us.*

As we ride, other memories from the last week also flit through my mind, though I cannot remember what order they happened in . . .

The night we spotted the mysterious, scattered luminosity of the Northern Lights oozing from behind the clouds.

The evening when, as we came down a hill, Al's bike slipped over and he landed with his whole face in a snowdrift. I let out a brief chuckle at the absurdity of it all but Al scowled at me and rode on into the night without a word.

The day we were riding through a series of empty, white fields and I heard a shriek pierce the emptiness behind me. I looked over my shoulder and saw that Al had been riding with one hand while tuning his long-wave radio with the other. It was 3 November 2004 and he had discovered that George W. Bush had just been voted in for a second term.

The night we were climbing a hill and I had run out of water. I was very thirsty and I started to get a craving for fruit juice. I promised myself that, when we reached the next town, I would buy myself some fruit juice. I saw a car coming and flagged it down to ask if they had any spare water. 'Nyet,' *said the bearded Russian driver, 'but take this instead.' He handed me an unopened two-litre carton of fruit juice.*

There have also been several occasions when truck drivers have shouted down at us from their cabs to warn us against camping because of wolves. Having grown up in London, I have always been frightened of animals, so I was vexed by all of this wolf-talk. Al never tires of reminding me how I once ran away from a curious cow when we were hiking in Scotland. Last night while we were staying with another wolf-paranoid host, I asked how often he had actually seen wolves in the area.

'Never,' he said.

'Have you ever heard them howling?'I asked.

'No.'

'Do you know anyone who has heard or seen a wolf around here?'

'No. But you should not camp; there are wolves!'

And now, it is getting dark and we know we must keep riding into the night yet again. The road ahead is bleak. There are no cafés for 50 miles, so we will be in the tent again tonight. All of a sudden, we see a convoy of Land-Rovers emerging hazily out of the snow-dusted horizon and driving towards us. As they draw closer, we see they have stacked roof-racks and are covered in corporate stickers and logos. They stop and an assortment of men and women climb out.

'Well, hi there!' says one of the men, in an American accent. 'Where are you guys heading?' Al and I have not seen a foreigner since leaving Magadan. It sounds strange to hear our own language.

We introduce ourselves and say that we trying to cycle to England. We discover that the dozen men and women who have climbed out of their cars to say hello are part of an American expedition sponsored by Land-Rover. With the help of an entourage of local translators and fixers, they are attempting to drive around the world.

A man about our age says, 'Wow, just now we were saying to each other how adventurous this feels, driving out here on a road that few foreigners have ever been on, in such crazy, cold conditions. But then we saw you guys coming over the brow of the hill on your bicycles!'

They cannot believe that we do not even have a support team and they suddenly feel rather out-toughed.

But I do not feel tough.

I just envy their being able to cover in one hour's driving, sitting in their warm cars, what it takes us a whole, long, crazy day of frozen sweat and miserable cold to accomplish. The Land-Rover team thrust a can of Red Bull into our hands and before we can say 'But isn't this stuff incredibly bad for you?' they take a photo for their high-octane-drink sponsors, pat us on the backs and wave a cheerful goodbye as they zoom off to their next hotel. We stand there shivering and frightened as we watch them go, distinctly unenthused about the prospect of what still lies ahead for us that night: four more hours of riding through blackness, at ever slower speeds, until we reach our magic number of miles. Only then will we allow ourselves to throw up the tent and briefly sleep.

Three days later, we are excited to at last be getting closer to the railway. The cafés and villages are becoming more regular, but we are also noticing that with the increased 'civilisation' there is a growing roughness among some people. I am shocked when a passing car rolls down its window and the skin-headed youth inside sticks up his middle finger at us. That night, we are invited by a café owner to stay in his house in the village. It is less a house than a cluttered, wooden room lit by a single dim bulb, which hangs from the ceiling. I roll out my sleeping bag on the mattress and am surprised to discover a huge machete under the pillow. Why on earth would anybody need a machete in a quiet roadside village like this, I wonder?

We will soon find out.

14
Vodka and the handgun

Distance to home = 32,887 miles

Everyone says forgiveness is a lovely idea, until they have something to forgive
C. S. LEWIS

Al threw a triumphant arm up at the giant, hundred-wagon freight trains as they clattered past us. The pair of drivers blew their powerful air-horns and waved back. The afternoon we reached the Trans-Siberian railway was a great boost to our morale. We had stuck to our 67-miles-a-day target and made noticeable progress south. Now the bright sun was out and the temperature on my thermometer, to our total disbelief, was rising to nearly zero °C. The road ran exactly alongside the rail tracks, which stretched behind us all the way to Moscow and ahead of us to the coast – from where we hoped to catch a ferry away from dark, bleak Russia, to bright, technological Japan.

At last, we believed not that we might make it, but that we should make it. Although we were weary, believing it was possible gave us strength. The road surface was improving and there was now considerably more traffic. Most notable were the regular convoys of second-hand cars, which had been imported cheaply from Japan and were being driven across to the rich cities of western Russia. As dusk arrived, although we had already passed our magic number of miles, we agreed that we would press home our advantage and ride into the night until we reached the next town.

While we rode through the dark, I listened to minidisks and dreamed of the hot showers, big pizzas and long sessions watching DVDs we would enjoy when we eventually reached the end of Siberia. After two hours, I saw the lights of the town, glimmering into the coal-black sky like a celestial city. I was tired, but all seemed fine and calm and good.

As we turned up a track leading to the town, I saw a car idling in the middle of the road 100 metres ahead of us. Conspicuously, it had only one headlight, and as I drew closer I noticed that it had a number plate with 'Nevada' written over the top of it. Two men stood leaning against the car. I glanced over my shoulder to see Al riding through the snow 50 metres behind me. As I approached, the men beckoned me to stop.

I had grown used to friendly, inquisitive Russians flagging us down for a chat, so I stopped and said, '*Strazvitya*' (Hello).

The snow on the road was glistening in the headlight as the two men walked over and stood on either side of me. They were in their early twenties, wore woolly hats and had tough, pale faces. They reminded me of shifty characters from a comic book.

They mumbled hello and asked what I was doing. I noticed they were slurring their words.

I replied with my usual rough Russian sentences and vague hand gestures, pointing towards the coast 500 miles away. Al drew up alongside me. The two men did not seem particularly interested in my replies so, because we were worn out from the long day's ride, we said goodbye and Al rode off in front. As he did so, I looked down to see that the taller of the two men was holding firmly onto my handlebars so that I could not leave.

He leaned towards me and I could smell the vodka on his breath. Then he said: '*Dengi.*'

I knew that *dengi* meant 'money' and my first thought was that this was the first time we had met people scrounging for money in Russia. I smiled at the man, pretended I did not understand, said goodbye and tried to leave again.

The man did not let go.

Al turned round to see what was wrong.

The tall man said *dengi* again.

I said no.

Then, as Al wheeled his bike back towards us, he suddenly froze. 'Rob, that guy's got a gun.'

I looked down to see that the small man was holding a handgun in his left hand, near to his jacket.

A fix of adrenaline rushed into my bloodstream and my temple started throbbing.

'Show them the magic letter,' whispered Al.

I pulled the letter out of my bar bag and, noticing that my hands were shaking, gave it to the tall man along with a torch for him to read it with. He glanced momentarily at the letter and then snorted and handed it back to me. Using the torch light, he began to rummage through my bar bag. My breathing quickened though I did not move.

The man found my wallet and began to flick through it. He found the roubles (worth about £100) and then the dollars (worth about £50) and put them in his pocket with a smirk. Handing the empty wallet back to me, he pointed to the town and told us to go.

The two men climbed back into the car and drove off fast, their backlights disappearing into the night. Al and I stood silently, watching them go. I suddenly wanted to cry.

And then we were pedalling madly up to the town, afraid the men would turn round and come back to rob us some more. I could not believe what had happened, how quickly the mood of the night had turned around. We reached the town, Magdagaci. Shadows hung from the walls and dark alleys closed in around us. The old man walking alone down the road suddenly seemed threatening; the group of kids laughing outside their flat, menacing.

We asked the way in a shop and found the police station. We tried to explain the robbery, though the policeman in reception did not understand. An older policeman walked in and they had a gruff, noisy conversation, which ended with them insisting that we leave our bikes there and follow the older man. We thought he was going to take us somewhere to find out more about the robbery. A moment later, though, we realised he had still not understood because, like the many other hospitable Russians we had met, he took us back to his home to stay the night. We were too tired out to worry about the robbers now, and just felt relieved to have somewhere safe to sleep. The policeman lived with his teenage son in a bungalow. He said we could sleep on the tatty sofas in his living room, which was dominated by a large television blaring Russian MTV.

As we sat down, Al told me that he was sad that his record of being un-mugged on his round-the-world-by-bike journey had now been blemished. He was especially annoyed that it had been blemished in Russia, a land where, contrary to the propaganda we grew up with, the people had proved themselves to be so kind. We talked through what had happened. I regretted having had so much money in my wallet. It seemed likely that they would have been satisfied with half as much. Al wondered aloud whether he would have been robbed if he had been alone.

'When you are alone,' he said, 'you are seen as a kind of nomad, a wandering, searching adventurer. As soon as you start travelling in a pair, you begin to look like tourists. And tourists are usually the ones to get robbed.'

After that our conversations fell to silence and we sat there, in front of the television, lost in our thoughts. I started to pray. I tried to be grateful that neither of us had been harmed and that the thieves had taken only some money. They could have taken everything. They could have killed us. We had been fortunate. But the sneering face of the tall thief kept flashing into my mind. He seemed so self-satisfied, so ugly. What right did he have to steal my money, especially after all the gruelling hardships that we had put ourselves through? Bitterness rose in me and I started to force myself to pray for the two thieves. I prayed that God would help me forgive them.

The image of the tall man flashed before my eyes again and I wanted to curse him. I imagined myself, Bond-esque, wrestling the gun from the little man's grasp and hurling him to the ground. But then I caught myself in this adolescent fantasy, remembered that forgiveness was a choice and again tried to pray for them. But the anger surged back again. It was as if I was fighting with myself.

After a struggle, I breathed out deeply and let go of the hatred. I believed again that, although bad things had happened and bad things would continue to happen, God was still with us. He still cared. He still understood. He still even cared about my attempts to forgive our thieves. And that thought comforted me enormously. The evening drew to a close and I fell asleep, still shaken, but less confused than before.

Before we left, we looked at our maps again. In ten days' time we would be reaching the huge, ex-military city of the east, Khabarovsk. From there we had two options: the first and easier option would be to head directly south to the giant port of Vladivostok on paved roads, with regular, guaranteed ferries to whisk us to Japan.

The second and harder option was to turn north again and then eastwards through one more wall of mountains to bring us to a coastline that faced the oil-rich island of Sakhalin. Al had somehow managed to discover that an old school friend of ours, Alexis, was working for Shell on Sakhalin. Neither of us had seen him for half a decade but he had told Al by email that he had not received a single visitor since moving out to the bleak island two years previously. This reason alone made up our minds. If Alexis had never had visitors, then it was high time he had some, even if it meant one last, ridiculous detour through some final, blizzard-harassed mountains for us.

But before we had made it there, something terrible would happen.

15
The fire

Distance to home = 32,100 miles

In the world to come, I shall not be asked, 'Why were you not Moses?'
I shall be asked, 'Why were you not Zusya?'
RABBI ZUSYA

The next morning we rode out alongside the railway and for the next week our progress was faster and easier than it had been on the entire journey. Most days we were able to confine our riding to luxurious daylight. The road was now marked with signposts telling us how far it was to the next town, though the marked distances were sometimes grossly inaccurate.

Six days after the robbery, we completed our 67 miles by 4 p.m. and were pleased when shortly afterwards we arrived at a roadside café. It was a wooden cabin set back from the road behind some trees. We leaned the bikes up outside and went in to get some soup.

We were met by three friendly faces. First, there was Lena, a cheerful lady in her mid-thirties who was in charge of running the café. Second, there was Vladimir, Lena's husband, who was in his early fifties. Like many Russian men we met, he had a firm handshake and a welcoming smile. Third, there was a smaller man who told us he was from Uzbekistan. He worked for Lena and Vladimir, helping with general tasks around the café. He was in his fifties and had a weather-beaten face, wise eyes and a slight limp. The three of them were delighted to have a visit from some English cyclists and, while we drank coffee and ate snacks, they read through our magic letter several times, chuckling and exclaiming enthusiastically as they did so.

'Well, tonight, you must stay the night with us,' said Vladimir.

'We have a spare cabin in our field, which is warm and comfortable.' He pointed out of the window. 'Before that, though, we would love to treat you to dinner. Lena is an excellent cook, and she is cooking some chicken tonight.'

We spent the next two hours relaxing happily and enjoying their hospitality. Lena was highly amused to see the number of books we were carrying. She weighed our copy of *War and Peace* on her kitchen scales to prove how silly we were to lug so much extra weight all the way from Magadan. While I wrote my diary, Al sat by the fire, chatting with the Uzbek. Then, over a tasty dinner Lena told us, with smiling eyes, how grateful she was to her husband.

'It has always been my dream to run a roadside café,' she said. 'And now Vladimir has built it for me. We opened one month ago and you are our first foreign visitors, so we are very happy.'

They also told us that they had two young children living in her family village up the road. Throughout the evening, plenty of truckers stopped by and they too obviously enjoyed the welcoming, jovial atmosphere. It seemed the café would turn into a successful business. Before we went to bed, Lena and Vladimir insisted that we sign our names on the wall of the wooden building, so that they could remember our visit. At about 10 p.m. the Uzbek showed us to our hut, in which he had already stoked up the fire to make it warm and cosy. We stretched out our sleeping bags on the bed and fell into a contented slumber.

I first heard the screaming while I was asleep and the noise broke into my dreams as if I was underwater, filtering through in a muffled blur, until suddenly I woke up sharply and heard the sounds clearly. They came from outside; it was Lena, she was screaming for help. I sat up abruptly and looked out of the window, and the image of what I saw is still imprinted on my mind.

Huge yellow flames were roaring out of the windows of the café. The inside of the building was completely ablaze and black smoke poured towards the sky. The field was lit up by the glow from the fire and Lena was running around shrieking, '*Ploha, ploha*' (bad, bad).

'Al, wake up! The café's on fire!' I yelled.

Al sat bolt upright and we threw on our boots and sprinted out of the door. We ran over to the café and found Vladimir standing next to Lena about 20 metres from the fire. Vladimir was badly burnt and had bleeding feet. His thin night-clothes hung from him in tatters. He had only just made it out. Lena, although distraught, was unhurt. The café roared ferociously and three of its wooden walls were ablaze. The roof was starting to catch fire as well.

Lena and Vladimir were both crying and shivering. It was at least –20°C, so we urged them to come into our hut. Once they were inside, we shut the door behind us. Vladimir sat down whimpering on the bed. Al turned to Lena and asked where the man from Uzbekistan was.

Lena shouted at Al that he was inside. Al immediately took a step towards the door, but Lena jumped in front of him and yelled. '*Nyet! Nyet! Gasoleen, gasoleen.*'

I was in a state of shock and barely understood what was going on. Then Al shouted across to me that he wanted to go and try to rescue the Uzbek from the fire, but that Lena did not want him to go because of the gas tanks, which fuelled their cooker.

I stepped towards Lena, trying to calm her down while Al attempted to slip past. But Lena blocked him again and kept shouting about the gas tanks. They argued for several minutes, but Lena was adamant and hysterical and Al eventually agreed that he would not go into the blaze as the risk of an explosion was too high. He was firm with Lena that he must at least go to the road to try to stop a passing car. She looked at him hard before stepping aside quietly so he could leave. Al told me to help with Vladimir's wounds and keep them both warm and then he ran back outside and up to the road.

I stood feeling helpless. Vladimir sat, mostly naked, on the bed, shuddering and crying. I tried to wrap a sheet around him, but it kept slipping off. As I stoked up our little wood stove, I could see his feet were badly burnt and I did not know how to treat them. Lena and Vladimir sobbed and talked to each other about how their whole lives had been wrapped up in that café. I could pick out the words they were saying in Russian: money, papers, passports, all lost in the fire.

After a few minutes, feeling helpless, I left the hut and ran up to the roadside. Al stood waiting on the empty road. It was 3 a.m. and there was no traffic at all. I told him that I would take over waiting for a car and Al said he would go back to see if he could help Vladimir.

I watched him run back through the darkness. But, as he passed the blazing café, he suddenly stopped running. He hesitated and then turned to look into the flames. To my disbelief, he started to walk slowly towards them. His steps were tentative at first, but grew increasingly determined as he edged closer and closer. The scene was unfolding in slow motion. Al glided through the night, the flames raged up above him and I saw that he was going to go in to try to save the Uzbek after all.

But all of a sudden, like a thunderclap, a sharp, booming roar ripped through the night and an immense fireball erupted out of the far end of the café. The building exploded into pieces and, out of the corner of my eye, I saw the image of Al sprinting with flailing arms away from it. He escaped just in time. However, without a doubt, all hope for the man from Uzbekistan was now gone. He was dead.

Sometime later, I managed to flag down a truck that was passing. Stupidly, rather than asking them to take Vladimir with them to the next town, I asked them to alert the hospital and police. It was probably at least another hour before a small ambulance van arrived. Three medical staff ungraciously bundled Vladimir into it and drove him to the hospital. We managed to wave down another car to take Lena and the two of us to her family's village. We must have looked like refugees from some terrible war, with our pale, shock-filled faces, the exploded café still smouldering behind us. We reached Lena's home and sat stupefied and miserable as the night dragged on and Lena wept and told her people what had happened. At daylight, we were driven with Lena back to the site of the fire. A fire engine and two police cars were waiting for us. We sat inside one of the police cars and a bright, clean-shaven young detective interviewed us and seemed to enjoy practising his English. He told us that that the fire had probably started because of a faulty stove.

As we climbed out of the police car, we saw Lena sitting inside her friend's car, her face leaning against the window, staring at the smoking wreck in disbelief. The policeman told us that now we could and (he implied from the tone of his voice) should go. Before we left, we put some money in a plastic bag and passed it through the window to Lena. She took it with a perplexed look on her face as we said goodbye. Her eyes were red with tears.

It felt so wrong to get back on our bikes and pedal onwards, leaving Lena to grieve behind us. Every pedal took us further away, but what else could we do? Our ride suddenly felt like a ridiculous self-inflicted melody of pain and ambition. Our quest for adventure and our race against the visas was suddenly void of meaning. We had been seeking the thrills of danger and adventure, had taken risks with our lives and taken a battering with our bodies. But, all the while, people were suffering and we were doing nothing to help them.

We rode hard and fast that day, barely speaking to each other. I wanted to talk about it, but Al was internalising his pain. Again and again the memories and regrets of the previous night played through my mind like a videotape. I pondered on how unexpected tragedy can be and how devastatingly irreversible – nothing on the other side of it can ever be the same. I also contemplated my cowardly and confused actions. I wondered whether I could have saved the Uzbek if I had acted fast enough. When we stopped for a break, I tried to tell Al how brave and strong and clear-headed he had been. He was silent. Later, that evening, while we stayed in a villager's house, Al finally started to open up. He read me an excerpt from his diary, which he had written the night before. There was a whole page describing the little man from Uzbekistan. We realised we had never even found out his name.

16
Alive

Distance to home = 31,720 miles

We walk away from our dreams afraid that we may fail.
Or worse yet, afraid we may succeed
SEAN CONNERY, *Finding Forester*

We were exhausted and sad, but we knew we had to keep going. The road fell alongside the frozen banks of the giant Amur River and we saw China on the opposite side. We reached Khabarovsk, turned north and headed onwards towards the port of Vanino. The road surfaces were better now and we increased our daily distances to almost a hundred miles a day to make up the time we had lost because of the robbery and the fire. We met some policemen at a checkpoint who, after trying to give us a baseball bat in case someone else tried to rob us (we politely declined), told us of a shortcut through the mountains to the coast. Although this shortcut was not marked on our maps, when we arrived in the town they had indicated, the turnoff was there just as they had said.

The snowy track twirled over slippery passes and down beside half-frozen rivers. It should have seemed beautiful – the icicles on the pines, the snow on the slopes and the huge slabs of ice rushing down the river towards the sea – but I was sick of the winter and just wanted to escape from the Russian weather. We encountered several hours of blizzard one morning. It felt like a final, sinister attempt by Siberia to prevent us from escaping. But we kept going and eventually, unbelievably, crested a final pass and were able to look out onto a much-anticipated view of the open sea. After the months of snow and ice, the expanse of empty, grey water was a strangely soothing sight.

*

A few hours later, in darkness, we wheeled our bikes up a ramp and onto the night ferry. We slept and ate for most of the crossing and the following evening we landed on Sakhalin. We camped for a final time in the Russian snow before cycling the last 50 miles to the city where Alexis lived.

When we arrived at his expat apartment complex, the receptionist gave us the key and we let ourselves into his luxury flat with whoops of joy. That night, when Alexis returned from work, he took us out for a big Indian curry to celebrate both our survival and the fact that he was at last receiving some visitors. Because of the shortcut through the mountains we had ended up arriving early, so, for the next three days, while Alexis was out at work, we relaxed at his flat, took gloriously long, hot showers, ate seriously tasty meals and indulged in ridiculously long email sessions.

Having noted down the address of each of the families we had stayed with, before we left, with the help of Alexis' Russian secretary, I wrote to thank them all. I heard nothing back until two years later when my parents received a handwritten letter from Siberia. I was still on the road in Asia at this point so I asked my father to send it to a Russian-speaking friend in London who then forwarded me a translation. The letter was from Lena, from the café. She thanked Al and me for doing what we could to help on that dreadful night and expressed her gratitude for the money we had left her. She also told us that, sadly, unbearably, after six weeks lying in hospital, Vladimir had died of his injuries, leaving her to care for their two young children alone.

The day the ferry for Japan departed was my twenty-eighth birthday, but we had to get up at six in the morning because it was a 20-mile ride to the ferry terminal and the ferry left at nine. We arrived at the port and I wheeled Alanis ahead of Al to the passport control counter. I handed my passport over to the young, crew-cut immigration official and waited contentedly for the definitive stamp that would allow me to leave. However, rather than stamping it and handing it back, the official began to scrutinise the passport, looking carefully at my face and then back at the passport. I smiled back at him confidently. I had calculated and recalculated our daily distances so many times over the past few months, I was positive that we were leaving the country on time. Eventually, with undue reluctance, the official stamped my passport and let me through. He did the same for Al and we wheeled our bikes onto the ferry and went upstairs to the passengers' lounge.

Before falling asleep, I pulled my passport out and opened it to have a look at that visa one last time. As I flicked through its pages I noticed that, strangely, I suddenly had a lot of visas from Africa and South America, including some from countries where I had never been. Turning to the back page where my photo was, I saw why the official had been confused. It was not my passport – it was Al's. Somewhere along the ride we must have mixed them up. We had raced our bodies to the bone in order to leave Russia legally and then managed to pass through immigration using the wrong passports.

*Statistics for Parts 1 & 2 (Siberia)**

Dates:	September–December 2004
Distance flown:	4,500 miles to Magadan
Total distance covered from start:	4,019 miles
Distance left to reach home:	31,159 miles
Distance covered by bicycle:	3,315 miles
Distance covered by boat:	704 miles
Age:	27
Maximum distance in one day's effort:	105 miles
Minimum distance in one day's effort:	26 miles
Most punctures in one day:	5
Coldest temperature:	-40
Coldest temperature in which puncture fixed:	-36
Bars of chocolate eaten:	189
Most consecutive days without a shower:	12
Arguments with Al:	2
Goldmines visited:	2
Packets of instant noodles consumed:	Over 100

*Some of these statistics are estimates. Figures are given for the end of stage.

Part Three

Japan–South Korea–China–Hong Kong

December 2004–October 2005

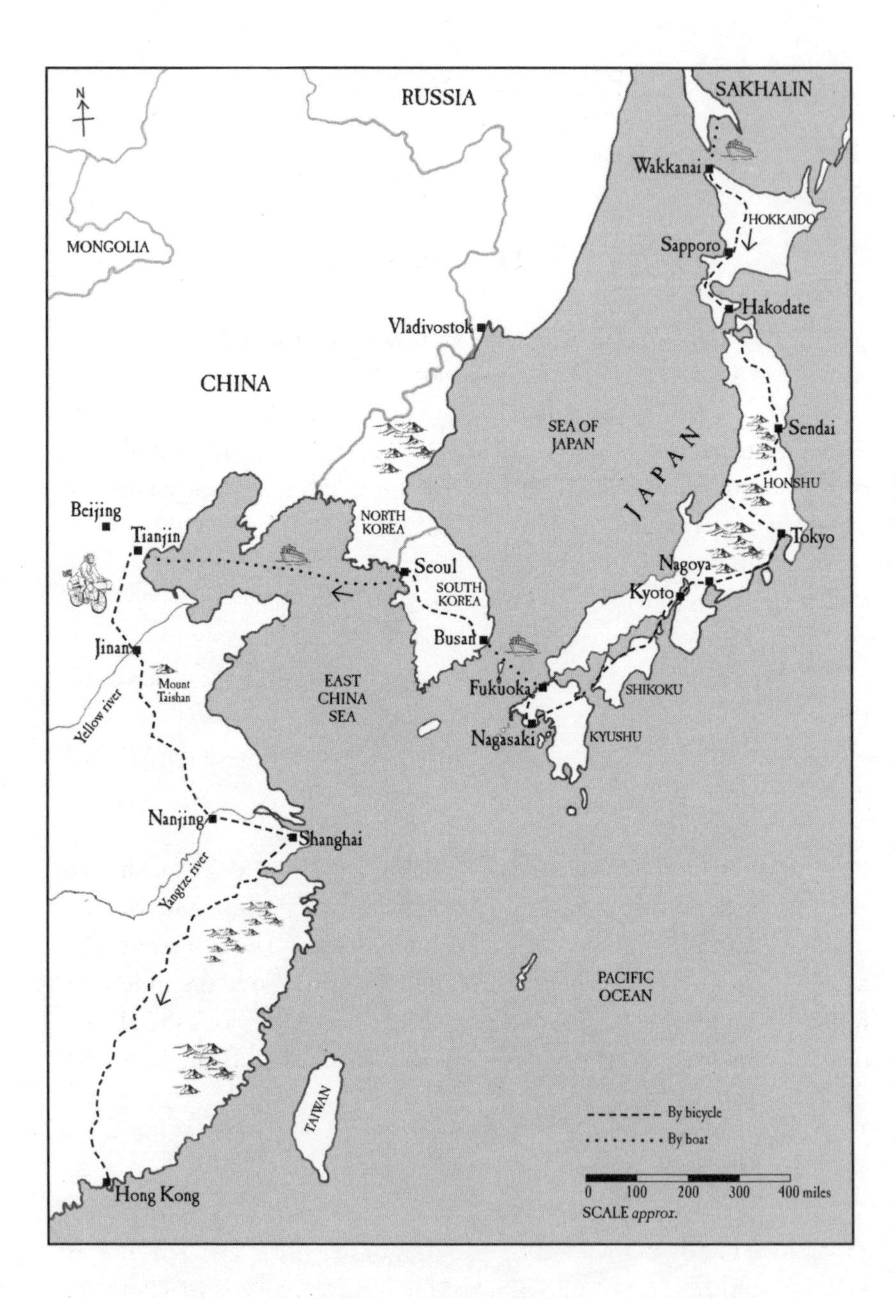

RUSSIA
SAKHALIN
MONGOLIA
Wakkanai
HOKKAIDO
Sapporo
Hakodate
Vladivostok
CHINA
SEA OF JAPAN
JAPAN
Sendai
HONSHU
NORTH KOREA
Beijing
Tianjin
Tokyo
Seoul
Nagoya
SOUTH KOREA
Kyoto
Busan
Jinan
Mount Taishan
EAST CHINA SEA
Fukuoka
SHIKOKU
Yellow river
Nagasaki
KYUSHU
Nanjing
Shanghai
Yangtze river
PACIFIC OCEAN
TAIWAN
By bicycle
By boat
0 100 200 300 400 miles
SCALE approx.
Hong Kong

17
Bienvenu au Japon

Distance to home = 31,159 miles

One kind word can warm three winter months
JAPANESE PROVERB

As we wheeled our bikes out of the Japanese immigration building, our first surprise was to see a tiny, middle-aged Caucasian nun waiting to meet us.

She took a tentative step in our direction.

'*Bonjour! Je m'appelle Marie-Louise.*'

'Excuse me?' I said.

'Is that French she is speaking?' asked Al out of the side of his mouth.

'I think so.' We both smiled politely at her and wondered what would happen next.

Five minutes later we were cycling behind the nun's car as she led the way back to her house. She had invited us to stay and we had managed an adequate response in our GCSE French to gratefully accept. She drove with her hazard lights on at about six miles per hour. 'I wonder if she is driving this slowly for us, or does she always drive at this speed?' Al pondered aloud, 'and how did she know we were coming anyway?'

'I don't know,' I said. 'I think she must be a friend of John Hamilton.'

John was the father of a friend from England. He worked in Japan and I had emailed him from Sakhalin to say we would shortly be coming through on our bicycles. He had replied enthusiastically, saying he would contact a few people who might invite us to stay.

I recalled now that he had mentioned some French nuns, but I had not expected one to be waiting to meet us the moment we stepped off the ferry on the remote north coast of Hokkaido Island.

The nun's car turned onto the main street and suddenly our senses, which had been so deprived of colour among the endless black and white of Siberia, were bombarded with a cacophony of reds, blues, yellows and greens. The whole street was lined with flashing vending machines, giant billboards and neon-lit shop fronts. We saw more traffic lights in the next ten minutes than in the whole of our time in Russia.

We reached the house and two middle-aged Japanese nuns bowed and welcomed us inside. We bowed in return, feeling faintly absurd. We sat at the dining table, and the sisters began to bring us endless plates of meat, vegetables and biscuits. After the feast had ended, their friend drove us to the local *onsen*, the Japanese hot springs. As I submerged myself in the steaming water my muscles were soothed, and the past months of stress and strain began to slip from my face like the dawn.

When we returned, dinner time arrived. The nuns had now discovered it was my birthday and, like mother hens, they clucked around us feeding us more and more, including a big home-made cake and a bottle of red wine.

'*Spasiba*,' I said in Russian, leaning back, very full, in my chair.

I remembered I was no longer in Russia and corrected myself, 'I mean, thank you . . .'

No one spoke English.

'Errr . . . I mean *merci beaucoup*.'

'*Arigatou gozaimasu*,' said Al smugly, showing off a sizeable percentage of his Japanese vocab.

The nuns smiled and we kept eating.

In Siberia, we had been so absorbed with trying to survive that we had given little thought to what we would do if we actually made it to Japan. We had convinced ourselves that it would be a high-tech land of easy riding and luxurious living. However, as we prepared to leave the nuns' house, it dawned on us that it might have challenges of its own. The nuns' friend had a computer, so the next day we sent emails to contacts we had further south, and also received a translation of our magic letter into Japanese. Then we laid out our map on the floor and made a rough plan. We were currently on the north-western tip of the northern island of Hokkaido. From here we would need to ride 1,300 miles south through the four principal islands, via Tokyo, to the southern port of Fukuoka, and then catch a ferry back to the Asian mainland.

Then we said goodbye to the nuns and wobbled back into our journey. The road from Wakkanai took us inland and, as the town fell behind us, the temperature dropped. The smooth highway went through bare, snow-dusted fields, while a bulge of damp, green hillocks protruding in the distance looked across at us like a regiment of samurai guards. Occasional cars passed by in both directions. In contrast to the drivers in Russia, who stared, stopped and offered us vodka, the drivers in Japan looked straight ahead and pretended not to notice us.

We made slow progress and did not reach the next town before nightfall. As it grew dark, an icy crosswind began to blow across the fields. It cut through my coat and I began to feel cold again. I felt dismayed that we had not left nasty weather behind in Siberia. The thought of spending that night in the tent was unappealing, but we had no choice. We started scanning the roadside for a suitable spot. A service station came into sight. We pulled in and Al suggested pitching the tent beside a wall to shelter us from the wind. While he scouted around, I excused myself and went to visit the toilet block.

In Siberia, our lavatory experiences had been bottom-numbing; in Japan, our lavatory experiences were to be relished. Inside the spacious cubicle, the toilet resembled a small spaceship. When I sat down I was delighted to discover the seat was heated. On the armrest, I saw a control panel. I started to experiment with the buttons. One of them made a digital flushing noise, presumably to drown out the loud, embarrassing sounds I was making. The next button gave me a shock as a jet of hot water shot up my behind. The next dried me with hot air.

I was still laughing when I emerged and saw Al preparing to put the tent up on some snowy concrete. I told him about the control panel and joked that the large disabled toilets were easily large enough to sleep in.

Al shuddered in the wind and chuckled before saying quite seriously, 'Actually, that is a very good idea.'

We looked at each other for a moment and then, making sure there was nobody watching, we wheeled our bikes inside. Giggling like children, we locked ourselves into the largest cubicle and then cooked some food the nuns had given us, read our books and settled down to sleep on the floor.

When we awoke the next morning, we felt very pleased with ourselves for discovering such a luxurious place to sleep. We agreed that it was actually a good deal cleaner and more comfortable than the more dilapidated hotels we had stayed at in other corners of the world and, as Al pointed out, it was even en suite.

Over the next few days the brief, empty wilderness of far northern Japan began to disappear behind us. In the first sizeable town, we remembered the nuns' reassurance that crime was rare in Japan so we left our bikes unattended against a wall and went into a 7–11. Our hearts sank as we scanned the aisles for cheap food and saw that even biscuits and rice were expensive. At last we saw something we could afford, though unfortunately it was instant noodles, the same food we had been eating in Siberia. We bought 15 packets, costing us £2.

The towns then became ever more regular and it started to feel as though we were riding through a continuous corridor of convenience stores and vending machines. We often passed road works, crowded with busy Japanese road builders wearing smart overalls and hard hats. 'They remind me of Lego men,' said Al. 'They seem so eager to work.'

On the following nights, rather than public toilets, we slept in train-station waiting rooms. We thought we might be thrown out or told off by the man in the ticket office, but he did not even look in our direction. One morning in a train station, we were woken up by a uniformed team of Japanese factory workers. They were lined up in tight formation in the waiting room. Suddenly, with some loud yells, they began to move their arms and legs in time with one another, stepping forward and back and raising their hands to the ceiling before dropping them down again. It made me think of a military display combined with an aerobics dance routine. Their faces were bright and unembarrassed, their arm movements synchronised and wide-ranging, and their shouts authentic and enthusiastic. This was the famous Japanese corporate team warm-up exercise. Was it any wonder, I thought in geography-teacher mode, that this group of islands flung out on the eastern edge of Asia, of which only 20 per cent of the land area was habitable, which had virtually no natural resources and plenty of natural disasters and which had been totally devastated in a war less than 60 years beforehand, should have been able to recover and become the world's second-largest economy in just a couple of decades?*

*Other reasons for Japan's miracle economy include the generous support of the victorious Americans in the early post-war years, the high demand for Japanese exports created by the Korean war and the great Japanese knack for technological innovation.

18
A fracturing friendship

Distance to home = 30,886 miles

Let him who cannot be alone beware of community . . . let him who cannot be in community beware of being alone
DIETRICH BONHOEFFER

Al had been in touch with a network of JET teachers* by email and, as a result, when we reached Sapporo city, we had an invitation to stay for two nights with an American–Vietnamese girl called Kelly. Kelly smiled politely though she looked alarmed as we tumbled through her door with arms full of panniers. Like most flats in Japan, Kelly's flat was very, very small. We felt we were overwhelming the whole home, especially as the only way to store our bags was to pile them up in the bathtub. We slept that night on the floor, squeezed between pieces of furniture.

The following night, Al and Kelly went out to meet her friends in a bar. I said I would rather stay at the flat and rest. I was feeling exhausted, and had still not recovered properly from Siberia. Over the previous week, I had found myself tiring quickly on the road as well. Al was faring much better and was back to full strength already.

I spent my evening in Kelly's flat feeling sorry for myself and went to bed early. The next day Al told me he had enjoyed his evening out. 'It was great to spend some time laughing again,' he said. Was he implying that I was not a very fun travelling companion these days, I wondered.

*

*Japanese English Teachers: a teach-abroad programme for young graduates from North America and the UK.

The following week, on Christmas Eve, after big distances on fast roads running between snowy fields and identical towns, we reached Hakodate. It was a city set on a curling promontory on the southern coast of Hokkaido. A JET teacher from England had invited us to stay in his flat while he was away for the holidays. We could hardly believe it when we let ourselves in. The flat had a hot shower, high-speed internet access and a huge DVD selection. Surely this is what we had been looking forward to for months.

However, the next day, Christmas Day, although spent sleeping, eating, and watching DVDs, was not a happy one. Our different speeds had continued to cause us both mutual aggravation over the past few days, and petty annoyances that had been building ever since we had left Magadan were now becoming more serious. Furthermore, as we sat eating our Christmas dinner together in silence, it was obvious that, after four months of being continuously together, day and night, we had run out of things to talk about.

Two days later, tensions between us were running at an all-time high. As usual, I was slow getting ready so we arrived late at the ferry terminal and missed our boat to Honshu. Al was clearly annoyed with me, but he did not say anything. We waited two hours until the next ferry departed. When we landed on Honshu, it was dark and there was a heavy blizzard blowing. We cycled through the slippery streets and eventually found a train station. After cooking up more tasteless noodles, we sat in our sleeping bags on opposite benches, reading our books in silence. Rather than two young explorers, we resembled a grumpy old couple.

On New Year's Eve, things started to reach crunch point. We were staying with another JET teacher, this time a young American girl whose name was America. She said we could call her Merica for short. We went out to a bar to celebrate the New Year, but Al and I spent the whole evening glowering at each other. Poor Merica must have wondered what was wrong with us.

The next day, I tried to cheer us all up. First of all I went for a noisy swim in a cold, nearby river. Uncharacteristically, Al said he did not want to join me. When I got back to the flat I bleached my hair yellow with some peroxide dye from the supermarket. Al did manage to laugh good-naturedly at the result, but it was not enough to thaw the ice between us.

As we departed again, it was raining hard. The snow was melting quickly and water poured off the roads into the storm drains. We climbed a grey-walled gorge all afternoon and a giant motorway bridge spanned the gap above us. That night we rolled out our sleeping bags in yet another train station. I read my book while Al cooked dinner. It was silent in the empty waiting room, but I could hear the wind howling down the valley. A draft was coming in under the door, so we were both wearing our coats. We had hardly spoken all day, and we knew we needed to talk. As we started eating, it was Al who started the conversation.

'Rob, I thought that we were just getting grumpy with each other in Siberia because it was so difficult. I thought that we would start having fun again in Japan, like we used to on our other adventures . . . but really we both know that we are not.'

I was glad that Al was broaching the subject and it was good to be talking more openly. It felt as if we were a married couple talking through a long-brewed but unspoken feud.

'Yes, you're right,' I agreed quietly. I waited for him to continue.

'We are having no fun together any more,' he said, 'and if we keep riding together we will just end up hating each other.' He paused, and the wind rattled the windows. Then he added fatefully, 'So I think we should split up.'

Split up? I knew things had been going badly, but Al's sudden suggestion was a shock. In my mind, I had still been thinking that things would improve again. I was not prepared for us to go our separate ways, or at least not quite yet.

'Yes, maybe you have a point,' I said.

'We will have a much better time on our own . . . and we can meet up in other cities as we head through Japan.' There was still friendship in his voice. This was not an acrimonious suggestion.

Rather, it was a carefully thought-through solution for the problem, as was always the case with Al.

'Yes, you are probably right.'

'Will you be okay riding on your own?'

The thought of riding alone actually terrified me. I had been on a few short solo trips before, but they were minuscule compared to the task I would face of cycling thousands and thousands of miles to get home on my own. Over the past four months I had become far too reliant on Al, whether it be for fixing things that broke, making decisions about the route, or putting the tent up when we were exhausted. I had no idea if I would be able to cope by myself.

'Yeah, sure.' I forced a smile. 'I'll figure it out.'

As we continued talking, we brought up other reasons why riding separately from now on made more sense. After our experience at Kelly's tiny flat, we knew we would be less intrusive on future hosts if they would have to put up with only one cyclist (plus luggage), rather than two. We also admitted that even in Siberia we had both wondered whether we would ride all the way home together. The first seeds of suspicion were sown when we realised that we had different ideas about what route we should take across Asia. Al wanted to head directly west across northern China, then traverse the 'Stans' and ride up through Eastern Europe to get home in time for tea, medals and his twenty-ninth birthday.

In contrast, I had started to talk of an implausibly *indirect* route home, which included a detour to the southern hemisphere. I wanted to ride down through China to Hong Kong, before somehow finding boats via the Philippines to Australia. I would then cycle halfway around Australia before catching a boat back to Singapore and heading home via the mountainous spines of South Asia and the Middle East. I did not know why I wanted to take this route – the idea had just slipped into my mind unawares – and now it was there I could not get rid of it. I did feel that having torn up my roots and left home, there was no harm in being away for longer.

At the same time, I could understand why Al was not keen on my suggestion. He had been away for three years already and was starting to suffer from 'the law of diminishing returns' – appreciating life on the road less and less the longer he was away. His more direct route would take only nine months, a short sprint in comparison to my 'slight detour'. In some ways, although the idea scared me, I had also started to think that some solo riding might be good for me. Ever since Magadan, I had been impressed by how Al had matured while he was on the road. Perhaps riding through hard places and testing myself with frightening challenges might make me grow up too.

In the early stages of deliberating about whether to do the ride, I had mentioned it cautiously to my father. He had generously agreed that it sounded like a good adventure, but also encouraged me to think of other projects I could undertake at the same time, so as to gain as much as possible from the experience. I had taken his advice and thought of several goals to set myself: to raise £10,000 for the children's charity Viva; to become fluent in Russian;* to write a website; and to give interviews for local media whenever possible. Similarly, as an extra project on his ride, Al had been giving slideshows about his journey in schools en route to raise money for charity. A few days before our 'splitting-up' discussion, a JET teacher had emailed Al, inviting him to give a talk at her school on the opposite coast of Japan. It would involve a long detour on the way to Tokyo, so he did not want to go. He now asked if I wanted to go instead, to get my public-speaking career off to a start. It was a good idea, so we agreed to ride together for two more days, after which I would cross the Japanese Alps to reach the school, and Al would head directly to Tokyo.

Now that we had admitted it was time to part, there was a strong sense of relief. We suddenly found ourselves able to joke about how out of proportion our grievances had become. Al said that even the sound of my breathing was starting to annoy him. I admitted that the way Al packed his panniers so neatly made my blood boil. I also confessed that when I had agreed to do the journey I had imagined us as two heroic adventurers, laughing in the face of danger and dropping ice cubes down the vest of fear. As it turned out, I

*Unfortunately, though perhaps understandably, I abandoned my attempts to learn Russian when I reached Japan.

said, I felt that our expedition consisted more of one heroic adventurer (Al) and one pathetic, irritating sidekick who did nothing but cause problems and complain (me).

'Well,' said Al, smiling, 'maybe now you're going to do some riding on our own, you'll be able to feel more heroic.'

'I certainly hope so,' I replied.

19
Alone

Distance to home = 30,620 miles

8 JANUARY–2 FEBRUARY 2005

Al and I shake hands outside his host's house and I set off towards the mountains, alone. Within half an hour I am lost in a maze of traffic lights and billboards in the first town. It takes more courage to ask directions from strangers now that I am by myself, but eventually someone directs me to the right road. I climb steadily for several hours in a low gear and the snowy peaks loom into sight once again.

As I climb, doubts and questions begin to dance through my mind like ghosts:

> *When you signed up for this thing you were going to do the whole ride with Al.*
> *You were supposed to start riding from Shanghai, not Siberia.*
> *Now you are your own in Japan and you are planning a detour to Australia!*
> *What on earth are you doing?*
> *You are out of your depth and you are a fool.*

I am genuinely surprised by how things are turning out. A part of me just wants to turn around, ride back to Al and beg that he might accept my company for the pedal home on whichever route he prefers. But my legs just keep turning and as the distance between us grows so too, slowly, does my confidence.

I ride past Aizu-Wakamatsu, the Alpine town where the last samurai took their stand, and then night arrives and it starts to snow. I have left the tent with Al, so I have no choice but to press through the thickening darkness in search of shelter. I am relieved to come to a village and find the train station. I wheel the bike inside, and look around the empty, plastic benches. It seems much more frightening to sleep in a train station now I am alone, but I keep myself busy with the usual routines: I roll out my sleeping bag; I cook some noodles; I read my book; I write my diary. I write about how scared I feel, but also how free I feel. I am now able to ride at my own speed without feeling guilty for slowing us down. I go on, noting that 'it is a strange kind of thrill, being so totally alone in a land full of humans. No one on this planet knows where I am, can picture this scene – me in a station with Alanis in the mountains of central Honshu.'

I had better get used to no one knowing where I am. There will be hundreds more nights like this before I reach home.

The next day I freewheel out of the mountains and reach the Sea of Japan. The nationalistic writer Yukio Mishima described the Sea of Japan as 'the source of all my unhappiness, of all my gloomy thoughts, the origin of all my ugliness and all my strength . . . a wild sea'. Riding alongside it for two days, with angry waves lashing the cliffs, and hailstones, rain and bitter winds beating my face, I begin to understand what he meant.

I reach the town of the JET teacher Jen, who welcomes me in and lets me sleep on her floor. The next morning, before a large audience of her smiling Japanese students, I show slides of Al and me cycling through Siberia, and tell the story of the journey so far. I weave in some honest messages about the fears I face and how I keep going. Because it is my first ever 'Cycling Home From Siberia' lecture, I am encouraged that the students laugh at my jokes and are inspired to treat life as an adventure themselves.

The next morning, I wave goodbye, climb back onto the bike and pedal away, alone once more.

The traffic around me builds and together we wait.

Then the lights turn green and I am away: pedalling, accelerating, trying to keep ahead of the cars behind me. They approach rapidly and roar past in a blur of sudden wind and heavy fumes. I spin past a grassy field full of electricity pylons and out of the corner of my eye see more 7–11s, more sushi bars, and more billboards advertising businesses I do not understand. I whiz past another succession of green lights. To break up the monotony of riding into another big city, I have set myself a challenge of counting the traffic lights today, and I am already over 100. I see a Coke can lying in my path, and glance back over my shoulder to check for cars before swerving around it. Up ahead, a rising tide of angular urban sprawl is growing close: Tokyo.

Eventually, at nightfall, I roll beneath a swirl of footbridges, metro bridges and neon signs and arrive in the downtown district where I have been invited to stay. I have survived my first week of riding on my own, I am in the middle of one of the world's great cities. Things are looking up.

I stay in Tokyo for a week, with a half-Japanese, half-Polish friend of a friend. Prior to his current job as an investment banker, Kiyoshi was a conflict-zone cameraman for the BBC. Showing me into his small flat, he says he knows what it is like to live off a couch in a foreign country. He gives me a set of keys and tells me to stay for as long as I like. Welcomes such as this still astound me.

Tokyo is a futuristic city, a place from a science fiction film. Streets full of cars and people whoosh past in every direction. Beautiful women clatter down the street in high heels. Men in business suits burst in and out of tall buildings. At night, I sometimes see them getting so drunk that they fall down in the street, still wearing their suits and ties.

I have plenty of contacts here, so each day I am out and about meeting new people. Al is also still in Tokyo and one night, together with a Japanese friend, Michitaka, we go for a meal and compare experiences from our first week alone. Al tells me he has been busy since arriving. He has given lectures in many of the capital's top schools and has been interviewed about his ride by an array of impressive-sounding magazines.

'Yesterday I was interviewed by a magazine called Tarzan,*' he*

jokes. 'I offered to do them a photo shoot wearing my leopard-skin Y-fronts, but unfortunately they turned me down.'

The plate of slimy seafood arrives. Both Al and I have grown used to eating Japanese food and agree it always tastes good as long as we do not find out what it is. However, Michitaka then announces that we are eating octopus balls. My face freezes in mid-chew. Al and Michitaka start laughing at me. I suddenly realise that he meant balls made of octopus rather than balls belonging to an octopus.

The next evening, I stay in the flat on my own. It is hard to believe that six weeks ago I was spending my nights in a tent in an empty Siberian forest. All of a sudden, living in this intense city, I feel homesick. I long to see some old friends who really know me rather than new friends who think I am a crazy English cyclist. Will it always be the busy cities where I feel most lonely during my ride home?

I start scrawling in my diary with agonised introspection. I reflect on my tendency to regret missed opportunities and to compare my own achievements with those of others; namely, at that moment, Al's notable success as evidenced by his interview with Tarzan. *I have enjoyed some good adventures on this journey so far, but what is the point of adventure?*

I remember a past conversation with Al about how the number-one aspiration of people surveyed in Britain was to travel the world. And yet now I find myself out here living that dream, I still feel confused and unsatisfied. I remember what someone once said about how 'the trouble with the rat race is that even if you win, you are still a rat'. Although I have declined to enter the rat race of climbing a conventional career ladder, maybe I am just in a different sort of rat race to become a daring explorer. I wonder what the actual point of my journey is. All I am doing is seeing one very narrow corridor of the earth – the field of vision that I see from the saddle of a bicycle.

All I know is that I do not want to give up now. After all, if I did, what would I do instead?

20
The naked cyclists

Distance to home = 29,948 miles

Once, as I was pedalling nowhere on a computerised bicycle, I thought of Kierkegaard's comment that the knowledge of one's own death is the essential fact that distinguishes us from animals. I looked around the exercise room wondering just how distinguished from the animals we modern humans are. The frenzied activity I was participating in at that moment – was it merely one more way of denying or postponing death?

PHILIP YANCEY

I headed south from Tokyo and the rest of Japan passed in a blur of main roads, 7–11s, and sprawling cities. The winter was now drawing to a close and the warm air was more pleasant to ride through. Having emailed various friends of friends from Tokyo, I now had a long list of kind people to stay with en route. My hosts varied from a teacher in Nagoya, to a mechanic in the town of Toyota; from a scholar in Kyoto to an acupuncture student in Osaka; from a salaryman* in Kobe to a biochemist in Korume. Their hospitality was humbling, but apart from offering to give my slideshow in the local schools, there was nothing I could do to repay them. One school gave me a small Japanese flag. A few days later I snapped a bamboo stick from a roadside forest and strapped it to the back of my bike as a flag pole. From then on, I tried to add a little flag in each country I went through.

Hosts often took me to visit their local *onsen*, karaoke bar, or

*Japanese middle management.

Zen Buddhist temple with its exquisite gardens. Japan was far removed from anywhere I had been before but despite all these experiences I felt I was only skimming the surface. I joined the ranks of foreign visitors who have found the Japanese culture somewhat inscrutable. Perhaps, one person told me, this was because of the Japanese distinction between *honne* (one's personal views) and *tatemae* (the opinions demanded by your position within the group or society).

When I reached the southern island of Kyushu, I coasted down a tree-clad hillside and entered the tropical port of Nagasaki. Even after visiting the memorial museum it was impossible to fathom what had happened on that quiet August morning in 1945. It was shocking to find out that a key criterion by which Nagasaki had been chosen as a target was that it had not been seriously bombed before. This would allow a better assessment to be made of the atomic explosion's destructive power. Japan was now so peaceful I could hardly believe that the horrors of that war were still in living memory. One middle-aged Japanese lady I stayed with told me of how her father had been trained during the war to sit on a torpedo and steer it into American ships. Fortunately the war had ended before he had had a chance to put the training into practice, but he was haunted for the rest of his life by the guilt of having survived when so many of his countrymen had not.

For our last few days in Japan, Al and I rode together again, one last time. As we had both been growing bored with Japan's smooth, easy roads, we decided to manufacture some adventure by cycling through a town without any clothes on. After all, we told ourselves, the Japanese love crazy things like that, so surely they wouldn't mind.

We chuckled as we stripped off our clothes and pedalled madly past another string of 7–11s and sushi restaurants. To our surprise, the Japanese drivers stopped pretending not to notice us and looked out of their cars with shocked stares as they overtook. After a few minutes, we thought it might be prudent to put our clothes back on.

Just as I had zipped up my coat we saw the first police car appear around the corner. It drove up to us and stopped, and two uniformed officers climbed out.

We looked at them blankly.

Another police car and two more officers pulled in.

We smiled sheepishly.

A third car arrived, this time unmarked, containing two plain-clothes detectives.

In a land with such a low crime rate, our escapade was obviously a case for the best men in the force. It began to dawn on us that we might be in genuine trouble. Fortunately, none of the policemen spoke English and, as Al was our Japanese speaker, I let him do the talking.

He tried to explain, with various arm gestures, that it was a very hot day, and so we had needed to cool down. The police frowned at us. Then Al explained that it was actually normal for the English to ride naked. The police were unconvinced. Finally, he admitted that it had actually not been a very clever idea, and it was a bit cold for naked cycling after all. The police told us off and let us go, and we rode away laughing with relief.

We pedalled on, fully clothed, through some forested hills, until we reached Fukuoka, where we had been invited to stay with another English teacher. From here we would be catching ferries to our next countries. Al's ferry was bound for China. It left very early, so the next morning he rose while it was still dark. From my sleeping bag on the floor, I watched him quietly pack his bags. I realised that I really would be on my own once he left, and that I would not see him for two years. I braced myself to get up and shake his hand and wish him Godspeed on his homeward leg.

But, before I managed to stir myself, I fell asleep.

When I woke up a few hours later he was gone. It was just Al's way to leave quietly and without a fuss. I said a prayer for him, packed my bags and headed out of the door to catch my own boat. It was bound not for China, but for South Korea.

21
A cyclist's revenge

Distance to home = 29,011 miles

I thought of that while riding a bicycle
ALBERT EINSTEIN (ON THE THEORY OF RELATIVITY)

South Korea felt instantly different from Japan. Even before the ferry docked I observed a middle-aged man talking loudly and jovially to his wife. Then, to my astonishment, at the culmination of their conversation he slapped her cheerfully on the bottom and they both burst out laughing. This, I thought to myself, was a seriously un-Japanese way to behave in public.

Riding through the town where we docked, Busan, I noticed other differences. The roads were not as smooth as in Japan. There were sizzling, greasy food stands and gritty street stalls, mixed in among the glass-fronted shops and restaurants. When I asked for directions, the people were more boisterous and less formal. Continuing into the countryside, at my peril, I learnt that Korean drivers were not as careful as the Japanese. Passing through a sleepy, grey village, a truck reversed into me and knocked me over. Fortunately a couple of passing locals yelled at him before he drove over the top of me, and I was not hurt. As I rode off again, still trembling, I told myself that an occasional near miss was not a bad thing if it reminded me to be more careful.

A kind host in Japan had given me an old tent, so once again I could camp. With spring now in the air, I enjoyed sleeping in the wild again, on the side of quiet, green mountains. On my way to Seoul, several expatriates had invited me to stay. First was an Englishman called Dunc in the ship-building port of Ulsan. For dinner, Dunc and his Russian wife took me to a Korean restaurant.

I jumped at the opportunity to try Korea's most infamous dish, stewed dog. I once heard Benedict Allen say that, after eating his own dog (which he was forced to do because he was starving to death in the Amazon), he had found its flavour was easy to describe to others because it tasted almost exactly the same as cat. I was more inclined to say that it tasted like beef, though a touch more chewy. I liked dogs, but I felt justified in eating a dog on this occasion because, during previous bike trips, I had often been chased by them as I passed through their villages. I expected it was only a matter of time before I was chased on this expedition as well.

After Ulsan, a tailwind carried me smoothly to Daegu. My next host was Sebastian Eissing from Germany. Seb was famous on the cyclists' grapevine as an intrepid and outstanding cyclist–explorer who had cycled through many of the craziest parts of the world. I was apprehensive about meeting him but hoped that, having crossed Siberia in winter, I might earn his respect. I arrived at our arranged rendezvous early and started to rehearse what epic lines I might use to greet him: the great English cyclist–explorer meeting the great German cyclist–explorer; both have survived the trials and tribulations of the badlands of the world and now, in a back-country town in the wilds of South Korea, they will meet face to face at last; this would indeed be a moment of destiny . . .

Suddenly I heard a German accent behind me:

'Ahaaaaa . . . I zee yoo have a *vooman's* saddle!'

I turned to see Sebastian. He was my height with thinning brown hair, a kind face, and a v-shaped beard. He grinned and pointed to my cushion-like bicycle seat. I corrected him that it was actually a very comfortable unisex saddle, and we both laughed.

We went back to his flat where I met his girlfriend, Kirsten. That evening, over dinner, we exchanged tales from the road. He explained how he had first caught the cycling bug during a backpacking holiday in Syria during his first year at university. After buying a £15 Chinese bike on a whim, he subsequently decided to ride to Egypt. However, once in Cairo, he made up his mind to abandon going home and instead ride all the way to Cape Town. After that, he had gone from one extraordinary ride to the next: across the

Sahara (twice); across Iraq (twice); and, most daring of all, across Afghanistan during the Taliban era.

'Afghanistan was pretty crazy,' he admitted. 'One night, while I was camping next to a stream, hidden from the road, I was attacked by three men. They dragged me out of my tent and beat me with sticks. Then they ran off, taking my two panniers with them.'

'What did you do?' I asked.

'Well, if I didn't get the panniers back, then my trip was over, so I got up and started to chase them. I found a ridge above the path they were on, so I ran along it and started to throw stones down on them. They threw stones back at me, but I had the higher ground. Eventually they dropped the bags and ran off. I ran down, grabbed the bags and cycled to the next town, where the local mosque let me stay until morning.'

I listened, wide-eyed, and wondered whether this guy was incredibly brave or amazingly irresponsible. Shuddering, I decided that I would never be courageous or loony enough to cycle across Afghanistan.

On the day I aimed to reach Seoul, I rose early and braced myself for a long day's ride. I had been finding that it was rare for me to lose my way when travelling between cities, but that when I actually reached a city I was very likely to get lost.

Gradually the countryside disappeared and the roads converged into a series of clogged-up traffic jams, which merged into the heart of Seoul. The buses that day were the worst I would ever encounter. They did not even notice me as they scraped against my panniers while overtaking. I dragged Alanis over some pedestrian bridges to cross a 14-lane highway beside the river and then, finally, worn out yet relieved, found Richard and Hannah's flat. They had emailed a few weeks beforehand to invite me to stay. I had still not worked out how they knew me, but they welcomed me inside like an old friend.

22
The biggest church and the tallest flagpole

Distance to home = 28,737 miles

When whales fight, shrimp get hurt
KOREAN PROVERB

Ding!

Cheeo! Cheeo! Cheeo! (Lord! Lord! Lord!)

Waaaaaaaaaaaaaaaaaaaaaaaaaaaaaa

At the sound of the bell, like at the start of a boxing match, the crowd erupted.

It was Sunday morning, and I was with Richard and Hannah in the Yoido Full Gospel Church. With more than 700,000 official members, it was the largest church in the world. We were sitting in an auditorium, packed with 16,000 people, and every seat was occupied. Another 16,000 people were participating in the service in outlying buildings, and this service was just one of the day's seven. Compared to England, where it seemed a miracle to find a church where all the seats were full, in Korea it was a miracle if you found one empty place.

The most remarkable part of the service was the prayer time, which began with the sounding of a bell, followed by impassioned praying. The people's faces and voices were earnest as they cried out their requests to God simultaneously. They were so enthusiastic that there was another bell, which went off a few minutes later to tell them to stop so that the rest of the service could proceed. The sharing of communion was also a moving time and incredibly well organised. Everyone present was able to receive the bread and wine in less than five minutes. Although this was the largest church in Korea, it was not unique. Eleven of the 12 largest congregations in the world were in Seoul. Outside, as I explored the city, the most notable features of the otherwise bland skyline were the dozens of red neon crosses emblazoned across it.

I later read that nobody really knows why Christianity has thrived there. Missionaries did not arrive until the 1780s and by the start of the twentieth century Christians still made up less than 1 per cent of the population. But in the 1950s, the trickle of growth turned into a flood. By 1960 the Protestants alone had grown to over 100,000. By 1990 they were over ten million. In attempting to explain the growth, sociologists have suggested that similarities between Christianity and some of the traditional Korean beliefs gave a natural point of contact on which to build. They also highlight the significance of the Christian relief agencies that provided essential help, both during and after the war. Perhaps most important, though, was that, unlike in other Asian countries where Christianity was seen as the religion of the imperial Western oppressors, in Korea Christianity became associated with the causes of liberation and freedom. Traditionally, the greatest enemies of the Koreans were not the Europeans but the Japanese, and it was often the Christians who showed most courage in resisting them. They refused Japanese demands that they should worship the emperor, and they often defied their oppressors to the point of death. The non-Christian Koreans were thus able to see beyond the foreign origins of the faith and, instead, gained respect for it, and began to accept it as their own.

There is undoubtedly some merit in these theories, but a more common explanation given by the Korean Christians themselves is far simpler: 'It is because we pray,' they say.

A day before I had reached Seoul I had received a shock as I crested a quiet hill: a vast convoy of tanks and armoured personnel carriers was thundering towards me. It reminded me that I was now nearing the most heavily militarised border in the world. North Korea begins less than 40 miles north of Seoul. The border had been agreed upon as the thirty-eighth parallel in an armistice in 1953, after three years of bloody conflict with almost three million dead. In the border region there was also a four-kilometre area of no-man's-land, known as the Demilitarised Zone (DMZ), to act as a buffer. Since then, although there have been occasional rapprochements, an actual peace agreement has never been signed. The two halves of Korea are therefore still technically at war, the million or so troops stationed either side of the DMZ testifying to the fact.

Because entering North Korea was therefore not allowed, I would need to catch a ferry to reach China. However, I did hear that foreign tourists were allowed to visit the border with a tour group. It sounded interesting, so I paid my money and joined a busload of Americans for the day trip.

We drove through a succession of checkpoints and eventually arrived at a military compound. After being ushered into a lecture hall, Specialist Pipkin from the US army introduced himself as our guide for the day. In a military-style bellowing, he went on to brief us with the following mandatory orders:

'You'll see North Korean soldiers at the border. Don't attempt to communicate with them in any way.' We nodded.

'The area we're taking you to is militarily sensitive. Don't take photos unless we tell you you can.' We looked at each other, then nodded.

'If you need to use the bathroom, please go and do so now. You won't be allowed to go once we reach the border, unless,' he paused earnestly, 'it is a *must-go* situation.'

He also told us that there continued to be occasional confrontations at the border. There had been an incident in the 1970s when a troop of North Korean commandos had entered the South disguised in South Korean uniforms, and proceeded to try to assassinate the then president, Park Chung Hee. On another occasion, a Russian soldier had defected across the border, provoking a fire fight between the two sides.

With this advice echoing around our heads, we were marched into the Truce Village of Panmunjon in the DMZ. There were several pale-blue huts straddling the border and two tinted watchtowers looked down at us from the North Korean side. No guns were allowed, but a number of unarmed South Korean guards stood facing across the border. Rather than standing in a conventional sentry pose, they were poised with bent arms, aggressive expressions and dark glasses.

We followed Specialist Pipkin into the Truce Hut. It had pale-blue walls and was mostly bare, apart from a varnished wooden table in the middle of the room. It stood exactly astride the border itself, so that when the two sides met for occasional summits, representatives from each side could remain sitting in their own country. It was precisely here that the armistice had been signed half a century before. A South Korean soldier stood with a leg on each side of the border and we were briefly allowed to step onto the North Korean side of the table and have our photo taken with him.

Back outside, the bus took us to a viewing platform from where we could look across at a North Korean peace/propaganda village (depending on whether you were from North or South Korea) named Kijong-dong. No one lived there and the windows did not even contain glass. Most of the DMZ around us was covered in a wild meadow and the smell of pollen drifted past us.

'Do not step off the platform onto the grass,' said Pipkin. 'You are surrounded on three sides by a minefield.' A tourist behind me said that the DMZ was one of the richest ecosystems on this side of Asia because it had lain completely untouched by humans for so long.

'That,' continued Pipkin, pointing to an enormous flag fluttering above the village, 'is the world's tallest flagpole.' He told us that after the South Koreans had put up a 100-metre-high flag pole in the 1980s, the North Koreans had been determined to go one better and had built their own flagpole. It was a staggering 160 metres tall, proving that even if North Korea was one of the poorest and most totalitarian countries in the world, they could at least boast the tallest flagpole. It would have been funny, if it was not so tragic.

Pipkin also said that until a few years previously the two sides had waged a cross-border propaganda battle. For up to 20 hours a day the North Koreans used to blare self-aggrandising misinformation about their Northern paradise through loudspeakers. In retaliation, the South had played pop music.

I asked whether it was true that the South Koreans had previously used giant spotlights to beam the message 'We have rice' up onto the clouds above North Korea.

'I can neither confirm nor deny that,' said Pipkin, 'but I can say that it was a relief when both sides agreed to stop the propaganda war in 2004.'

Finally, our bus took us to the site of a secret infiltration tunnel. The tunnel had been discovered in the 1970s when a routine South Korean patrol had seen steam rising from the ground. We walked down some steps, past some well-constructed walls and into the base of the tunnel.

'When the tunnel was discovered,' said Pipkin, 'it also had a narrow-gauge railway. Two thousand soldiers per hour could have come through.'

The North Koreans had subsequently denied that the tunnels had been built to mount an invasion, and instead came up with the impressively implausible excuse that they had been building the tunnels as part of a coalmine. Three other tunnels have also been discovered since, and it is suspected that there are several more undiscovered.

A tourist asked Pipkin if he thought the North Koreans would ever actually try to invade.

'Well,' he said, blank-faced, 'I certainly hope not.'

I felt strangely emotional as we drove back to Seoul. I thought about the shadow of hills that had loomed over us, to the north, throughout the tour. What was life like for the North Koreans, living unseen on the other side? It was tragic that Korea had been the battlefield for the ideological conflict of the world's superpowers, and yet, a decade after the Cold War ended, it still remained divided.

23
Rivers of jostling spokes

Distance to home = 28,113 miles

8–11 APRIL 2005

Two hours before my ferry is due to dock, I walk out onto the deck. I expect to see an empty grey sea rolling away towards a misty horizon. Instead I see a vast armada of freight ships queuing up to deliver their goods to the hulking port in the distance. After lumbering past a long line of floodlit docks we berth and I stumble down the ramp with Alanis. I am nervous at the immigration counter because I have heard rumours that tourists are not allowed to bring bicycles into China, but the officials stamp me through without a fuss. I follow an empty road for ten minutes through the night before arriving in a deserted but well-lit street. It is lined with blank-faced buildings and I see three students walking towards me.

I can say only four phrases in Chinese:

Ni hao – *Hello, how are you?*
Wo hen hao – *I'm fine*
Wo bu hao – *I'm not fine*
Xie xie – *Thank you.*

As the three students approach, I pull Alanis onto the pavement and dig out my new magic letter. Then, giving them my biggest smile, I say, 'Ni hao' *and, pointing to myself,* 'English!'

They are alarmed and look at me as if I am dangerous.

I hand them the letter, hopefully. Once they have read it I point to the phrase that says: 'I am looking for a cheap place to stay, please.'

In turn, they look at the bike, me, the letter and each other. They have a brief conversation that I do not understand and then one of them points down a side road and says, 'This way', in English.

We walk together for several minutes and come to an unmarked building with an open door. The students speak to a lady inside. She is in her fifties and not at all pleased to see me. She scowls and shouts at the group. I pass the magic letter. She reads it, but keeps scowling. The students continue advocating for me and several gruff men appear. They read the letter and join in with some shouting as well.

I feel strangely calm and try to charm the caretaker lady by smiling at her. She sees me smiling and pauses her tirade briefly, but then starts shouting again. Eventually, probably more due to the students' perseverance than to my smiles, she gives in. It will cost me £1.50 for the night. I thank the students and stagger up the stairs behind the lady, carrying Alanis.

Inside my room there is a bed, a sheet, a television and a desk with a drawer full of playing cards. I sit on the bed and flick through the TV stations. Several of them are covering the wedding between Prince Charles and Camilla Parker Bowles which, until then, I had not realised was occurring that day.

The next morning, I wheel the bike out of the hotel for my first glimpse of daytime China. I had been expecting a country where the people are dour and sombre and clad in grey-blue Mao suits. But now the gloomy street from last night has come to life. Bicycles, cars and overloaded trucks hurry in all directions. Men and women in colourful T-shirts bustle out of the shops. They are chattering and full of energy. The buildings in the main street are old and the T-shirts have been mended, but behind them I can see cranes putting up new buildings.

I look down at my country-scale map of China and wonder which way I should go. A group of men with scrutinising faces gather around me. They start to ask me questions in Chinese. I produce the magic letter. It is eagerly passed around. They smile at *me with toothy grins. Someone writes something on a piece of paper and hands it to me. It is written in Chinese and they seem to assume that because I have a letter written in Chinese, I should be able to read Chinese.**

I need to get going so I say to them: 'Tianjin?' – the name of the first city I am aiming for.

Mandarin is a tonal language, with four distinct tones. The meaning or comprehensibility of every word is dependent upon using the right tone. The growing crowd stares at me blankly so I repeat 'Tianjin' in several different tones:

Tiiiiianjin.

Tiaaaaaaanjin.

Tianjiiiiin.

I notice that, with each tone, I am contorting my face in a different direction. The crowd looks at me as if I am mad for a while. Suddenly one of them understands what I am saying: Tianjin!

Ah, Tianjin, everyone acknowledges together, laughing at me as if to say, 'Why didn't you say that in the first place?'

Together they point down the high street and shout at me enthusiastically. I say 'Xie xie' *and start my ride across China.*

The main road quickly turns into a three-lane highway which is shared by motorised vehicles, donkeys, pedestrians and bicycles. Just before I left Seoul, I received an email from Al. He has now left Beijing and is riding west on a road beside the Great Wall. He warned me that the drivers in China were crazy, and pointed me to some helpful advice on his website:

*I found out later that the long-lived Chinese Empire had not been administered with a common tongue, but with a common written language. This meant that if a government official was sent to a far-flung province where he could not speak the local dialect (of which there are still several thousand in China), he could at least still communicate by writing.

Al's ten rules for driving in China

Chinese driving is among the worst I have ever seen. It is easy to drive Chinese-style; indeed, you could even try it out this evening on your way home from work. Here's how:

1. *Set out to be as annoying as possible. Bear that in mind at all times. Now enjoy some or all of these strategies, either one at a time or simultaneously:*
2. *Meander from lane to lane as your fancy takes you.*
3. *Drive very fast in the slow lane, or very slow in the fast lane.*
4. *Beep your horn at all times, especially when it is completely unnecessary.*
5. *Never use your mirrors.*
6. *When you have to pull out into traffic, do just that. Pull out into the traffic. Waiting for a gap is for wimps – it is much easier to let the fellow driving at top speed on the highway hoot in panic and swerve wildly out of your way.*
7. *Occasionally drive the wrong way down the carriageway.*
8. *Get annoyed if people get annoyed at you.*
9. *When you tire of these games go fetch your flock of sheep and wander with them down the road.*
10. *Have fun!*

Al was absolutely right. Everyone is in a hurry, and there is no such thing as cruising – everyone swerves, brakes, accelerates and honks continuously. As I duck and dive down the road I decide that Al's ten can be simplified into one principal unifying theory: do not crash. The key to obeying this rule is to keep your eyes on what is in front of you at all times. It is the responsibility of those behind to take evasive action.

I approach the outskirts of Tianjin. The number of cyclists swells, and I find myself riding among a river of jostling spokes and pedals. We flow together in harmony with blank faces. Our number is made up of young and old; smart and haggard; peasant and student. I am the sole foreign devil. And we are silent, save for the gentle sound of chains rolling over cogs, and the noise of an occasional hack and spit.

With our superiority of numbers, we can even challenge the dominance of the car. When we approach a set of red traffic lights, we do not stop but instead plough onwards. Despite riding through six lanes of moving traffic, we somehow slip through the gaps, like water, and emerge unscathed on the other side.

I stay two nights in Tianjin where I buy a road atlas from a bookshop so that I can now decipher the cryptic characters on the road signs. After that I join the road south across the floodplains of the Yellow River. It is early April and a warm spring wind is blowing gently against me. Ploughed fields spread away from the road to a flat horizon and the roadside ditches are half-filled with rubbish. The traffic is more agricultural now: tractors, trucks, trailers and bicycles, many of them piled high with brown sacks of produce.

On these rural roads, the people have rarely seen foreigners. My untidy beard and over-laden bicycle must make me look even stranger. They stare and point at me as I ride past. Maybe it is not rude to point and stare here.

I stop and another crowd gathers. I point to the phrase: 'I would like something very cheap and filling to eat, please' on the letter and am directed with lots of prodding into a dirty white building. Inside, the room has stained walls and cheap wooden tables. A wrinkly cook coughs and spits while frying dishes on a flaming stove. A middle-aged waitress, in a drab apron, brings me a big bowl of fried noodles and a cup of green tea. While I eat, I write my diary and several children, scruffy and whispering, gather around and watch my strange, alien scrawl. When they start asking questions, I show them my map and point out my route through China. Pointing to the various cities I will ride through, I let them teach me the Chinese pronunciations: Nanjing, Shanghai, Hong Kong. My lunch finished, I ask how much it costs and am humbled when the waitress tells me the meal is on the house.

Before I leave I need to fill my water bottles. China is the first country where I think the water might make me ill. I will have to use my bottle of iodine to purify it. Only two drops are required for one litre of water, but they still make the water taste as if it's come from a swimming pool. However, instead of cold water, the waitress brings me a thermos of boiled water and encourages me to use that. Boiled water is safe (all the germs are killed by the heat), so I fill my bottles and let it cool down as I ride away. I am grateful that I have no need for the iodine yet.

*That night, I find another cheap hotel. There is no shower in the communal bathroom beside my room, so I fill a bucket of cold water from the tap and pour it over myself. I am now carrying just two sets of light clothes. The first is a set for riding. They have already become encrusted with grime and dust from the day's ride. The second is a clean set for the evening. After eating, I decide to explore the town. Rasping men with cigarettes hanging out of the sides of their mouths sit around barbeque street stalls. They sip tea, spit and chew on sticks of meat. Walking on, I see families window-shopping in glass-fronted department stores. After a while, I come across an internet café. Inside, it is musty and full of clunky computers. Pre-teenage boys are playing zombie shoot-'em-up games and shouting at each other. For 10p, I am allowed to go online for half an hour, so I check my emails and do some research for the route ahead.**

'China, China, China,' I write in my diary before I sleep, 'one of those places I always knew about as a child, but it did not seem real until I got here. It is different. Vast. With its own mysterious history

*As the trip progressed I would be surprised by how easy it was to find internet cafés, even in smallish towns in backwater countries. I would also discover that internet cafés across the world were pretty much the same: musty and full of clunky computers and pre-teenage boys playing zombie shoot-'em-up games and shouting at each other. I suppose the boys playing zombie shoot-em-up games in internet cafés I visited in China may well have been playing against the boys playing zombie shoot-'em-up games in the internet cafés I visited in India and Iran two years later.

and civilisation. And now it bounds into the 21st century . . . proud, confident, energetic.'

I realise that where I am right now, in a cheap hotel in a Chinese town (whose name I do not even know), I feel happier than I have done for a long time.

24
'Very boring with a lot of French kissing . . .'

Distance to home = 27,175 miles

Gone are the days when Shanghai was a paradise for imperialist adventurers

ENGLISH TEXT BOOK IN A CHINESE BOOKSHOP (THIS PHRASE WAS USED AS A BASIS FOR EXERCISES TO PRACTISE ENGLISH GRAMMAR)

After a week of riding south, I crossed the Yellow River. It was dark brown and churning. In centuries past, the river had been known as 'the sorrowful river' because so many people drowned in its annual floods. Now, with falling water tables, I heard that some years it only just reached the sea.

On my map, on the other side of the river, there was a town marked Jinan. When I crossed the bridge, I found it was not a town, but a city of five million people. Some friends had invited me to stay in Jinan. But when I arrived, I left Alanis at their house, went down to the train station and caught a train to Beijing. My parents were coming on holiday to China and I was going to meet them.

I met them at their hotel near Tiananmen Square. They looked well and were excited to be in China for the first time. In order to combine sightseeing and some time together, we signed up for a no-frills tour group, and travelled by train around some of China's great historical sites. As we spent time talking, I was able to catch up on news from home, including more news of my dear cousin Rossie, who had been seriously injured in a traffic accident while I was in Korea. I also told them more of my experiences, including what had happened on the night of the fire in Siberia. I knew it could not been easy for them having a son who went off on such escapades, but I was grateful that they were letting me choose my own path in life.

After three happy weeks, it was time for them to return to England and for me to return to the bicycle. An electric storm flashed across the skyline as I hugged them goodbye and boarded the train back to Jinan.

I left Jinan and the Yellow River behind me and lumbered further south through fertile floodplains and undulating, green hills. I still had plenty of contacts, both expat and Chinese, to stay with, and on other nights I stayed in cheap hotels. One evening, I stayed with a Chinese surgeon at the foot of ancient, sacred Mount Taishan; another, in a hostel in Qufu, the town where Confucius was born. I found it hard to grasp the age of the Chinese Empire, so I tried imagining that something even older and bigger than Europe's Roman Empire had actually lasted until modern times.* Thinking of China's more recent history, I sometimes wondered what terrible experiences the older, more wrinkled faces by the roadside might have witnessed first-hand: the Japanese invasions; a prolonged civil war; Mao and his disastrous policies. I had been reading of how, when Mao finally died in 1976, tens of millions of Chinese people had perished in his inadvertent famines, the intelligentsia had been wiped out, and China's economy was smaller than Belgium's.

I continued to find China both a lot of fun and completely confounding. As I rode down a dusty, potholed road one afternoon, a car overtook me at high speed, honking its horn and showering me in

*Throughout most of its history Chinese civilisation had, by many measures, been far superior to its Western counterparts. It pioneered countless innovative technologies centuries before Europe: for farming, the wheelbarrow was invented; for administration, paper and ink; for exploration, the compass; for education, examinations; and, for warfare, gunpowder. Such technological superiority should have set China easily above outside aggressors, but owing to a lack of practical application and a tendency to isolate themselves from the rest of the world, by the time the European 'foreign devils' arrived, China had fallen badly behind. Using wily diplomacy and strategic military force, the Europeans soon bullied the ancient empire into opening its ports for trade.

gravel. I scowled at the car as it disappeared in the dust. Two hundred metres further on, I saw that it had stopped. I pedalled up to it, bracing myself to tell the driver what I thought of his driving. But, as I drew alongside, the driver leant out of his window and with a broad grin handed me a bottle of cold water and gave me the thumbs-up sign. I could not help smiling and giving the thumbs-up sign in return.

After two weeks, the road slid down to the Yangtze River. I turned left and followed it downstream for three days until I arrived in Shanghai. Taking a week off, I spent my days exploring the streets where many different worlds met: old and new; East and West; rich and poor. The street levels were filled with tourists, businessmen and local workers jostling together past Burberry, McDonald's, and cinemas screening *Star Wars III: The Revenge of the Sith.* On the side streets, beneath the shadow of construction cranes, Chinese markets carried out their business as they had done for centuries, though perhaps with a few new products on offer.

One day I walked into a large indoor market where stalls spilled over with clothing, electronics and household products. Passing an area of tables spread with pirated DVDs, I saw that the selection included some films that had only been premiered the previous week in Hollywood. The DVD cases looked quite genuine, so I picked one up and read the review on the back. It was the Denzel Washington film *Man on Fire*, and the first soundbite review stated that: 'This movie is a lesson to any aspiring filmmaker. It has a very nice script, acting and direction.'

It sounded odd for an endorsement. The next one ended in mid-sentence: 'No amount of plastic surgery can save the plot or the creaky ending of this plodding . . .'

The pirates' production line seemed to be using Google to find reviews on the internet, though they clearly did not understand what they meant. I looked through more of the DVDs and their reviews. My favourite one was for the Pierce Brosnan movie, *After the Sunrise*. A bold statement on the case proclaimed that the film was 'Very boring with a lot of French kissing . . .'

Another part of the market displayed outdoor clothing and equipment, mostly manufactured by North Face. Everything was extremely

Year One *Russia*

Year One *Russia*

ear Two *Pakistan*

Year Two *Australia*

Year Three *Malaysia*

Year Three *Tibet*

Year Three *Greece*

Two months past 3rd anniversary on the road *London*

Me, Al and Lenin, the day we set off from Magadan
Russia

A Siberian campsite wearing Siberian gear (note the Royal Mail trousers)
Russia

Day four – we woke up to snow
Russia

The bottom of the scale and it is only October 24th (–40 is the point where the Centigrade and Fahrenheit scales converge)
Russia

Al has a runny nose
Russia

Ve shared the road with
ome unusual vehicles
ussia

Yakut Man
with pony
Russia

Al
Russia

Not quite what I had
anticipated: pushing the
bike through a frozen,
muddy forest
Russia

We must keep going
Russia

The nuns of
Wakkanai
Japan

Inside the Truce Hut in the DMZ.
The soldier is straddling the border
with one foot in North Korea and the
other in South Korea. I am standing
in North Korea
North/South Korea

A farmer takes his products to market
China

Errr... see page 123 for an explanation of this one
China

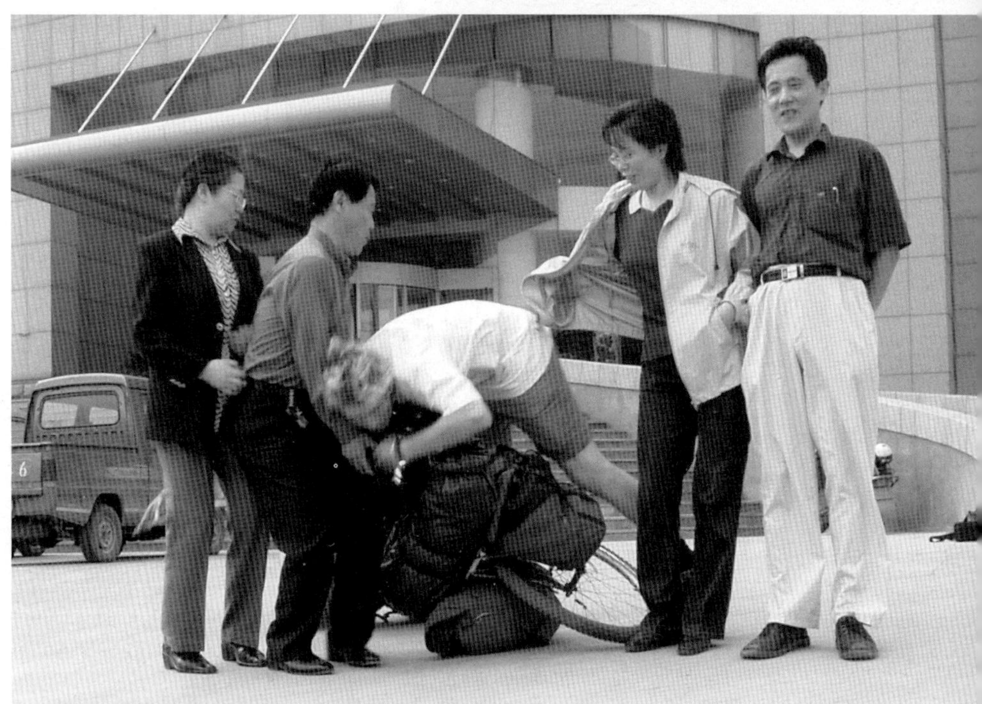

Crossing the South China Sea on *Talio*

A slum in Manila. The round black shape in the water is the back of a man's head. He is swimming in the water, looking for materials to sell for recycling. In the middle of the photo is a little boy with bare feet
The Philippines

The beach road
Papua New Guinea

Carrying the bike through a sea inlet
Papua New Guinea

A track through the jungle
Papua New Guinea

Catching a canoe across a river
Papua New Guinea

John carries Alanis across a
swollen river on the Kokoda Trail
Papua New Guinea

cheap. A Gore-Tex jacket which might have cost £100 in England was selling for £10. I looked more closely at a rucksack and noticed that the stitching was coming undone on one of the straps. Once again, these were imitations. I congratulated myself on spotting the fakes and walked on. It was only later that I began to reflect on my own North Face jackets. I had purchased them cheaply from eBay before I left for Siberia. But, once there, I had been infuriated when the zips started to break in the middle of cold, dark evenings on the road. It dawned on me now that the eBay entrepreneur had probably sourced his products from just such a market as this in China.

Just as Shanghai was famous for attracting adventurers, merchants and other seekers of fortune in the nineteenth century so, in the early twenty-first century, expats were again arriving in huge numbers. One day I met a fellow adventurous English cyclist, Edward Genochio. Edward had cycled out to Shanghai from England the previous year and was now living in the city for a while before cycling home again. On his outward journey, he had received a flood of media attention after his bike was stolen in an unusual manner while he was pedalling across Mongolia.

'I was just going to sleep in my tent in a field near the road,' he said, 'when suddenly I heard a horse neighing outside, and a ripping noise. I unzipped the tent and saw a Mongolian horseman galloping away. My bike was bouncing along behind the horse, tied onto it with a rope!'

The robbery turned out to be great publicity for Edward's ride. As a result, he had been given a new bike by a British bike company, and made good money writing articles for the tabloids. Unrelated to his fame as a cyclist, he confessed that, while in Shanghai, he had also earned some cash by acting as a model for a Chinese toilet-seat manufacturer.

In the plush bars of the city centre I also met the international high-fliers who had come to China for more glamorous work. Many worked for big multinationals. One English girl working for a British advertising firm told me that her job was to persuade the Chinese to consume more. Her new assignment was to persuade them to stop eating their traditional rice porridge breakfast and to try Kellogg's cornflakes with cold milk instead.

Besides those who worked for foreign companies, there were those who had come to China to found their own businesses, with varying degrees of success. A few days beforehand, in the city of Nanjing, I had stayed with a British architect called Rupert. He had come to China to set up an architectural company and told me how tricky it was doing business here. 'Sometimes, when we are commissioned to design just one building, we later find our blueprints being used in the construction of a whole set of buildings!' he laughed good-naturedly. 'But it's not just other companies. Once when we were interviewing a graduate for a job, he produced his portfolio, which included plans that our own company had designed!'

Others had experienced a more trouble-free ascent to wealth on the back of the economic boom. Josh, a young American, had initially come to teach English. While teaching, however, he had become friends with some local Chinese factory owners. The owner of a glass factory told Josh that if he could find clients in the West then he would earn a commission.

'I spent a couple of days surfing the Web and emailing all of the sheet glass wholesalers I could find in Europe,' said Josh. 'I received one reply from a German wholesaler. They asked for a sample, so I sent them one and they liked it. They put in a big order. I now send them a batch of glass every two or three months and make about US$5,000 profit each time.'

In China, this amount of money was a fortune, enough to live like an emperor. Impressed, I asked: 'How many hours a week do you have to work to earn that?'

'Well, most weeks,' said Josh casually, 'I work for about five minutes, maybe ten.'

Glimpsing the world of the 'work hard, play hard' expat life was exciting and made a welcome change from my evenings sitting in village restaurants being stared at. In the villages, where people were so unaccustomed to seeing foreigners, I had constantly been the centre of attention, like a large, colourful and odd-looking fish in a series of tiny ponds. In Shanghai, by contrast, I was a tiny, unnoticed fish, swallowed up in an ocean of glamour and excess.

25
Mr Bean on the back roads of China

Distance to home = 27,175 miles

It is an unnatural business to find yourself in a strange place
with an underutilized brain and no particular reason for being there
and eventually it makes you go a little crazy
BILL BRYSON

On the journey so far I had often faced the dilemma between taking the smooth, direct main roads (which were fast, but tended to be boring), or taking the hilly back roads (which were much slower, but far more interesting). In Japan, South Korea and the first part of China, I had usually stayed on the main roads. As I cycled out of Shanghai, destination Hong Kong, I decided to take the back roads through the mountains. I hoped I would see a different, more traditional, side to China. Having made it beyond Shanghai's vast suburbs on a main road, I stopped at a junction to survey my atlas. A tangle of little red lines wove their way south-west across the pages, so I picked a route, turned off the highway and cycled up into the hills.

As I descended into the next valley, I entered another world. The flat, agricultural plains were replaced by rows of lush, terraced paddy-fields. They climbed the hillsides in steps until near the top they merged with pale-green bamboo forests, or ridges of pines. The air was sweet with the fresh aromas of rural life – a combination of flora, dung and the occasional wok of noodles. The roadside villages were lined with little white houses with black-tiled rooftops. Young women crossed the street in front of me, carrying heavy loads on their backs. Children in bare feet gawped at me from doorways. After the hustle and pollution of the cities, the picturesque countryside made the lives of these peasants seem quaint. But it was clear the people here worked hard to survive.

Old men, shaded by wide-brimmed, cone-shaped hats, stood on the back of wooden ploughs being pulled through the mud by oxen. There was far less traffic around me, and it was a relief to ride in peaceful surroundings. Occasionally the old men yelled or cracked their whips, and the oxen snorted reluctantly as they strained forwards, but otherwise I was riding in near silence.

My daily target was now 65 miles a day, but I was now fit enough to spin through the hills and cover the distance without being too drained. There was little to worry about here and I felt myself beginning to relax and enjoy the ride. I fell into a routine of riding hard all day, taking generous lunch breaks, and staying in a string of towns and villages I'd never heard of in the evenings: Jiaxing, Anji, Sanyang, Yuquin, Sanyang, Dexing, Yugan, Yong Feng, Ji'an, Guidong, Ruchang, Yizhang, Lian Xian.

It was now June, and the temperature was rising steadily. Some mornings, before the sun became too fierce, I rode without a shirt on. Other days, a series of epic thunderstorms rumbled across the valleys. The rain was intense and the cliffs above the road began to crumble and spit muddy, head-sized rocks down into my path. At the sites of bigger landslides, teams of peasant workers used shovels to clear the mud from the road. They did not seem to mind working in the wet conditions, but perhaps they had no choice. Down in the valleys, some of the rivers burst their banks and I had to climb off and wade through the knee-deep water, while crowds of waiting Chinese laughed and cheered me on.

Despite feeling so fit and carefree, I tried to take one day off each week, ideally in a larger town and on a Sunday so that I could visit a local church. When, after a good deal of gesturing and asking around, I finally found it, I would discover that the majority of the congregation were elderly and there were no children at all. I later heard that this was because people under 18 were not allowed to go to church in China.

There were also other laws governing religion in China. The

most significant one was that worship was permitted only in the state-sanctioned (and thus state-monitored and state-controlled) churches. Prior to communism, China had been a popular place for Western missionaries. The growth of the church had been slow but steady, until Mao came to power and all missionaries were forced to leave. It was widely believed that, as had happened in Japan in the seventeenth century, Christianity would then die out, or at least decline.

However, when China began to open up again in the 1980s, Christians outside China were astounded to discover that the church had actually been growing at a rate faster than any church had grown at any time in history. Furthermore, much of this growth was not in the controlled state churches, but in the highly dynamic, illegal and underground 'house' churches. The Christians who joined the underground church faced real danger if they were caught, and thousands were imprisoned or tortured for disobeying the state. However, this seemed only to strengthen their faith and resolve.

Before leaving England, I had seen an exiled Chinese house-church leader, Brother Yun, speaking at a church in Oxford. While in China, he had been imprisoned and beaten many times for his faith, and once he had even had his legs broken by the prison guards. He claimed, however, that in these times of great danger and persecution, God had helped him, and that he had often seen people healed when they were prayed for. The most remarkable incident in his own life had happened while he was serving a long sentence in a maximum-security prison. He had one day found his cell mysteriously unlocked and suddenly felt that his God was telling him it was time to escape. He proceeded to walk through one unlocked door after another until, unseen by the guards, he strode out of the front gate and jumped into a taxi.*

I would have loved to visit a house church while in China, but I knew that, even if I could find one, it would not be a good idea because I would probably draw dangerous attention to the local members. So, instead, I usually went to the official churches. The

*His book, *The Heavenly Man*, recounts these experiences in detail.

services were in Chinese, so I did not understand what was being said, but I was content to sit through the service praying on my own. I could also still enjoy the sense of friendship and fellowship with the elderly people who took my hand and smiled at me before I left.*

From the continuing reaction of people in villages crowding round me whenever I stopped, I presumed that it was rare for foreigners to pass that way. Certainly, for three whole weeks, until I descended to the southern coast opposite Hong Kong, the only non-Chinese face I saw was when I caught sight of my own dishevelled reflection in a grubby hotel mirror. It was also rare to meet someone who spoke English and I noticed that, as a result of all the time on my own, my behaviour was starting to become decidedly strange. In the end I was embarrassing myself on such a regular basis that I came to see myself as a cycling version of Mr Bean.

The first serious Bean moment was the first day I tried wearing my new SPD shoes.† SPDs are the special cyclists' shoes with a metal cleat which clips into a specially designed pedal, thus enabling you to 'pull' as well as 'push' as your legs go round. They increase the efficiency of riding by 10 per cent. After a morning of smooth pedalling, I arrived in a village at lunchtime. As I slowed to a halt, I realised I was unable to pull my feet out of the pedals and so, to the bafflement of the watching crowd, I crashed over onto my side in front of them.

Other Bean-like moments followed on a regular basis. One day, I grabbed hold of a passing tractor to give me a tow. This was a sport that Al and I had attempted before in Peru. We called it trucksurfing. However, on this particular day in China there was a

*In the big cities, there was also a third type of church: the expat church. These were run by foreigners, and permitted by the government provided that Chinese nationals were not allowed in; I had to show my passport to gain admittance.

†My parents had brought me the pedals from the UK and given them to me during their holiday.

strong head wind and, as the tractor accelerated, the wind buffeted my wheels sideways and – like a speeded-up video clip – I shot straight into the drainage ditch. The middle-aged couple driving their tractor up the road behind me laughed and pointed at me as they overtook. A few evenings later I managed to set the flags on my flagpole on fire while I wheeled the bike around some roadside barbeque stalls.

On another occasion, having stopped to ask a throng of people for directions, I swung my leg back onto the saddle in order to set off again. But as I did so I heard a loud ripping sound. The seat of my trousers, which had been wearing increasingly thin in recent weeks, had ripped cleanly open, revealing my very white English bottom to the astonished onlookers.* I quickly sat down and pedalled away without looking back.

Probably most embarrassing of all, though, was the morning I said goodbye to some new friends I had made at a Chinese university. The friends were a mixture of students and officials, and the previous evening they had hosted me in a smart university hotel. They gathered outside the hotel to see me off, and I suggested taking a final self-timer photo of us all together. I put my camera on a wall, started the timer, and ran to pick up Alanis from behind the line-up. As I pushed her into position I realised, too late, that my grip did not allow me to reach the brakes, and I had too much momentum to stop with my feet. I careered into the back of one of the university officials and, at that very moment, the shutter clicked.†

*I had stopped wearing boxer shorts in China as they made me sweat too much.

†See photo pages.

26
The boat and the girl

Distance to home = 25,886 miles

God made man because He loves stories
ELIE WIESEL

The ferry docked and I wheeled Alanis out into the street. Hong Kong! A crowd swept past in both directions and old green trams clattered along the clean grey streets. Air-conditioning blasted from the doorways of fashionable shops and up above there were glittering skyscrapers, interconnected by sky bridges. As I had no Hong Kong money to use a callbox, I asked a passer-by if I could borrow their mobile phone, as had become my habit in mainland China. When three people all said no, it dawned on me that I was now back in a westernised environment where people were naturally suspicious of wild-looking men on bicycles. Eventually a South Asian money-changer said I could use his phone so I called my friend, Chi, who said he would meet me on the harbour waterfront.

Chi was a British-born Chinese, who had moved out to Hong Kong several years previously to work as a banker. We had been friends since working on the same gap-year teaching programme in Zimbabwe. After my month alone in rural China, it was a relief to see someone who knew me.

Chi took me to his apartment. It was on the twenty-third floor of a tall block of flats shaped like a cigarette packet. The block was perched on the side of Victoria Peak, among many other similar buildings which, shoulder-to-shoulder, climbed up the slope like mountaineers. With over six thousand skyscrapers, Hong Kong has more people living and working above the fourteenth floor than anywhere else in the world.

We left Alanis in the basement and caught the lift to his floor. As he opened the door, he gave me a set of keys. 'Treat your time in Hong Kong like an oasis in the midst of your long journey,' he said.

Chi had a lot of friends and enjoyed partying. That evening, to celebrate my arrival, he took me to a night club. Music blasted around disco-lit walls and the sweaty dance floor heaved with drunken energy. It was packed with happy, young professionals of my age, but I felt out of place. My head started to spin and I huddled behind a table in the corner. Within a few minutes I had fallen asleep. Brave explorer though I may have aspired to be, I was clearly no party animal.

Australia was over three thousand miles across the sea from Hong Kong. For a few months I had been doing sporadic research on how to get there. I did not want to fly because it was too easy and I wanted to experience the whole of my route from ground level. But my usual method for crossing long stretches of water – a ferry – would not work either, because there were no ferries from Hong Kong to Australia.

I spread out my map and looked for ideas. There were various exotic-sounding island nations scattered around in the sea to the south of Hong Kong. Even if most of these islands were unconnected by ferries, I thought, there must at least be other vessels such as yachts, fishing boats and cargo ships travelling between them. And so a plan began to emerge: first of all, I would find a passage on a yacht from Hong Kong to the Philippines. Once there, I could cycle and catch local ferries to a southern Filipino island, hitch on a cargo ship to Indonesia and then take another ferry to Papua New Guinea. From there I had to somehow cycle through 500 miles of mountains and jungles to reach the capital and thence hitch one last boat to Australia.

It was a daunting plan with great potential for getting me stranded, so I decided to approach it one step at a time. My initial task was finding a boat to the Philippines. I set about meeting yacht-club representatives and sent out lots of emails. Eventually I was put in touch with a man called Jon.

I went to meet Jon in the sleepy Hebe Haven yacht club, 90 minutes' bus ride from the city. I found him on the pontoon in his shorts and sandals. He was about to take early retirement, he said, and in six weeks would set off in his yacht, *Talio*, to sail her home to England. His first stop would be the Philippines. Because it was typhoon season, he did not want to take his wife and two children on the first leg. He was therefore looking for an adventurous pair of hands to join him. If I was prepared to take my turn on watch, pull the right rope when he asked me to and, by implication, did not mind dying in a typhoon, then I'd be welcome to come on board.

I returned to Chi's house that evening with a huge grin. I had found my first boat.

The following weekend I went with Chi to meet some of his friends at another bar. It was a more stylish venue than the previous week, and had muted lights, low glass tables and ambient dance music. When we reached our table, Chi's friends stood to introduce themselves. I shook their hands and sat down next to a Chinese girl called Christine.

'So what do you do?' I hadn't intended it, but I opened the conversation with my demon chat-up line.

'I'm just finishing training to be a lawyer,' she said, speaking with a slight North American twang.

'I never really understand what lawyers do,' I said, 'but it sounds like a very glamorous job.'

'It is not as glamorous as it sounds,' she said, smiling.

She had skin that shone and smooth black hair. Her eyes were deep and full of kindness. She started asking me about the bike trip. I was used to answering questions about why I was cycling across the world and how I coped with being alone in wild places. But instead of my usual rote answers – wanting to learn about the world and test myself – I found that I was able to talk more freely and honestly with her. I said I actually had no real idea why I was doing the journey, I just was.

We started talking about England. It turned out that she had been studying at Oxford the same year that I had been a teacher there. We discovered that we had once even been at the same church service at the same time. It was a small world, but this was the first time our paths had crossed. Although her family was in Hong Kong, she told me that she was moving to London in three months' time to work for a corporate law firm.

'Well, if you're still there when I get back in two years' time, maybe you could come to my homecoming party,' I said.

'Yes, maybe,' she smiled again.

Her smile was beautiful. I took an awkward sip of my drink, and smiled back. I was suddenly conscious of my huge out-of-control hair, and the fact that I had arrived in the bar wearing my fluorescent yellow windbreaker.

The music continued in the background and the waiter brought more rounds of drinks. The hours flew past and we chatted until 3 a.m. But then it was time to go, so we went our different ways.

I did not know if I would ever see her again, but for the next week I could not stop thinking about her.

Jon had told me that it would be at least another six weeks until the boat was ready for departure. As well as heading down to his yacht club on a regular basis to help out, I found some work on a children's holiday camp. The camp was based on a sandy beach on an island a half-hour's ferry ride from the city centre. My job would be to take groups of ten-to-15-year-olds camping, surfing and mountain biking, and in return I would receive living expenses.

The children who came on the camps were mostly 'city kids' who had never spent a night in a tent before. I got the impression that they had never exerted themselves beyond a mild sweat and had certainly never enjoyed the thrill of plunging their heads into a mountain stream having just dragged their mountain bikes up a steep slope.

On the first night, six of the 20 children were in tears. The next night, there was less crying, but several boys complained they were missing their computer games. On the third day I took them on a longer bike ride, and the complaints were balanced out with laughter and even signs of determination. By the end of the week, the children were full of smiles and sorry to be going home. I enjoyed doing some useful work again and it was good to watch the children learn about adventure, risk-taking and the buzz of pushing themselves outside their comfort zones.

The weekend after my first week on camp I went to another bar with Chi to meet his friends. I had told myself to forget about Christine but the moment I saw her walk into the room I felt my pulse quicken.

Keeping my cool was never my strong point. When she sat next to me, I found myself asking her a barrage of questions. We talked for most of the evening before saying goodbye again.

The following week, I managed to get hold of her email address and wrote, asking her if she would like to have dinner. I knew I would be blowing a month's budget in one evening, but could not miss the opportunity. It was the price of chivalry.

A few days later we found ourselves in an Italian restaurant. Christine said that she had been looking at my website. (A good sign, I thought.)

'I heard about you from Chi before you arrived,' she said. 'Initially, I wasn't too keen to meet you, as I thought because you were cool and well-travelled you would find me too boring as a lawyer.'

'Don't be silly, that's not true,' I said, putting down my fork for a moment.

As the evening continued, Christine started to talk about her real passions in life. She said she wasn't really interested in corporate law and had got into it only after being offered a job while doing well at university. Deep down, she wanted to work with street children in the Philippines, something she had already spent time doing in her holidays.

At the end of dinner, Christine insisted on paying for the meal as she had just received her bonus. I gave in quite gladly.

After walking her back to the foot of her block of flats, we said goodnight.

She's an extraordinary girl, I thought to myself as I walked home, but my circumstances are just not right to start anything. I had a rather counter-cultural view about relationships instilled in me by my faith and so, although from time to time on my journey it had been tempting, I was definitely not looking for a quick fling.

I told myself I had been stupid to even let my emotions get as far as they had.

If I was to see her again, it would be because I was trying to start a proper relationship.

Which given the circumstances was pretty unlikely.

But, knowing how rare it was for me to meet someone I really liked, and aided by my increasingly 'of course it's not impossible' attitude to life, I persuaded myself that I had to see her again.

The day after the meal we arranged to meet again and ended up meeting almost every day that week. The following weekend I bought her a bunch of flowers and that evening, sitting on the rocks on Stanley beach in the typhoon rain, I kissed her for the first time.

Because of delays with making the boat ready, the six weeks that Jon had predicted ended up doubling to 12. Now that I had met Christine, I was glad about having to wait. We saw each other most days. When we met for lunch outside her skyscraper she would arrive looking smart and beautiful, while I turned up covered in salt and sand, fresh from the kids' camp. We went for long, late walks, we talked for hours and we visited many of the outlying islands by ferry. They were special days, but we knew that in no time at all reality would have to kick in.

As the time neared for me to go, we began to be filled with angst about what we should do. I had spoken to enough older, wiser people to know that, however permanent it felt, falling in love was a temporary thing. We had known each other for only eight weeks, and while I would soon be departing on a yacht for the Philippines, Christine would be flying thousands of miles in the opposite direction to London. It would probably take me two years to get home. That was a very long time. Waiting for each other would be a huge and difficult risk to take. I had been living a life full of physical risks over the past year, but taking a risk with my emotions seemed even more difficult.

Discussing our options, sitting at a tram station late one night, we knew that, apart from just breaking up now, we could put it on hold for two years, or we could try and keep it going long-distance. While my emotions definitely wanted to keep it going, and the thought of breaking up pained me very much, I also knew there were no guarantees it would work out even if we did stay together until I got back. I said all this to Christine.

Christine's pretty forehead furrowed for a moment. Then she replied, 'I guess there are no guarantees of anything in life, are there?'

We sat in silence for a while. Then I tentatively asked Christine if she might be able to come and visit me on a holiday when I reached Australia. We could then reassess how things were, and plan to meet again if we wanted to.

'It would be quite a risk to take,' I said, 'but if we're prepared to take the risk, then we could try and keep this going . . .?' Christine had recently been telling me that she was naturally risk-averse, so I was not sure how she would respond.

She smiled at me. Then she nodded.

Statistics for Part 3 (Japan–Hong Kong)

Dates:	December 2004–October 2005
Total distance covered from start:	9,292 miles
Distance left to reach home:	25,886 miles
Distance covered by bicycle:	4,343 miles
Distance covered by boat:	930 miles
Age:	28
Number of traffic lights went through in Tokyo:	Over 100
Nights in train stations/public toilets:	10
Nights in tent:	5
Average cost of a hotel room in China:	£1.50

Part Four

Hong Kong–The Philippines–Indonesia–Papua New Guinea

October 2005–March 2006

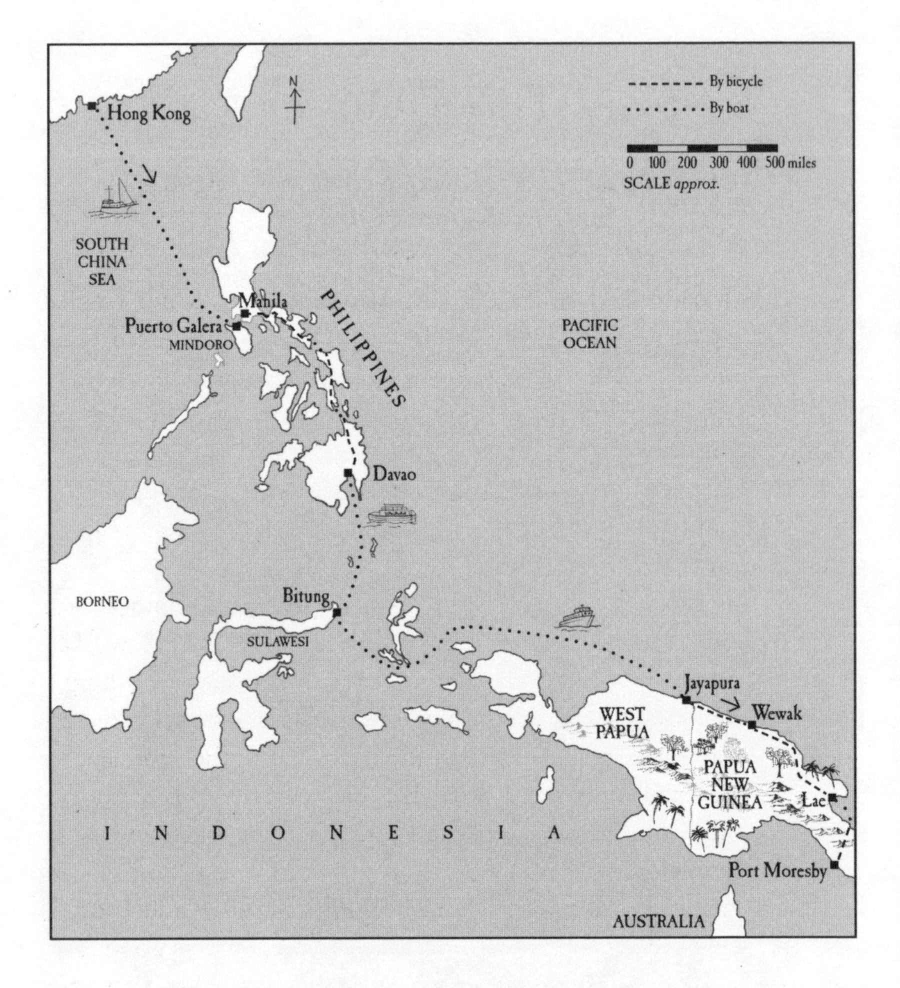
By bicycle
By boat
0 100 200 300 400 500 miles
SCALE approx.
N
Hong Kong
SOUTH
CHINA
SEA
Manila
PHILIPPINES
Puerto Galera
MINDORO
PACIFIC
OCEAN
Davao
BORNEO
Bitung
SULAWESI
Jayapura
Wewak
WEST
PAPUA
PAPUA
NEW
GUINEA
Lae
I N D O N E S I A
Port Moresby
AUSTRALIA

27
Six days in the life of a Siberian sailor

Distance to home = 25,886 miles

. . . but I would be content with nothing but going to sea
ROBINSON CRUSOE

Sounds of drilling, hammering and occasional swearing rippled across the pontoons of the Hebe Haven yacht club on the Sai Kung peninsula. The sweltering noontime sun beat down and the summer haze drifted out across the sea, merging with the sky on the horizon. We were hard at work making *Talio* ready for the voyage. We equipped her with new radars on her mast, extra food supplies in her holds and spare fuel cans strapped to her deck. It felt as if we were preparing for battle.

With his casual confidence and easy swagger, Jon reminded me of an un-institutionalised version of James Bond. As we worked together on the boat, he told me that after 'being a bit of a hippy' in his student days, he had stumbled into an international career as a geological surveyor, working in Lesotho, Colombia and Papua New Guinea. He married a local Papuan journalist, Liz, and 13 years ago they had moved to Hong Kong where he started work as a landslide engineer.

'I was 37 when we moved here,' he said wistfully, 'and I didn't expect we would stay for very long. But the money was good, and then we had a baby, so we stayed for a while. Then we had another baby, so we stayed a while longer. Now I'm 50 and I wonder where the time has gone.'

As well as taking early retirement, Jon and Liz wanted to move back to England to put their boys through secondary school. Thus Jon now had the perfect excuse to sail *Talio* home.

Apart from some messing about in dinghies as a boy, I was not an experienced sailor. I was in good company with Steve, the only other crew member. Like me, Steve was English, in his late twenties, and always struggled to remember how to tie a bowline. He was an engineer in Hong Kong, but spent weekends paragliding, scuba diving or trying some other extreme adventure sport.

Eventually, on 8 October 2005, with the boat fully loaded and my dismantled bike squeezed into a spare sleeping hold below deck, we were ready to leave. I had left Hong Kong Island for the final time that morning, hugging Christine goodbye at the gate of a subway station. I felt excited to be getting on with the journey again, but my heart was heavy about leaving her. Al, who had now made it to Turkey, sent me a chirpy email saying 'I have been looking at my atlas and worked out that if you continue to cross the lines of longitude at your current rate, you will not arrive home until 2018!' The future seemed a strange mixture of sadness and excitement.

At the yacht club, Jon started the engine. We waved heroically to the small crowd of well-wishers as we cast off the bow ropes and chugged towards the open seas. After a three-month break, the next leg of my journey was finally under way.

As we left the shelter of the mainland, the wind became stronger. The hull leaned over steadily: crash, whoosh, bounce; crash, whoosh, bounce. We ploughed through the waves and the sea thumped and splashed against our side. I was perched to the right of the cockpit, while Steve was on the left, and Jon, captain-like, sat behind the wheel. He steered us confidently through a line of supertankers, giving us sporadic orders to tighten a rope or check an instrument.

After an hour under sail, an awareness began to silently creep through me: I was feeling seasick. The ominous sensation of tingling fingers and a tightening oesophagus made me shuffle towards the cabin door. I leaned out to breathe the fresh air. Steve noticed that I was turning pale and called across to ask if I was all right.

'I'm feeling a bit siiiiiiiurggghhhhhwerrrwerwg . . .' A sudden convulsion stirred deep inside and, with a loud groan, my guts hurled a mixture of that morning's breakfast and last night's dinner up out of my mouth and over the gunwale into the sea. I sat gasping for breath and vomiting for an hour, fearing that I would feel like this for the whole week. Occasionally I spat to try and remove the taste of vomit, but mostly I concentrated on trying to be completely still. Even moving my eyes set off another bout of nausea. My discomfort was exacerbated further by being embarrassed that I could not help with sailing the boat. Jon suggested that I lie down below. Lying horizontal helped and I slept until the next morning.

When I awoke I could hear the sound of knocking and rushing water under our keel. I climbed up to the cockpit and saw that the outlying islands had now disappeared. The sea had turned dark and sank away below us like a chasm. I was feeling better and took my first shift on watch behind the wheel that morning. As the day wore on my nausea disappeared entirely, and I ate a hearty meal before bed. At 4 a.m., Steve woke me for my first turn on night watch. Under the darkness, I felt as if we were in the middle of an epic poem: our 17-tonne, 36-foot steel craft crashing through the deep seas, an empty, endless horizon stretching on forever in every direction.

The next three days passed by easily. We were kept busy, either taking our turn on watch, or doing chores. The most dramatic task was cooking. Below deck, with the boat keeling over at 45 degrees and continuing to bounce violently over the waves, I secured myself by wedging my legs between the sink and the galley panels as if attempting the splits. Lighting the stove, I tried to keep the pan of chicken sizzling while simultaneously avoiding getting boiling fat thrown all over my sweaty, bare chest. As I reached over for the pepper, the boat lurched sideways and under the force of gravity I lost my footing and tumbled backwards across the cabin and landed with a crash against a cupboard. A kitchen drawer slid from its holding and emptied cutlery all over the floor. I could see Jon and Steve looking down at me lying on the floor with concerned expressions on their faces. Mr Bean at sea, I thought to myself.

As the days passed, the GPS showed that we were travelling at a good rate. By our fifth morning, the wind died, the skies cleared and the ocean turned turquoise. We began to see signs of land. First of all it was the precarious little Filipino fishing skiffs with home-made wooden outriggers, darting around in the distance. Then I noticed some coconuts in the water. One coconut floated past with a little crab sitting on top of it. The wind dropped and for the next two days we continued under engine power. However, the engine had a tendency to break down every three or four hours. This required Jon, who was the only person who knew how to fix it, to squeeze his head and torso through a small hatch under the cabin stairs into the oily engine compartment. Once there, he had to 'bleed' the engine. Jon's profanities drifted up to the cockpit where Steve and I sat, raising our eyebrows at each other and trying not to smile. With all the constant maintenance, I reflected to Steve that sailing the high seas on a long-term basis was probably not the type of exploring for me. I had just read a book by a famous solo round-the-world sailor, Webb Chiles, which described his impressive jousts with wind and waves over many years. However, for me, the most interesting part of the book was when he had been shipwrecked on a Pacific island and was taken care of by the local people. For me, I said to Steve, it was people and land, rather than fixing things and being alone at sea, that made me come alive.

On our sixth day at sea, we sighted grey shades of mountains rising from the edge of the world. A puff of onshore wind began to blow. With stubbled grins on our faces, we raised the sails and steered *Talio* into a bay of sandy beaches and tropical palm trees.

28
The street children of Manila

Distance to home = 24,949 miles

If we do not act, we shall surely be dragged down the long, dark, and shameful corridors of time reserved for those who possess power without compassion, might without morality, and strength without sight
MARTIN LUTHER KING JR

19–31 OCTOBER 2005
Thursday morning, 6 a.m., Puerto Escondido: I wrap my trousers, passport and wallet inside a bin bag and throw it overboard, before shaking hands with Jon and diving in after it. We arrived two days ago and anchored in the middle of the bay. Last night I took Alanis ashore in Jon's dinghy and locked her in a restaurant storeroom. I now feel that swimming to the beach would be a fitting way to begin the next leg of the journey. As I near the land, I push the bag in front of me and a narrow ferry boat skids across the still morning water. The passengers are school children in smart, yellow uniforms, and they look down at me as they motor past.

I reach the shore and set off on Alanis, but instead of following the chain of islands directly south in the direction of Australia, I ride north for a day to Manila. I want to visit the capital because there are a number of children's projects there which are linked to Viva, the charity I am raising funds for. They had invited me to come and spend some time with them to see their work first-hand.*

*

*The projects are linked to the Philippines Children's Ministries Network, Viva's Filipino partner organisation.

Sunday morning in Manila: smog and noise rise from a vast, elongated traffic jam which snakes between a glamorous shopping mall and an ugly slum. I am struggling to push my way through the mass of people and keep up with my Filipino friend, Pastor Romi. He walks ahead of me through the jumble, leading the way to church. We cross the main road on an overpass and are funnelled down a one-way staircase. Halfway down the steps I notice a collection of children sitting against the wall by our feet. They have dirty baby faces and unevenly shaved heads. They are between four and ten years old and their grubby hands hold up broken plastic cups for money. For a moment my eyes meet theirs, and then I look away.

But one little boy has spotted me and now he hops to his feet and runs up beside me. His little hand takes hold of the side of my trousers as I walk and he offers his cup up towards me. He does not say anything, but his face is a contorted scowl and his big brown eyes are imploring.

'I cannot give to you, little man,' I think to myself. 'You may be being asked to beg for someone else. I have heard all about the begging cartels which use street children to do their begging. Anything I give you may be snatched away, meaning you never get to see it.' But the little boy keeps walking with me, and now his hand is pointing not to his cup but to a convenience store stacked with cheap food. But I will not stop. I cannot lose my guide. We are already late. Suddenly the boy turns and leaves me with my excuses, and walks back with a bowed head to his begging spot by the stairs. He is still hungry. I continue on my way, feeling tearful and guilty.

*Wednesday morning: the car pulls up outside a cemetery. 'We're here,' says Craig, an English man in his early forties who works with street children in the city.**

We walk through a rusty gate into a maze of stone slabs. Twenty metres ahead of us, three boys are leaning against a wall. They watch us approach. They recognise Craig and are pleased to see him, and he speaks to them calmly in Tagalog. The boys stare at

*I had been introduced to Craig by a teacher in Manila. The website of his charity is www.ascf.ph

me and seem to be asking Craig who I am. They wear ragged T-shirts and shorts and have infected wounds on their legs. The pupils of their eyes are dilated. In their hands they clutch balls of tissue which they periodically hold up to their noses and sniff.

'They're inhaling glue,' Craig says, looking at them sadly. 'It's cheaper than food and suppresses their appetite. It is a way for them to escape their pain, but over time it will destroy their immune system and give them brain damage. Drugs, crime and violence are daily experiences for these children.'

One of the boys clasps hold of my hand. His grip is sweaty, and I can smell that he has not washed for a long time. Together, the boys and I follow Craig further into the cemetery. Rounding a corner of tombstones we see many more children, though these seem to be too drugged-up to notice us. Some of them are young, maybe five years old. Several are asleep, lying on top of the gravestones in the burning morning sun. A young teenage girl shares ones slab with a pale, feverish-looking baby.

When I ask Craig why the children live here, he says that at least in the cemetery they are usually undisturbed. He says that some are from very poor families whose parents have thrown them out, some are orphans and many have been so badly abused at home that they ran away.

Behind the graves, I see a ten-year-old girl sitting alone in the shade. Her elbows are rested on her knees, and she is staring forward into space. Her eyes are empty. Something about her gaze makes me think, not of a child, but of an 80-year-old who is tired of life.

I had several such brief glimpses into the world of the street children at risk in Manila. After my daily excursions, I could go back to my American host's air-conditioned apartment on the rich side of town. The children had nowhere to live, no one to look out for them except each other, and they had no possessions but the ripped clothes they were wearing. And this was the tip of the iceberg. There were over 50,000 street children in Manila and, according to UNICEF, over 100 million in the world as a whole. They also state there are over one million child soldiers, two million child prostitutes and 40 million children working in exploitative workplaces.

But it would be wrong to suppose that people in Manila were unmoved by suffering children. Many, such as Pastor Romi and Craig, worked night and day to help them. They ran day-centres offering health checks, food and clean clothes. They supported poverty-stricken families so that they could take their children back, or not have to throw them out in the first place. If it was dangerous to reconcile children with their families, they provided residential homes where the children could come to live, be educated and find a new family.

I went to visit some projects. They were full of laughter and happy smiles, and felt more akin to loving homes than institutions. 'You can tell if the children in a home are happy by how much noise they make,' said one staff member. 'Noisy children are happy children.' Many of the staff members were ex-street children themselves and their dedication and care were amazing to see. They were the true heroes and heroines of the world. However, I also noticed they were often exhausted. It was understandable. Street children, with their incredibly pain-filled backgrounds, cannot be easy to work with. I found being a teacher of 'normal' English children was tiring enough – to look after these children must have required superhuman strength. They also worked very long hours, sometimes 12 hours a day, 365 days a year. I heard that projects were often started by churches or local people who could not bear to see the misery on their doorsteps. But, untrained, under-resourced and out of their depth, these projects frequently floundered and closed within a couple of years, as the severity of the issues was too much to handle.

Viva are deeply involved with working to help children around the world, but, rather than opening new projects, they work to strategically help the projects that already exist. They do this by helping to network projects together so that they can pool expertise and resources. They also channel funding to the best projects and support the staff by running retreats, providing training and giving encouragement.

What I saw in Manila convinced me of the impact of their work in helping more children to be reached more effectively. Through giving slideshows at schools and rotary clubs, and through donations via my website, I had recently passed my original fund-raising goal. Now I was even more determined to reach double that target.

29
The Al-Jamar

Distance to home = 24,011 miles

If we don't offer ourselves to the unknown, our senses dull . . .
we wake up one day and find that we have lost our dreams in order
to protect our days
KENT NERBUR

The cargo ship *Al-Jamar* was 40 metres long, with a yellow-painted hull, two decks and a roof. The captain, who had a three-day stubble, and chest hair emerging from his shirt, accepted my 50-dollar bill and ordered a teenage boy to carry Alanis into the hold. I took my panniers onto the upper deck, lay down with a book, and waited for the boat to depart. It was my twenty-ninth birthday that day. Exactly a year previously I had been with Al on the boat from Sakhalin to Japan.

I thought back on the past few weeks during which I had cycled and island-hopped down through the humid tropics, the length of the Philippines. The roads had been mostly smooth, though often congested with noisy traffic, especially the Filipino public buses – *jeepneys* – so called because they resembled long, stretched jeeps. The people in the towns had looked after me well. Most nights I was invited to stay in the roadside Catholic churches, though sometimes the evangelicals took me in. On one occasion, I was hosted by the Seventh Day Adventists. I liked staying with priests and pastors both for practical reasons – they were likely to speak English and they were hopefully trustworthy – and also because I enjoyed talking about deep issues with them.

One night my hosts contacted the local TV studio, who turned up in a large car to interview me and filmed me riding around the town's main street. The feature was broadcast on the national news programme. From that point on I received many more invitations to stay.

When I reached the southern island of Mindanao I waited two weeks for the *Al-Jamar* to depart. I was invited to stay in the spare room of a household of Filipino graduates. Unfortunately, after I had been staying there a few nights, I was robbed for the second time on my trip. I had woken up in the middle of the night to see someone in my room. I assumed one of the graduates had left something in the closet, but when I mumbled a sleepy hello the man suddenly turned and ran out, slamming the door behind him.

I frowned, clambered out of bed and walked into the hallway. The man had gone, but I saw my trousers lying in a heap on the floor. I picked them up and noticed my wallet was missing from the pocket. Downstairs I found the front door was open and the thief had fled. I woke the household and everyone expressed their shock. After a discussion the housemates concluded that a thief must have broken in from the outside and stolen my wallet.

I felt angry that I had been robbed again, but tried to be grateful that I was unharmed. Night-time robbers were dangerous in the Philippines. A pastor in Manila had told me that his brother's throat had been slit by such an intruder. I had also not lost much money because the wallet that had been stolen was my 'mugger's wallet' – my day-to-day wallet, which contained only a small amount of money and an out-of-date credit card. After the robbery in Russia, I knew this would be enough to keep most would-be robbers happy. My real wallet, with the genuine bank cards and more money, was hidden deep in my panniers.

For the remainder of my nights in that house, I pushed my bed against the door before I slept.

A few days later, while I was still waiting for the boat, Christine happened to be back in Hong Kong for work. She managed to take some time off to fly over to meet me. I was so happy to see her and we went to a beach for three days to chill out and catch up.

In the taxi on the way back to the airport I was trying to put on a brave face, but I saw she was already crying.

I didn't know what to say at the departure gate, so I just said, 'I'll miss you.'

'I'll miss you too,' she said. 'I'll be praying for you.' And then she turned and was gone.

I sat down in the car park outside the airport, and my eyes started to brim over. I would not see her again for at least four months and even that was assuming she would come to meet me in Australia. It dawned on me how different and how much more difficult the rest of the trip might be now I had a girlfriend.

A few days later I rode down to the quayside and boarded the *Al-Jamar.*

The tranquil sea lapped gently against our hull as we chugged southwards, while I lay on the deck reading my book. The sun sauntered across the blue sky at a leisurely pace and we passed beneath a chain of green volcanic islands releasing twirls of black smoke into the atmosphere. Sometimes I caught sight of fishing boats or freighters shifting across the still horizon. The Indonesian crew spent their time smoking cigarettes on their hammocks or playing cards. At mealtimes they shared their plates of rice and fish with me. Each day at dusk, they lined up and knelt down, bowing their faces Mecca-wards, towards the boiling sun as it slipped beneath the western horizon. Indonesia would be my first Muslim-majority country of the expedition.

We sighted land after four days of relaxed voyaging. Apprehension began to rise in me again and a few hours later we pulled into Bitung, a port on the Indonesian island of Sulawesi. I slept on the floor of the port police station for three nights until the ferry to New Guinea arrived. It resembled an enormous metal anthill with people swarming in and out through a mass of little doorways. A young Indonesian policeman called Ratul helped me carry Alanis up a broad gangway and we pushed through the crowds and into the warren of compartments. Finding some floor space, I laid out my roll mat once again. This would be my home for five more days at sea.

The ferry chugged eastwards, stopping once a day at a different Indonesian island. Occasionally I took a walk onto the deck for some fresh air and to see our progress. As far as I could see, of the thousands of passengers, I was the only Caucasian on board. The other passengers were split between Indonesians, with their straight, black hair, and Papuans, with their tightly curled hair and very dark skin. The word 'Papuan' actually came from a Malay word meaning curly.

The island of New Guinea came into view on our fifth day. New Guinea was divided down the middle. The western half was part of Indonesia, and called West Papua.* The eastern half was a separate country, Papua New Guinea. Feeling a strong sense of awe, I looked across at the tropical waterfront. Mountains rose up out of the sea like a green wall, covered in rainforest. Clouds obscured the tops of the mountains and down on the shoreline smoke rose from a cluster of wooden houses. It looked mysterious and menacing. I wondered if my plan to cross the island overland would work.

*Formerly Irian Jaya.

30
'I don't mean to be negative but . . .'

Distance to home = 21,941 miles

I should warn you that travel in Papua New Guinea can be quite dangerous – I have been held at gunpoint and robbed 16 times, and have been caught in crossfire from warring tribes using M-16s and the like . . . I don't mean to be negative but I'm sure you would want to make informed decisions on where you travel

EMAIL FROM A MISSIONARY IN PAPUA NEW GUINEA

The air was warm and the night felt alive as I joined the jostling crowds and wheeled Alanis down a huge gangplank onto the concrete harbour. The ferry had reached Jayapura, the provincial capital of West Papua. It was 22 December and I had been invited to spend Christmas with some English teachers from America. I was looking forward to some time to rest on dry land after the claustrophobic ferry. After that, I would cross the border into Papua New Guinea, 20 miles away.

Four days later, on Boxing Day, I set off. The road wound along a cliff top and overlooked a long, empty beach. Then it turned inland and flattened into a swampy, well-populated valley. The village houses were raised three metres from the ground by wooden stilts and their sides were made of planks with corrugated iron roofs. Naked children laughed and jumped in and out of a shallow irrigation stream. I saw a bare-chested man in shorts standing poised above a large pond with his bow and arrow. He was staring intently into the water for fish and did not look up as I cycled past.

At the end of the valley I continued into some hills covered in jungle. A newly built bridge crossed a swollen river. As I neared the top of the hill, the jungle drew back to reveal a cluster of houses.

I always felt anxious when crossing borders that were off the tourist routes. The less significant the border, the more likely the immigration officials were to have delusions of grandeur.

Three Indonesian soldiers in combat gear rose to their feet and watched me approach. Their uniforms were clean and well ironed. The first was smoking a cigarette, the second was wearing a shiny digital watch and the third had a large machinegun hanging around his neck. They waved me to a halt. I showed them my best smile, and made a bad joke about how hot it was and how much I was sweating. They looked unimpressed so I used hand signals and mentioned place names to explain my journey. They gradually relaxed and, after another man had used my camera to take a photo of the four of us posing together, they let me through.

The newly built immigration building was large and made from glass and metal. I could see an empty hallway through the window, but the door was locked. Some men, playing cards in a hut beside it, told me that the immigration official was visiting his family because it was Boxing Day.

I asked them when he would be back.

They looked at each other and said, 'Soon,' though it was clear from their faces that they had no idea. When I pressed them further they admitted it would probably be the following day.

I had been thinking and worrying about entering Papua New Guinea for several months, and I felt impatient to get on with it. But I knew there was no point blaming the card players, so I accepted their offer to sleep on the floor that night. I sat on a wall to write my diary. A woman in a colourful dress and with Papuan hair walked past with her two children. The men did not even look up and she made no attempt to go into the immigration building. I saw several other women coming in from the other direction. For those whose villages straddled the border, it seemed that the international boundary was simply ignored.

A few moments later, a motorbike appeared. It was the immigration official. He had decided to come back from his holiday early. I dug out my passport and followed him into the building. He sat at his desk and started rummaging through his drawer. He found a stamp, took my passport and stamped it. I looked at it and saw he had given me another 'in' stamp for Indonesia. He thought I was arriving *from* Papua New Guinea. I told him that, actually, I needed an 'out' stamp. He rummaged through his drawer again, now clearly annoyed with me for making him do extra work. Finding the correct stamp, he stamped me 'out' and waved me through impatiently.

There was a mile of no-man's-land to ride across. It was a newly paved road, though it was not yet open to cars. The immigration building on the Papua New Guinean side was a simple brick hut. The border guard insisted that I wash Alanis with the tap as she was covered in mud. I took the opportunity to fill my water bottles. Beside the tap was a sign warning that the Agency for Environmental Health had tested the water tank and discovered that it was contaminated with *E. coli* bacteria. I would need to use my iodine to purify my water in Papua New Guinea.

I showed my newly cleaned bike to the official. He asked me where I was riding to.

'To the capital, Port Moresby,' I said, smiling.

'There is no road to the capital.' He was blank-faced.

'I will take my bike along the paths in the jungle, and I can use boats if I have to.'

The official shook his head. 'It is not possible.'

'Well, I would like to try,' I said.

He shrugged and handed back my passport. 'Welcome to Papua New Guinea, then,' he said. 'Be careful.'

I freewheeled away from the border and down to a beach. Children were playing in the surf, using pieces of driftwood to ride the waves. I followed the road back up into the forest. Walls of thick vegetation rose around me like barricades. I felt as though the trees were watching me. I reached the brow of a small hill and gazed up at the giant trees beside the road. Their strong, thick trunks rose boldly out of the undergrowth. I wondered what strange creatures might live hidden there. Glancing back at the road I suddenly saw a snake slithering across a metre in front of me. It was a foot long, and had a strip of bright yellow squares down its back. I closed my eyes, forgot to brake and yelped. Alanis rolled onwards and over the top of the snake. I opened my eyes and looked behind me to see the poor creature limping towards the side of the road in a series of jerks. I think I had broken its back.

'Concentrate, you idiot!' I said aloud, unnerved but relieved I had not been bitten.

Even though five of the world's top 20 most poisonous snakes lived there, snakes were actually fairly far down the list of things I was worried about in Papua New Guinea. While researching my route to Australia, I had received a wide range of reasons for pessimism from a wide variety of well-wishers. Many said it would be difficult, dangerous and perhaps even impossible country to cycle through. For some reason, however, I had felt strongly drawn to it.

My first worries were about which route to take. The rainy season was due to begin within a month. Many of the roads were unpaved or unbridged, or both; this meant they could be traversed only in the dry season. There were also parts of the country that, according to my vague, country-scale map, had no roads at all.

Higher than my route worries, though, was my fear of being attacked or murdered. I had received emails from a number of concerned expatriates who lived in the cities, or worked in the gold business or as missionaries. As well as the missionary who had been robbed at gunpoint 16 times, other warnings included:

*He is f****** mad. But then again mad dogs and Englishmen (where is he from?) . . . Please pass on my best regards if you see him before he heads off and attempts this and maybe take the contact details of his family back home in case he never arrives here in Port Moresby.*

I worked in the 'security' business over there . . . and it is the wild west, with no back-up.

The FCO website said: 'Law and order remains poor or very poor in many parts of the country; armed carjackings, assaults, robbery, shootings and serious sexual offences are common.'

More encouraging, though more elusive, was the email that simply said: 'Expect the unexpected . . . I mean it.'

The reason for the pessimism, I discovered, were the gangs of thugs, known as rascals. Their endearing title was deceptive because the rascals actually had a well-earned reputation for extreme brutality. In the villages they were armed with knives and in the cities, with guns. Often the guns were home-made and consisted of a pipe and a bullet, which they would set off by hitting it with a nail. They were infamous for hijacking cars and buses, and frequently murdered their victims.

When I stayed with the English teachers on Christmas Day, a middle-aged American lady who had come round for lunch asked me point-blank what I suspected everyone wanted to ask: 'What will you do when you meet the rascals?'

It was a good question. I told her that I had tried to make myself less of a target in lots of clever ways: I had sent home my digital camera and was carrying plastic disposable ones instead; I had grown a bushy beard, would wear only my scruffiest clothes and had natural dreadlocks in my hair – all of which would make me look like a vagabond. Furthermore, I explained, I had borrowed a paint brush and painted Alanis a dirty brown colour. Surely my unexpected and dishevelled appearance would stun any would-be attackers into stillness for long enough for me to nip past unharmed. As for the nights, could I not befriend the village chiefs and so stay under their protection?

The American lady nodded politely but looked very unconvinced. For some reason, when people thought I could not do something, it made me more determined than ever.

'But, above all,' I said, smiling, 'I suppose I hope I just don't meet any rascals.'

I continued down the road, and it was almost dark when it led out of the forest and up to the waterfront town of Vanimo. A police car drove up alongside me. They wanted to know who I was.

I explained I was cycling to Port Moresby, and asked if they knew where an Australian called John lived. They did, and escorted me to his house. John was about 40 years old and ran one of the town supermarkets. We had been in touch by email and he was expecting me. Over dinner, he was optimistic about my chances of getting through.

'Ahhr, you'll be fine,' he drawled reassuringly. 'Don't let those pansies who work for the mines and travel around in helicopters frighten you off. But be careful of the malaria. I caught it again last year, and it just sapped all the energy outta me. I could barely climb the steps of my own home for three weeks.'

I made a mental note that, as well as avoiding the rascals, dodging the snakes and not getting lost in a jungle, I must remember to take my malaria pills. With these thoughts swimming around my mind, I set off early the next morning along the 'loggers' road'. John had confidently assured me that, though he had never driven on it, this would bring me directly to the next coastal town of Aitape by nightfall.

If only it had been that easy.

31
Lost

Distance to home = 21,885 miles

For ten years we in the Tory Party have become used to Papua New Guinea-style orgies of cannibalism and chief-killing, and so it is with a happy amazement that we watch as the madness engulfs the Labour Party

BORIS JOHNSON, 6 SEPTEMBER 2006

I do not in any way wish to dissent from the proposition that the Papua New Guineans live lives of blameless, bourgeois domesticity . . . modern Papua New Guineans, that is

BORIS JOHNSON, TWO DAYS LATER
(IN AN APOLOGY FOR OFFENCE CAUSED TO THE PEOPLE OF PAPUA NEW GUINEA)

The loggers' road led inland, back into the jungle. Within half an hour, the paved tarmac surface turned into a smooth clay surface. I passed through several villages. The people stared at me. I gave them a friendly wave and rode onwards without stopping.

One solitary truck drove past me that morning. When afternoon arrived, there were no more villages. I ate some crisps and biscuits for lunch, Christmas presents from my American hosts a few days previously. Their safe, hospitable home seemed a long time ago now and I suddenly felt very alone. The forest was thick. I could not see into it. Occasionally, I heard the sound of heavy wings flapping and looked up to see pairs of birds with huge beaks shimmering across the hot sky. I needed to go to the loo, so I laid the bike against the verge, took some toilet roll from my pannier and ventured a few metres into the trees. It was dark under the canopy, and there were a few shrubs, but there was still space for me to squat. The forest was so full of life, with buzzing and humming, but it was not concerned by my presence. I felt threatened by it. As if it would consume me and nobody would ever know what happened to me.

As the afternoon wore on, I ran out of water. I had not filled my bottles in the villages as I usually would have done because I was feeling scared, and suspected everyone of being a rascal. I stopped in the middle of the empty road and pulled out my map of Papua New Guinea. It was not detailed, and was country-scale. The road was shown by a vague, red-dotted line through the forest. There were no villages marked at all. I finished the final trickle of water from my bottle and did not know what to do. I could hear some water trickling through the jungle nearby, but I did not feel brave enough to enter the undergrowth to look for it.

Increasingly hot and thirsty, I pedalled on. Passing some deep tyre ruts by the side of the road which were filled with murky water, I crouched down and used my sunhat to filter out the green slime and fill my bottle. I started to wonder what I would do that night. I had bought a small, lightweight tent in Hong Kong, and had a lightweight sleeping bag, but I had sent my stove home. With all my worries about rascals, I had forgotten to buy a decent supply of emergency food. The road led on, winding up and down through the forest. I had no choice but to keep going.

In mid-afternoon, I heard a car approaching. It was an open-backed jeep, carrying at least a dozen people. I flagged them down. They told me there was a village coming up and then drove off rapidly, leaving me on my own again. The village was much poorer than the ones I had seen by the coast. The corrugated iron roofs had been replaced by leaves. The children who stood staring at me were dressed in dirty, torn T-shirts. Several of them had skin rashes across their faces. A man who spoke English ordered the children to fill my bottles, and gave me some slices of papaya. The village did not return my smile as I waved and set off again.

Shortly before dusk, I reached a fork in the road and decided to follow the right-hand track because it looked much more worn. A few minutes later I reached a settlement of makeshift shacks. A man with a beard urged me to stop. He told me he was a logger, and his name was Bit. Bit lived here with his wife and three children. I explained where I was trying to go, and asked how far it was to Aitape. He said it was still a very long way, but invited me to stay the night in his shack.

While his wife prepared us a meal, I took my two anti-malarial doxycyline pills, tucked my socks into my trousers and doused myself in repellent. Bit nodded knowingly when I told him that I was hoping to avoid malaria. The disease was endemic in Papua New Guinea, almost like a common cold but much more deadly. Research in 2003 showed that 30 per cent of the population had come down with the illness that year, and hundreds had died from it. Although some of the wealthier villagers I stayed with in coming months did have mosquito nets, most people had no protection at all, and certainly expensive repellent was out of the question.*

The meal was white rice and tinned tuna. I got the impression that the tuna was a luxury. The logger told me that he worked for a Malaysian logging company. He had to work for 12 hours a day but was paid barely enough to feed his family. He hated his work, but had no choice but to continue with it.

One thing that did make Papua New Guinea slightly easier to travel through was that English is widely spoken, owing to its legacy as a British colony. At the same time, Papua New Guinea is famous for its linguistic diversity. Although its population is six million, there are over 800 distinct languages spoken. The language group a person belongs to indicates their tribe, which is referred to as their *wantok*, or 'one talk'.

The most common language used to communicate in Papua New Guinea is therefore a kind of combined, multi-sourced pidgin

*I later met a French malaria researcher in Madang who told me that the Papua New Guinean people, although suffering severely from the disease, did have something in their immune system that made them suffer far less than people elsewhere in the world, even Africans. He had recently received a grant from the Bill Gates Foundation to try to discover why this was.

language, with a lot of English influences as well. So *taim bilong masta* means 'the colonial period', *gavman* means 'government', *plismastas* meant 'the police', and *singsing* means 'pub'.

Bit and his family helped me learn some other phrases which might come in handy on my way through:

Me gola Port Moresby meant 'I am going to Port Moresby.'
Me borablong you meant 'I am your friend.'
Me kago was 'my luggage', and if Alanis broke, then, evidently, she was *bagarap*.

The next morning, I emerged from the shack to see the forest shrouded in an eerie, grey mist. After a breakfast of bread with Bit, I said goodbye and climbed onto my bike. A moment before I pushed off, Bit told me that I was going the wrong way. He said that I had to go back up the hill I had come down the previous night, and take the left-hand fork at the junction.

I pushed Alanis back to the junction and saw again that the left-hand road was less worn. There was grass growing up in the middle of it, indicating very few cars. I was very uncertain but what else could I do but follow it? After a few minutes the road became very muddy and I was forced to climb off and push. The mud stuck to the wheels and accumulated into a thick layer which jammed against the pannier racks. I scraped it off with a stick and kept going.

By lunchtime I had barely covered ten miles. I reached the top of a ridge and looked ahead. The road wound down and disappeared into a shroud of green tree tops. At the bottom of the hill, I came to a big clearing in the trees with a small brown river flowing through the middle of it. There were several clusters of wooden huts on stilts. A teenage boy in an old T-shirt and baseball cap stood beside one hut and watched me arrive. I introduced myself and he said his name was Anderson and that he had recently come down to this village to visit his cousins. He spoke good English.

I asked how far it was to Aitape, and he said he did not know, but that it was very far. I stood still, wondering what to do. I had no idea how far it was or where I was on my map. I had little food left. I had not seen a car for almost 24 hours. I was terrified that I would take another wrong turn and get lost in the jungle and that no one would ever see me again. At that moment, two men emerged out of the undergrowth ahead of us. One of them wore blue shorts and plastic sandals and was carrying a machete. The other carried a large bow.

'They are my cousins,' Anderson explained.

They walked up to us, and looked at me. I said hello, and asked what they had been hunting for.

'Tree kangaroos,' they said, 'but we have not caught anything.'

I told them that I was heading for Aitape and asked if they knew how far it was.

The two men looked at each other. Then the man with the machete, whose name was Yagi, said, 'It is very far . . .' and nodded his head along the road and added, 'and the road ahead is broken.'

'But I am on a bicycle,' I said, 'so I can push through the broken bits.'

'No, it is a bad road, and you may get lost.'

He exchanged a few sentences I could not understand with Anderson before saying, 'You should wait until tomorrow. Then we can come with you and show you the way to the beach road.'

'The beach road?'

'Yes, there is a road along the beach. You can take it to Aitape, and you cannot get lost on the beach road.'

'How long will it take us to reach the beach road?'

'If we walk from dark till dark we will make it. You can stay tonight with us.' Yagi indicated the wooden house.

I felt reluctant to stop so early in the day, but was already exhausted from the heat. I knew it made sense to accept their offer to take me to the beach road. I hoped I was right to trust them. That night we sat in a smoky room and cooked plantains in their skins on a fire. Anderson told me that he was 18, that he was good at hunting and that he had recently finished grade ten at the school in his home town, which was about a hundred miles away. He planned to live in this village for the next two years, and save up enough money to go to complete high school. He said he liked maths and that eventually he dreamed of becoming an accountant.

I smiled and nodded encouragingly, but I felt sad that Anderson's dream would prove so difficult to pursue. Although Papua New Guinea is rich in gold and other natural resources, the economy provides few other avenues for employment. I had heard that one of the main reasons for the burgeoning ranks of rascals was the widespread frustration about the lack of opportunities for young men. Becoming a rascal was the only option for an interesting life for many of them.

After we had finished eating, Yagi and Anderson started chewing some green stalks. Every few minutes they dipped them into a little pile of white powder on a leaf. As they chewed, their mouths turned red. After a few minutes they spat the red mixture out through a hole in the floor. They told me they were chewing betel-nut. As I would discover, betel-nut chewing was a popular national pastime in Papua New Guinea. Most days over the next two months I would come across people chewing it or cycle past red puddles of spit beside the road. The white powder was actually made from crushed sea shells which reacted with the plant stalk and saliva to produce the red colour. Apparently it gave a minor but very addictive 'high', though prolonged use had been shown to drastically increase the likelihood of mouth cancer.

Yagi offered me some, so I clumsily dabbed a stalk in the powder and took a bite. A bitter, disgusting taste flooded my mouth. I felt my pulse quickening and a slight headache, but I chewed it for two minutes before spitting it through a hole in the floor. I washed my mouth out with water while Yagi and Anderson laughed. I said it was not to my liking and smiled back at them with red teeth.

I retired to the room and laid out my sleeping bag. I started to write my diary:

Well, I'm sitting here under my mosquito net, kind of wondering to myself – how on earth did I get here? I am sitting in the middle of a vast and mostly unexplored jungle with a bicycle and a vague and untried plan to try and get to Port

> *Moresby [the capital city] . . . O Lord, I am sinking . . . give me strength and keep me safe . . . from snakes and illness and getting lost and bad people and traffic and falling off . . .*

The list just seemed to keep growing.

I also wrote a short letter to Christine and, after that, fell into a fitful sleep.

The next morning, we rose in the dark. Alanis was sitting beneath the house, leaning against one of the stilts. As I wheeled her back onto the road I noticed the handlebars were sticky and slimy. Using my head-torch, I saw they were covered in the red betel-nut spit. I had left her directly underneath the hole in the floor through which Yagi and Anderson had been spitting the night before.

As we set out, Yagi carried his machete and Anderson a one-litre plastic bottle of water and a large papaya. I did not have much food left and was concerned that we would not have enough to make it through the long day, but Yagi said we would find more food along the way.

I leaned into Alanis, pushing her in front of me while being careful not to hit my shins on the pedals. Walking was a pleasant change from cycling. The road rose into the hills, and the jungle, messy and brooding, continued to droop over us on both sides. We encountered more stretches of mud. Yagi told me no traffic had come along this road since it had been damaged in the rainy season last year. We reached a section that had slumped into a river, leaving a hole where the road had been. It was 20 metres wide and three metres deep. I used my hands to climb down, and Anderson passed me the bike. I could see why no traffic could pass this way.

In the afternoon, Anderson began to slow down. He was walking in bare feet, and they were becoming sore. I dug out a pair of flip-flops that I had bought in Manila and gave them to him. For lunch Yagi cut open the papaya with his machete, and we ate it sitting in the middle of the road. In the afternoon I shared out the remainder of my Christmas snacks. Sometimes, when there was a downhill stretch of smooth road, I freewheeled ahead of the others. One time

I rounded a corner to see a brown animal the size of a child hop out of the forest and across the road in front of me. It was a tree kangaroo.

When we reached a junction, Yagi and Anderson would have a short discussion that I did not understand. Yagi was elusive about how much further we had to go. I wondered whether they really knew the way. As evening drew close we reached a ridge, and far below us, on the far side of a sea of tree tops, there was the ocean. By the time we had descended the hill it was dark. In the distance we could see the lights of a village, and music was echoing quietly through the night. It was New Year's Eve.

32
The beach road and the rascals

Distance to home = 21,812 miles

2–4 JANUARY 2006

I am pushing Alanis down the beach road, though we have now discovered that it is not a road at all; it is a deserted, sandy beach. Anonymous lines of footprints lead, like Man Friday's, towards the horizon. Palm trees and bushes sprout in chaotic clumps by the high-tide mark, interspersed with giant pieces of splintered driftwood. The sea, ruffled with white horses, sends line after line of breakers crashing up the sand. Alanis's wheels plough into the soft sand as I push her and, even with Anderson's help, we crawl forward at barely one mile per hour. The sun beats down on my head and I am running low on energy.

In mid-morning we reach an inlet where a waist-deep river meets the sea. I give one of my disposable cameras to Anderson and ask if he can walk across ahead to take a photo. Yagi takes my panniers, and I lift Alanis over my head and wade through the water with the waves breaking around my armpits. As I have almost lost my balance several times, it is a relief to climb out onto the other side.

At lunchtime, we have no food, but Yagi walks into the bushes and returns a moment later with a pineapple. Although much of Papua New Guinea is mountainous and difficult for crops, here on the coast it is extremely fertile. I remember what John had told me in Vanimo: 'If you stick something in the ground here, it grows.'

Soon we reach a large brown river, meandering out of the jungle, and an old man in a dug-out canoe gives Alanis, Yagi, Anderson and me a lift across. In return, I give him my spare T-shirt.

The afternoon drags on and the beach now leads us past a lagoon.

Yagi says he has a friend in the cluster of huts we can see in the distance. The village is called Arup and the villagers welcome us to stay and cook us fish on the fire for dinner. A large crowd gathers around and stares at me. They tell me that this village survives by fishing and growing vegetables. It sounds like a tranquil existence. But then they tell me that seven years ago the beach was hit by a tsunami. They point to a palm tree with a sharp kink in its trunk where the wave had bent it over. A teenage boy speaks up about how, when the tsunami hit, he had been playing on the beach. The wave swept him, along with the entire village, into the lagoon behind us. He says that many people were drowned. After dinner I am invited to stay the night on the floor of a hut. I am extremely tired but it takes me a while to fall asleep. My skin feels itchy from the sand, and with the sound of waves crashing onto the beach I imagine another terrible tsunami is about to arrive.*

The next morning we reach a solid dirt track and it is time to say goodbye. Yagi and Anderson look protectively at me as we shake hands. I follow the track until it gradually turns into a dirt road and then I see bigger buildings and a proper street. Instead of one day, it has taken me five, but I have reached Aitape at last.

Huddles of people sit beside the main street selling fruit, clothes, batteries and betel-nut. I see the police station with a man holding a big machinegun outside it. I ride over and meet a policeman called Eddie. I explain that I am now trying to reach Wewak, a bigger town about a hundred miles away. Eddie draws me a map marking the local villages and tells me that the road will be mostly smoother now. He also says that it is safe.

'Are there any rascals around?' I ask.

Eddie stops smiling. 'Yes,' he says, looking suddenly serious, 'you should be careful because of the rascals. Last year, the rascals in this village', he points to the map, 'chopped down a tree to block the road, and robbed everybody who came through.'

*Some months later I found a minor headline from 1998 on the BBC website reporting that over two thousand people had died in the disaster.

I wonder why a minute beforehand he had told me it was safe.

'Okay,' I say, 'how can I be careful? What should I do?'

'If you see any young men drinking beside the road, and they shout at you to stop, it is better if you do not stop. Or,' he pauses, 'maybe you should take a truck.'

I do not want to wait for a truck so I climb back onto the bike and start riding. The jungle looms over me from the right, while on the left I catch a spectacular view of the empty beach and the wild blue sea. Although most people so far have been helpful and friendly, what Eddie said about the rascals has made me afraid again. I start thinking about Christine. Each night, by torchlight, I have been continuing to write her a letter. It is quite long now, and I hope there will be a post office in Wewak so I can send it. I wonder what she will make of my frightened scribbles from a Papuan jungle as she reads it sitting in her air-conditioned office in London. Our lives are so far removed from each other.

In mid-afternoon my daydreaming is disturbed as I approach a village. A line of wooden huts sits close to the road. On the short grass in front of them I see half a dozen young men sitting in a circle. One of them is poking the ground with a machete and several are holding bottles of beer. Looking up and seeing me coming they suddenly all point at me and rise to their feet. A cold chill of fear slips down my spine and the American lady's question flashes through my mind: 'What will you do when you meet the rascals?'

The men start running towards the road and I start pedalling harder. My heart is pounding as I watch them get closer and I hear them shouting at me to stop. I shout back, 'Hello, how are you?' in my friendliest voice, but then I accelerate frantically. I see a small bridge ahead. They are running towards it to cut me off. My feet spin faster and I swerve onto the other side of the road, bump through a pothole, and reach the bridge just before them. I ride across it hard, gasping for breath, and I can still hear the men running after me and shouting.

As I reach the other side of the bridge I catch sight of another group of young men sitting in the shade of a tree. They notice me coming, and a moment later they too are on their feet and running towards the road.

I keep up my fast pedalling and pass in front of them before they can block me. I think I have made it. I look over my shoulder and am relieved that they have stopped running and are looking after me angrily. And then, all of a sudden, with my eyes off the road, Alanis careers into the ditch. Both groups of men see what has happened and start running towards me again. I scramble up the bank, my feet slipping in the loose earth, and jump back onto Alanis. My legs spin wildly, but the men are gaining. I puff loudly, and gradually slip ahead. I do not look back again until they are far behind.

33
The Hungarian and the jet-ski

Distance to home = 21,707 miles

Papua New Guinea is a land of misfits, mercenaries and missionaries
A SAYING ABOUT PAPUA NEW GUINEA

'Welcome to Wewak,' said the chubbiest of the group of three. He was an Australian tuna fleet manager, in his fifties, and had a grey beard and a beer belly. 'What brings a crazy Englishman out here to the frontier, then?'

I was in the bar at the Windjammer, the premier hotel in town. I was not staying here – it was way beyond my budget – but it was a good place to meet the crowd of eccentric expats who still lived on this remote northern coast.

'I'm on my way to Australia,' I replied, feeling a bit like Tony Hawks when he had to explain that he was hitch-hiking around Ireland (with a fridge), except I was trying to get myself through the Papuan jungle (with a bicycle). I explained how I had crossed from Indonesia and made my way through the jungle and along the beach to get here.

They all laughed and the Australian slapped me on the back. He seemed pleased to hear that there were still some unconventional people in the real world.

'Twenty years ago Wewak was full of expats,' he said, 'but now it's only us crazy ones who remain. Hey, Ernie,' he turned to a short, thin man with glasses, 'why don't you tell Rob here what you used to do?'

Ernie took a swig of his beer and with a quiet laugh told us, in a Scandinavian accent, that during the Cold War he had been a spy for NATO. He said he had once taken a bullet in the leg as he fled from the East German police on the wrong side of the Berlin Wall.

Towards the end of the evening I asked the third man, a Hungarian called Peter, what he was doing in Wewak. He said he was there for the gold. I had heard about the mineral riches of the highlands. Several big foreign companies were based there. There was controversy about the environmental damage they caused. I asked if he worked for one of the companies.

'No,' said Peter, 'I work for myself. Those companies are raping this country.'

He explained that although the big mining companies mined for gold in the mountains, there was also a lot of gold that got washed down the rivers and out to sea. He had invented a panning machine, which he used in the smaller tributaries upstream, and claimed it allowed him to collect lots of gold. I was not sure whether to believe him.

'But I am not in this for myself,' he continued. 'Once I have perfected the design I want to give these machines to the villages so that they can find their own gold. I hate the big foreign companies who are stealing it all. The government are no better; they steal all the taxes that the gold brings in.'

I asked if he had a boat to take the machine up the river, and he said that he actually used a jet-ski, and towed it in a canoe behind him. I tried to imagine what the locals, and indeed the occasional luxury foreign cruise ship, must make of seeing a grey-haired Hungarian zooming up the remote Sepic River on a jet-ski, towing a big box in a canoe behind him.

Then he got to the crunch question. 'You should come with me and see for yourself when I go upstream next week.'

'Er . . .' I hesitated. It would be an utterly idiotic, but extremely fun thing to do – stopping in the middle of Papua New Guinea to make my fortune for a while. But regrettably I was not that sort of adventurer, so I turned him down and politely changed the subject.

34
The priest who dodged bullets

Distance to home = 21,656 miles

I get the feeling this is a rather dangerous town
FROM MY DIARY, 9 JANUARY 2006

From Wewak, the road led into some hills where the forest was replaced by sporadic stretches of rolling pastureland. With the open space around me, it suddenly felt easier to breathe. I did not see many people in the villages, though I could sometimes hear singing coming from the wooden village churches. My host in Wewak had advised me to wait until the Sunday before riding this road, because on Saturday the men went drinking and it was when they were drinking that they were most likely to engage in rascal-like activities. On a Sunday morning all the rascals were either hung over, or in church, or both.

After lunch, riding through a coconut plantation, I was running out of water again. I saw a man walking down the road towards me so I stopped to ask him how far to the next village. The man smiled enthusiastically and said, 'It is not far, but if you like I can fill your bottles here.'

'That would be very kind,' I said, wondering if there was a stream nearby.

Without taking the bottles, the man grabbed a tree with both hands and started to shinny up it. He turned to smile at me from the top and threw down five coconuts. He chopped them open, and poured the milk into my three plastic coke bottles.

I thanked him.

'It is my pleasure,' he said with another wide grin. 'I am a pastor and I am very happy to have been able to help you.' As I cycled off again, I tried to imagine an equivalent scene back home: a Papuan cyclist riding through my neighbourhood in London, and my vicar, Ian, cheerfully climbing a roadside tree in order to help him.

In the late afternoon, a smart, white Land-Rover coming in the opposite direction drew up beside me. A man wearing a police uniform leant out of the window to say hello. He was chubby, with a moustache, and he introduced himself as the regional police chief.

I told him that I was trying to reach the riverside town of Angoram that night, and from there I hoped to find a motorboat to take me through the mangrove swamps on the other side.

'You should be careful,' he said. 'I am returning to Wewak to write a report. We just recovered the body of a white man from the river. He was a student from New Zealand. He had been living in a village upstream studying linguistics.'

'What happened to him?' I asked.

'We think he was on a canoe with two local men. They were supposed to be taking him to the next village, but they murdered him to steal his computer.' He paused and then said, 'You must be careful in Angoram, it is a dangerous town.'

The sun dipped lower and my shadow lengthened on the road ahead of me. I arrived at a line of houses with grass roofs, which were spread across a field. I could see no evidence of modern technology apart from the road and a telephone line.

A man in a T-shirt watched me arrive. Someone in Wewak had told me I should try to stay with the priest, so I asked the man where the priest's house was.

He spat a jet of betel-nut onto the grass. 'Over there,' he gestured behind him with a backward tilt of his head.

I wheeled Alanis across the grass and past a mango tree where children were throwing stones to bring the fruit down. I saw a short man from the Indian sub-continent walking towards me. He was in his late thirties, and had a gentle face, a side parting and a neatly trimmed moustache. He was surprised to see me, but after I had introduced myself he shook my hand with a faint smile and said his name was Father Lawrence. Then he quietly invited me into his house.

After a much-needed shower, I sat in the middle of his living room. The table was scattered with theology books. Despite the nets on the windows, there were still mosquitoes inside with us. Father Lawrence came out of the kitchen with two cups of tea.

I said that Angoram seemed a difficult place to be based.

'Yes, it is not easy,' he said, taking a thoughtful sip from his cup. 'There were three old German priests living here when I arrived, but they found the local population difficult to manage. They said that this used to be a nice place – it had an airstrip and electricity and was reasonably safe. But law and order broke down and everything fell into disrepair. The local rascals started to intimidate them and in the end they were too frightened to leave the house.'

After the priests left Father Lawrence had stayed on alone, but, far from hiding in his house, he had been venturing out into the community, confronting corruption and challenging the rascals. This meant that he had made some enemies. A town like Angoram was not a safe place to have enemies.

'I saw there was a telephone line beside the road, so at least you are not completely cut off,' I mentioned optimistically.

'Well, there used to be,' replied Lawrence, 'but then someone decided to cut down a tree, and the tree fell onto the telephone line and broke it.'

'When was that?'

'About two years ago. You see, often the people in this town just do not think about the consequences of what they do. They think, "Okay, today, I will cut down this tree" and they do not consider the consequence will be that it will break the telephone line . . . and in a country like Papua New Guinea, once a telephone line is broken, it will not be repaired for many years. It is the local people who will suffer, but it is not in their culture to think about such things.'

I had heard it said that one root of many of Papua New Guinea's problems was that 10,000 years of stone-age technology and culture had been abruptly altered by one hundred years of modern technology and culture. Previously there had been no roads; now the roads had become rivers to carry the menace of AIDS quickly around the country. Previously there had been no towns; now the towns had become hotspots of crime as young men, separated from their tribal elders, found identity in the rascal gangs. Previously the tribal warfare had been carried out with bows and arrows, resulting in occasional deaths; now it was waged with M-16s provided by corrupt politicians and drug money, resulting in massive death tolls. The delicate checks and balances which had been built into the culture had been completely disrupted.*

Father Lawrence walked into the kitchen and returned with two plates of vegetables and rice mixed with Indian spices.

'Although it is difficult and I feel very isolated, I believe God has called me here to help these people. I have founded a school and I subsidise the fees myself. The local people still come to me if they are ill, as I am one of the only people with a car and I can drive them to the hospital in Wewak.'

'Has anyone ever threatened or tried to harm you?'

'Yes, the people here become very dangerous when they start drinking. In the last six months they have tried to kill me several times. The first time was last June. I was walking home and a drunken man started shooting at me with a home-made gun. I ran and dived into the cement water tank underneath my house. It protected me from the bullets until he finished his ammunition and ran away.'

I could not help smiling at the thought of short Father Lawrence leaping, Bond-like, into his water tank as bullets flew past. But it was not funny.

'I was attacked again last week by two other men. They were drunk and they knocked on my door and invited me to share a coconut with them. I went outside and one of them suddenly tried to strike me on the head with his machete.' Lawrence acted out a

*I later heard a story about a family in the capital city who hired a young man to cook and do their laundry. He had initially done the laundry by hand, heating water in a metal basin over a fire outside. But then the family had bought a brand new washing-machine and told the man that he should now use this instead. They returned from work the following day to find that the man had put the clothes into the machine, built a fire in the yard, and then put the washing-machine on top of the fire.

vertical blow. 'I sidestepped him and his machete got stuck in the wooden step so I ran back into the house and locked the door.'

Father Lawrence beckoned me over to the door of the house and showed me the nick in the wooden step where the blade had struck the porch. It was a centimetre deep.

'Why were they attacking you?' I asked, shaking my head.

'They are from other churches in the town,' he said. My heart sank. 'There is a lot of rivalry here and some of the churches speak against the Catholics. Even though most of them know I am trying to help, many are still opposed to me being here. In my New Year's sermon last week I explained to my congregation that I am not afraid of dying. I am not here for money. I am here because God has called me. If I am killed, I have no wife or children to mourn me and I will go peacefully and be with God. I think the sermon made quite an impression. But I am not optimistic about the future. Most of my congregation is old and in 15 years' time most of them will have died. I think it will be two or three generations before there is real hope for Angoram.'

The next morning I joined Father Lawrence and his small congregation of eight elderly ladies and one old man for the Mass. I felt moved to be sharing the bread and wine with Christians from such different backgrounds. My life and future felt far out of my hands and I thanked God that I had made it safely this far. I asked for his protection in whatever lay ahead and that it would not take me long to find a boat across the river. I also prayed for my sister. It was her thirty-first birthday that day. After Mass, Lawrence gave me breakfast and showed me down to the river.

He shook my hand, said goodbye and walked back into the town to the people whom he loved and whom he refused to give up on. I never saw him again. I sometimes wonder how he is now.

35
Kokoda

Distance to home = 21,211 miles

He's dreaming! There is not a hope of him cycling the Kokoda. The thing is vertical for 90 per cent and the rest is in a bog with far too many tree roots in the way . . . I reckon he is mad . . .

EMAIL FORWARDED FROM EXPATRIATE WORKER IN PORT MORESBY

Since leaving Japan nine months previously, I had been roughly following the route along which the Japanese army had advanced during World War II. Motivated by the belief that all Asia was its rightful property, the Japanese had annexed Korea, invaded China and then pushed south to take South-East Asia, the Philippines and Indonesia by 1942. Indonesia and its desperately needed oil had been Japan's original goal, but beyond these islands lay an even greater prize: the resource-rich but sparsely populated landmass of Australia. The ideal place from which to launch an invasion of Australia was the Papua New Guinean capital, Port Moresby, which was just 200 miles from Australia's east coast.*

The Japanese first attempted to take Moresby in a naval struggle, but failed. They next prepared to make an attempt by land. They had already captured the north side of the island, so to reach Moresby on the south side they would have to cross the Owen Stanley Mountains, which run like a backbone down the island's centre. No road existed through these mountains. Instead, there was a footpath used by locals – the Kokoda Trail – so called because it began

*Whether the Japanese actually wanted to invade Australia is still open to debate. Some historians argue that they wanted only to be able to attack its east coast, as well as control important shipping channels from Port Moresby.

in the unheard-of village of Kokoda. The trail led through thick jungle and over a series of huge ridges, swamps and unbridged rivers for a hundred miles.

The Australians knew that blocking the Japanese advance was imperative, but their best troops were fighting in Europe or had been captured in Singapore. A company of barely trained volunteers made up of farmers and tradesmen was all that could be spared. When they arrived in Papua New Guinea, before they had even reached their defensive positions on the trail, the majority were already weakened by malaria and dysentery. In contrast, the Japanese forces were highly experienced, well equipped and utterly devoted. They outnumbered the Australians by more than five to one. The onslaught began with waves of screaming Japanese soldiers charging at the Australian positions. They frequently broke through, resulting in vicious hand-to-hand fighting in the mud and the darkness. At risk of being surrounded, the Australians fought a rearguard action, retreating from ridge to ridge. After several months, they had been pushed back to a final ridge, less than 30 miles from the capital. But gradually the tables turned. Australian reinforcements arrived and the Japanese were driven back the way they had come. It was one of the first times in the entire war that the Japanese advance had been significantly reversed.

Fifty-two years later, I too was trying to reach the capital. There was still no road connecting the north and south sides of the island. The Kokoda Trail was one of the country's few successful tourist attractions, and had in recent years started to draw adventurous Australians keen to walk the historical route. However, the hikers all came in the dry months of April to September when it was still possible to wade through the mountain streams. I was arriving in January, in the middle of the rainy season, when the rivers were flooded. I did not know whether I would be able to cross the rivers, but I did know that the mountain trail would be unsuitable for riding my bicycle. I would have to push or carry it.

After saying goodbye to Father Lawrence I had paid 50 dollars cash for a motor-boat ride down the Sepic River and past the mangrove swamps. A better road then allowed me to make quick progress by bike to the cities of Madang, where I stayed with VSO volunteers, and then Lae, Papua New Guinea's second city. The roads east of Lae were impassable because of rain, so a local ferry took me along the coast for eight hours to Oro Bay. I then cycled up a flat, dusty road towards a barricade of hills, which looked smooth and green in the distance. The sky was full of clouds, but the sun broke through in streaky patches. The forest around me thickened and, as evening arrived, the road reached the base of the mountain. I drew up among a line of wooden houses. I was in Kokoda village.

I had decided to hire a local guide for the crossing to show me which paths to take and to help with the rivers. John, a local man, was tall and muscular with a bushy beard and had been working as a guide on the trail for 20 years. He told me that it was rare for anyone to attempt the trail in the rainy season, and that no one had ever taken a bicycle over it. He said that it would be very difficult, but that hopefully we should still make it in a week's walking.

After paying John his fee and squeezing our food supplies and all my things into a rucksack John had lent me, we were ready to leave the next day. Before I went to bed I admitted to John that I was developing a painful earache. John said we should delay our departure by 24 hours. When John's wife, a nurse in the village health centre, heard about the earache, she injected two shots of penicillin in my backside, and told me this would fix it.* John's mother-in-law also heard about my earache. She walked into the jungle and returned with a handful of special leaves. She boiled them up into a paste and poured it into my ear. I do not know which of these remedies did the job, but the pain eased, and I told John I was ready to go.

*

*The health centre had been funded by the Rotary Clubs of Australia, in gratitude to the people of Kokoda for the assistance they gave Australian soldiers during the war.

As we walked out of the village to the start of the trail, a man called Tom joined us. Tom had acted as a porter for tourists the previous year, and John was training him to be a guide. The path disappeared into the mountains ahead and clouds rolled over the ridge high above like a grey veil.

We wound upwards in a series of switchbacks along the brown-earthed, but mostly leaf-covered track. The air smelt earthy and rotten. John led the way, occasionally using his machete to hack down the branches that blocked the way. On either side of the path there was an impenetrable wall of green shrubs and vines. It was impossible to ride now, so I was wheeling Alanis, but occasionally I lifted her past fallen trees and large roots. Sweat poured down my back underneath my rucksack. After a four-hour climb we staggered onto the top of the ridge and looked back across the valley. From this height the village was now a scattering of tiny, brown rooftops. We would have to scale eight more such ridges before Moresby.

We stayed in a village on the ridge, and the next day the path contoured along the side of the valley. Another dense, leafy column of hills blocked the horizon and a dark shadow coming down the valley told us rain was coming. We stopped to collect some fruit in a village at lunchtime. The villagers told John that it would be difficult to cross the rivers up ahead, as the floods were even higher than usual that year.

The path led downwards and John and Tom walked on ahead of me, and were lost from sight. The temperature was cooler now that we were in the hills and the knowledge that I had a guide made the jungle seem less threatening. I felt confident that, if we plodded along at this steady speed each day, we would make it across in the week John had predicted.

At the bottom of the valley I heard the sound of rushing water behind a wall of trees. Tom was waiting for me on the path.

'The usual crossing point at the river is not possible,' he said. 'We must go this way.'

He led me down a small, freshly cut track which they had hacked off at right angles to the main track. The sound of the roaring river grew closer and suddenly the undergrowth drew back to reveal a foaming mass of angry white whirlpools thundering past. The torrent of water completely blocked our path. John was standing, barefooted, beside a branchless fallen tree that had been swept downstream and was now jammed against the bank on both sides.

'You must take your shoes off and walk across,' John shouted at me, above the roar. It was a dubious-looking bridge, and appeared far too slippery. John climbed onto the tree and, holding his hands out to balance himself, scampered quickly across it. Even watching him cross made me tense up. He had a rope with him and tied it to a tree on the other side. Then Tom walked across in front of me, holding my hand, and I tried not to look at the water rushing underneath me. John followed, carrying Alanis. There was no way I could have crossed this river on my own.

On the other side, the path had disappeared. Tom cut us a path through the jungle with his machete and I carried Alanis on my shoulder. It started raining and I started to stumble in the undergrowth, falling on my side and dropping Alanis in the bushes. As it grew dark we came to an abandoned grass shelter and stopped for the night. My sleeping bag had got wet that day, and for the first time in months I felt cold. Tom and John had not even brought a sleeping bag, and I saw Tom shivering as he tried to sleep.

At lunchtime the next day we reached another ferocious river. We waded upstream in the shallows but there were no trees to walk across this time. John used his small axe to chop down a tree to make our own bridge. The tree fell, cackling through the leaves, and landed on the water with a smack. It did not quite reach the other side and so, caught in the current, it twisted downstream and was dragged quickly away by the rushing white-water. Night was arriving so John said we should camp and hope the river was lower the next morning. It started to rain again as we cooked dinner on a sputtering campfire. This was our second night of sleeping rough when we had expected to be in a village further up the trail. I noticed that our food supplies were beginning to run low.

*

The next day the river was even more flooded. We stood side by side, in silence, watching it roar past us and down into the jungle below. The opposite bank was only ten metres away, but there was no way to get across. I was cold and wet and distracted by pangs of hunger.

Tom said he wanted to jump in and swim across with the rope.

'You cannot do it, Tom,' John said, 'that is a suicide mission.' I was inclined to agree.

'I have been walking the trail for 20 years,' said John, turning to me, 'and I have never seen the river so flooded. We have not brought enough food to wait here any longer. We must give up and go back.'

I had no choice but to do as he said. It took several hours of walking towards Kokoda before the fact that we had failed sank in.

36
'I've had enough of this stupid bike ride'

Distance to home = 21,211 miles

Never, never, never, never give up
WINSTON CHURCHILL

Two days later, with badly blistered feet, damp clothes and famished, worn-out bodies, we staggered back into Kokoda village. We had been gone only four days, and had made it over only one of the nine ridges that lay between Kokoda and Port Moresby. Even Tom and John looked exhausted.

'I am sorry we have failed,' said John. 'I think you should ride back to Oro Bay and try to find a boat to take you around the tip of the island to Moresby.'

I was too fatigued to contemplate going back into the mountains, so with a sigh I agreed that this was probably the best idea. I went and sat in John's spare hut to try to come to terms with what had happened. I could not quite believe that we had failed. Up there in the mountains I had felt isolated. The weather and rivers had felt merciless. I had thought that by paying for an experienced guide, everything would work out okay. I started to feel angry. I had worked so hard to make it this far. I had taken more risks than I was comfortable with. But now I had been beaten back by bad weather.

'I've had enough of this stupid bike ride,' I mumbled to myself. 'I am fed up with being tired, hungry, dirty, afraid and alone. I miss my family. I want to see Christine.' That morning, I had actually managed to get in touch with her. There were no phone lines this far up the road into the mountains, but there was a man who owned a two-way radio. He had patched me through to his friend with a computer in Port Moresby. This friend had kindly sent an email message to Christine to say I was okay. She had sent a reply saying, 'Good to know that you are alive, happy six months, Robbie.'

I began to deliberate about retreating to Lae and catching the plane to Australia. It would be so much easier.

For the first time on the ride I started to think seriously about giving up entirely. Why not just retreat to Lae and from there fly back to England? I thought to myself. True, *Cycling from Siberia to Kokoda* did not have quite the same ring about it as *Cycling Home from Siberia*, but there would be no shame in it. I had already achieved far more than I had dreamed possible when I started. I had always claimed that I was not doing the ride to prove myself to myself, or to anyone.

But, as I contemplated quitting, I considered how I would feel if I went home. I knew I would feel happy for a couple of days. I could have hot showers and eat big pizzas and see the people I cared about. I would feel safe again.

But how would I feel after that initial euphoria had worn off? I would probably regret quitting for the rest of my life.

In contrast, I started thinking about how ecstatic I would feel if I could still make it to Australia without flying. I wondered whether, as John had suggested, I could find a boat around the island to Moresby. Or, better still, whether I could make another attempt at the Kokoda Trail. This time I would take more food so that I could sit it out if the rivers were still impassable.

John said he did not want to try again, so I went to see Tom in his little wooden house with a leaf roof on the outskirts of the village. Tom told me that, if it stopped raining, he would be prepared to take me on a second attempt. I said I was running out of money. He replied he needed to go to Moresby anyway to visit relatives and that he wanted to gain some experience as a guide, so money was not important to him. Each morning for the next four days, we walked down to the village river that swept out of the mountains. Each day the flow was lower. Five days after we had arrived back from the first attempt, I gave Tom £60, apologising that it was all I could afford. Tom smiled and shook my hand: 'Let's go to Moresby,' he said.

*

It had stopped raining, the air was warmer, and we moved faster than before. Tom took my pack, while I pushed and carried Alanis. I liked Tom. He had a boyish enthusiasm and a happy-go-lucky attitude to life. After two days we reached the un-crossable river again. The flow was lower now, and we spotted a jumble of wedged trees and debris upstream of the trail. Scrambling across to the other side, we grinned at each other and pressed on up to the next ridge.

For the next week we battled past fallen trees and rushing rivers; we slithered down muddy slopes; we waded through lukewarm swamps; we hacked our way through sections of the trail where the jungle had completely overgrown. Carrying Alanis made me even more tired, especially on the big climbs, and I continued to trip over, dropping her beside me. Once when we sat down on a log in a clearing to have lunch, Tom scraped the ground with a stick and uncovered some old, rusty bullet casings left from the war. He picked them up and handed them to me. One day we walked through long grass in a swampy valley, and in the evening I removed my boots to find my feet covered in leeches and my socks red with blood. As the week wore on, I looked forward more and more to the moment when we would stagger into a village for the night. By day three my feet developed a string of blisters, which I popped and doused with iodine to prevent infection. I covered them in plasters and hoped they would not get so bad that I could not walk. My earache returned, but I was already taking antibiotic pills, so there was nothing more I could do. On several nights Tom asked if he could have a pill, so I gave him one. On our last night I asked him what was wrong with him, and he said his knees were aching. I said I didn't think antibiotics would do much good for his knees, but Tom popped it in his mouth anyway. We both laughed wearily.

As we neared the end of the trail, we passed through two villages which Tom told me had been fighting with each other. Apparently, although they were both making money from the tourists, they were eager to increase their share of the profit, and so had resorted to fighting. Three months beforehand, one village had attacked the other, burning down a guest house and murdering the owner. There had not yet been any payback so things were still tense. 'Payback' was an 'eye for an eye' approach to life, which was deeply ingrained in Papua New Guinean culture. If you took some land, then you had to give payback in some form. If you killed a man from someone else's *wantok*, then someone from your *wantok* must die, 'as payback'. It was very logical. Walking up a street with my host in Wewak, we had witnessed a bus driver run over a stray dog. The bus had then been surrounded with people, all claiming that the dog belonged to them, and that therefore the bus driver must give them payback.

Tom said that the villagers had better be careful with their feuding, or they would drive away the tourists altogether.

After eight exhausting days of walking, we waded through a final river and climbed a final ridge to reach a muddy road. A little

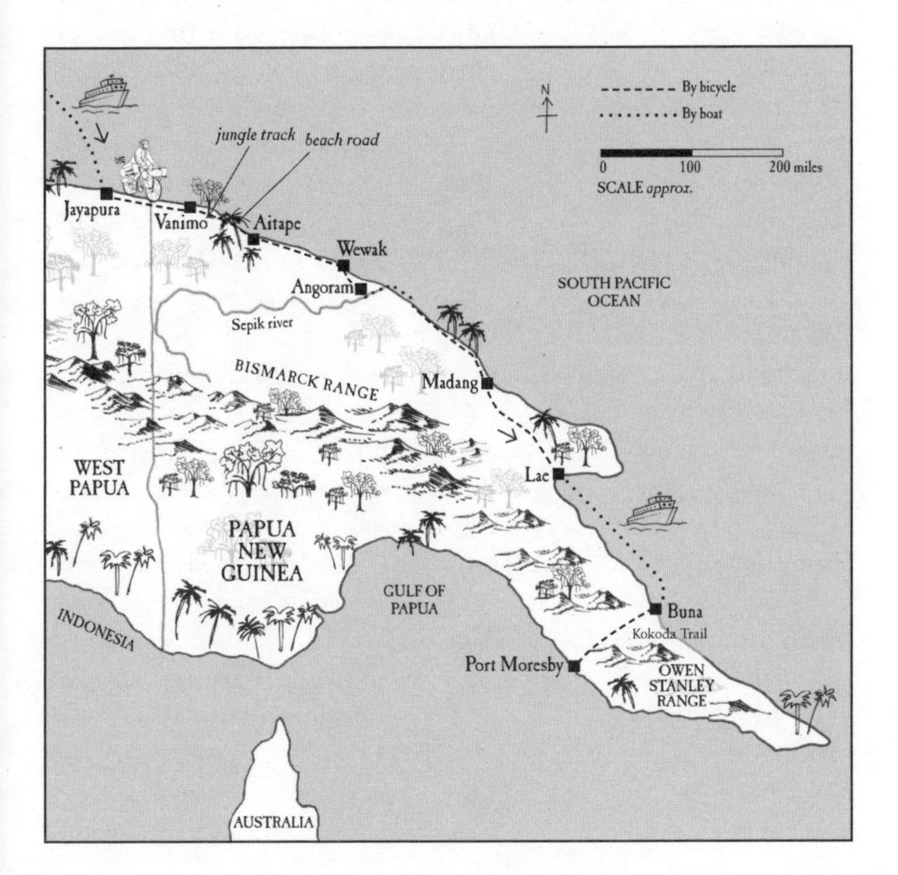

further on we came to a village where an asphalt road rolled down a hill for the final 20 miles to Port Moresby. A large tourist sign announced that we were at the end of the Kokoda Trail, so we took a photo of Tom and me standing side by side underneath it. My shirt was ripped, my beard was long, my hair was a mess. I was dirty, tired, and hungry.

But we had made it, and I felt great.

37
The worst city in the world

Distance to home = 21,121 miles

Out of 130 cities surveyed, Port Moresby was found to be
the least liveable in the world
The Economist, 2006

Work as if it all depends on you, and pray as if it all depends on God
ST AUGUSTINE

Two months prior to my arrival, the *Economist* had proclaimed Port Moresby the 'least liveable city in the world'. I had heard chilling stories about knife-point robberies in crowded markets and of thugs smashing down the gates of expat homes and murdering everyone inside. Recently, some rascals had hired a helicopter, landed on the roof of a bank and attempted to rob it, 'Hollywood-style'. A gigantic gunfight had ensued and the whole gang, as well as several policemen, were killed.

I rode quickly through the outskirts and when young men shouted at me to stop, I waved, smiled and accelerated. Shacks and half-built blocks were scattered along the roadside. As I reached the city centre, I reached the top of a hill and saw the Coral Sea stretching out beyond a hilly promontory. Sunlight shimmered off the water, and smoke from a cluster of hillside huts coiled up into the sky. I stopped pedalling for a moment and let myself take in the beauty. It seemed that Port Moresby combined a reputation for danger akin to Johannesburg with a setting almost as stunning as Cape Town.

Waking up the next morning in a comfortable bed in an air-conditioned flat was wonderful. I had been invited to stay by several kind expats in the city. I spent my first two days resting, and working through my host's DVD collection. I wanted to take a brief break before confronting the final, vital challenge that remained. However, after that, I had to make a start. I sat at the dining-room table and wrote in my diary:

As my visa ticks quietly away, I look out of the window of this apartment at the lazy sea stretching south to a dark and empty horizon, but which (according to my map) eventually reaches Australia. It is there where I hope to go . . . all I need to do now is find something that floats that will take me there.

My best hope for finding a boat to Australia was with a shipping company. I already had a number of contacts who worked in the industry, so I made arrangements to meet them. They were optimistic at first, but one by one contacted me to say a ride with their ships would not be possible. Since 9/11 there were severe security restrictions, they said, and insurance implications for taking non-staff passengers on their boats now made it impossible.

This was a terrible disappointment. I wondered what I should do. My three-month visa was almost expired. I agonised that, having come so far, I might in the end have to catch a plane. I made a decision to try my very hardest at this task, so that if I failed to find a boat, I would at least have tried every option. I did not want to fail because of being lazy or being a wimp. I brainstormed a list of possible ideas, and then set about the task in earnest.

I had a coffee with a yacht-club manager, who told me that because of the typhoon season there were no yachts sailing for several months; I gave a talk at the rotary club, but no one could help; I gave an interview for national TV news, but received no response. Increasingly desperate, I met the British High Commissioner at a social gathering. He was impressed that I had made it this far (and slightly put out that I had cycled across the country without informing the consulate) but, in the end, did not have any fresh ideas. Then I heard that the Greenpeace boat, *Rainbow Warrior II*, had docked in town. An Australian friend I was staying with,

Christian Loherberger, managed to talk us past the security guards so we were able to join an onboard VIP party. We made friends with the crew, but they were secretive about where they were heading next. They did, however, hint that rather than heading south to hassle Australia about their off-shore oil rigs, they would be heading north, to hassle Malaysians about their rainforest logging practices. It had been one more stimulating evening, but I had to cross off yet another possibility from my list.

I was out of ideas. But then at the start of my third week in Moresby a young British manager called Pete invited me to his tennis party. I had been put in touch with Pete by Julian, a man I'd met in Hong Kong (whom I got to know through Angus, who in turn was introduced to me by Edward Genochio from Shanghai). At Pete's tennis party, I met his friend Sam who introduced me to his girlfriend, Felicity, who put me in touch with Helen, a teacher at an International School in the city. Two days later, I visited Helen's school and gave three slideshows to her classes. At the end of each presentation, I asked the crowd of children if they could please go home and ask their parents if any of them knew anyone with a boat that was going to Australia.

The next day, Helen rang me up. She told me that Ashley, a boy in the third row in the second talk, had an uncle with a boat. It was leaving for Cairns on Saturday. If I still needed a ride, they would be happy to take me on board.

I was back in the game.

The name of the boat was *Golden Dawn*, and she was a luxury dive boat heading across to Cairns for her annual maintenance checks. I spent the three days at sea combining book-reading, diary-writing and sunbathing. Soon after the verdant hills of Papua New Guinea had slipped below the horizon, the barren cliffs of Queensland drew into sight. I thought back on the situations I had been through in the last three months. I felt sad that such a beautiful country as Papua New Guinea, with wonderful people, also had such a dangerous side. I wondered whether the young men who had chased me on the north coast really did have bad intentions.

Or perhaps they were just excited to see me and wanted to chat. I remembered a conversation I'd had with one village chief I had stayed with. He had reassured me that everyone in his village was friendly and safe, but the people in the village further up the road were dangerous. The next day, when I got to the next village, the people insisted that they were the friendly ones, and were amazed that I had made it through the previous village unscathed. But although I could dismiss some of the danger as exaggerated, sadly the rascal threat in Papua New Guinea was very real. One of my chief optimists, whom I was in touch with by email before I arrived, was a Papua New Guinean called Danny. Danny had reassured me that the rascals would not be a problem. However, when I finally reached Danny's house in the city of Lae, he confessed that he had been very worried about me, but had said it was safe because he did not want to make me worry. Twice in the last few months, he admitted, the bus he was taking to work had been hijacked by rascals.

Pondering these things, I wrote in my diary:

> *I cannot say how big the risk was that I took coming (to Papua New Guinea) alone and on a bicycle . . . I think it is a sad trait of human opinion-forming that the behaviour of the few will always shape the reputation of the many . . . thus I think that Papua New Guinea's dangerous reputation is based on just a small proportion of the population. The people I actually met took great care of me, without exception.*

But, still, I was thankful to have made it through unharmed.

Statistics for Part 4 (Hong Kong–Papua New Guinea)

Dates:	October 2005–March 2006
Total distance covered from start:	14,057 miles
Distance left to reach home:	21,121 miles
Distance covered by bicycle:	1,415 miles
Distance covered by boat:	1,085 miles
Age:	29
Types of boat taken:	
Yacht	1
Cargo ship	1
Ferries	5
Canoes	3
Motorboats	1
Rivers waded through:	6
Snakes cycled over:	1

Part Five

Australia

March–October 2006

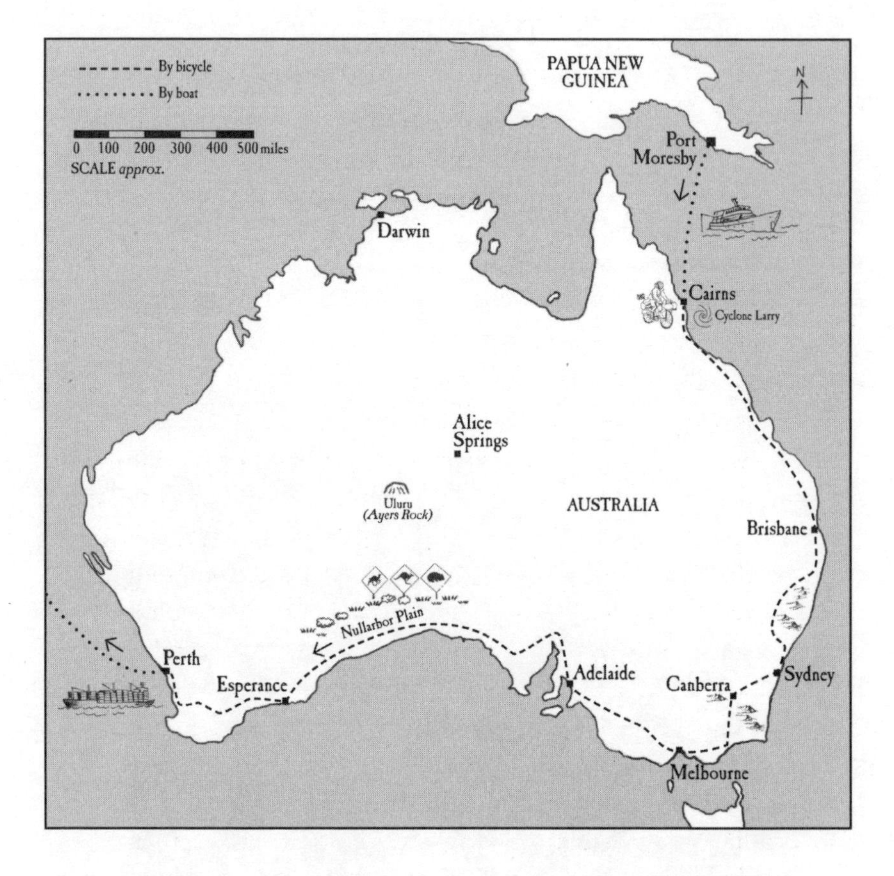
By bicycle
By boat
0 100 200 300 400 500 miles
SCALE approx.
PAPUA NEW GUINEA
Port Moresby
Darwin
Cairns
Cyclone Larry
Alice Springs
Uluru (Ayers Rock)
AUSTRALIA
Brisbane
Nullarbor Plain
Perth
Esperance
Adelaide
Canberra
Sydney
Melbourne
N

38
Cyclone Larry

Distance to home = 20,496 miles

To get back my youth I would do anything in the world except take exercise, get up early, or be respectable
OSCAR WILDE

I wheeled the bike off the waterfront and into Cairns. I could not believe I was there. The smooth, paved streets were lined with internet cafés, international restaurant chains and tourist shops offering dive trips to the Great Barrier Reef. Sun-tanned backpackers sauntered around beer gardens, and businessmen in suits walked serenely to their offices. After Port Moresby, where I was constantly looking over my shoulder, it felt strange to walk without fear. This was the first 'Western' country of my trip. English was the first language. Cars drove on the left. A big burden of stress slipped from my shoulders.

That evening, it rained heavily as I walked to the local phone box to make some calls. I spoke to my parents, who were relieved to hear I was safe. I called Christine. During my four days at sea she had been unexpectedly transferred to New York by her firm, and she seemed to be working even harder there than she had done in London. I was thrilled that she still wanted to come and visit me in Australia, so we began making a plan about where to meet. I also called my grandmother in Dorset. I had missed her hundredth birthday while I was in China, and that day was her 101st birthday. It reminded me that time was still passing at home, even while I was away.

Australia was the first country where I had a work visa, so as well as riding through the epic landscapes and visiting the landmark cities, another of my main goals was to earn some money. I had funded the journey so far with my life savings, most of which I had saved up during student summer jobs as a door-to-door salesman of children's books in California.* The journey had actually proved remarkably cheap so far – 18 months on the road had cost me about £4,000. I expected it would cost the same again to get home. My only costs were food; occasional maintenance; occasional accommodation; and visas. By cooking my own food and sleeping in a tent, even these costs were minimal. I think a journey by car or motorbike would cost at least ten times as much. As well as being cheap, the bicycle was also versatile. I could carry food and water for up to a week; I could travel a hundred miles a day; I could balance it on a canoe; I could carry it through a jungle; I could push it down a beach.

I was doing the trip without any 'corporate backing', although many people assume that this is essential for expeditions nowadays. That said, later on in the journey I was delighted to receive informal sponsorship from two companies. The first was from a Polish inventor in Melbourne called Michael, who, having seen me on Australian breakfast television, gave me a pair of his specially invented safeturn bike light indicators. These are worn on your wrists, and have sensors in them so that when you hold up an arm to turn left or right, the light is activated and starts flashing: essential gear for any aspiring cyclist–explorer.

My second sponsored item was a remote-control-sized gadget called a Dazer II. When you press the button, it emits a high-pitched noise. This noise is inaudible to human ears, but unbearable to dogs, and thus it is a brilliant way to prevent dog attacks. I would later use it to good effect against the big, angry dogs of Tibet.

But, despite my cheap lifestyle and this high-level sponsorship, I needed to earn some extra money in Australia. I initially considered

*As well as being a very lucrative job, this work had also prepared me well for the expedition, teaching me a great deal about perseverance, communicating with strangers, and the importance of having a healthy sense of the absurd.

traditional backpacker professions such as fruit-picking or serving coffee, but these were poorly paid and would require me to stay in one place. Then I began to wonder whether, after all my experience with giving slideshows in Asia, I could perhaps now start charging a modest fee to go into schools and give lectures there. I emailed some schools along my route and was pleased when over 20 schools immediately booked me to visit. The downside was that I had committed myself to reaching certain places by certain dates, which meant I would have to stick to a strict schedule of progress.

To further prepare for my ride through Australia, I shaved off my beard, bought a mobile phone and visited the supermarket. The choice of food in Australia was quite bedazzling after Papua New Guinea. After much thought, my staple evening meal in Australia would be: spaghetti or rice (cheap/compact/energy), tuna (cheap/protein), onions (cheap/vegetable), and tomato ketchup (cheap/flavour). For breakfast I would eat cereal with powdered milk as it was the food I had missed the most while in Asia. For lunch I would, where possible, treat myself to two-litre tubs of ice cream, which I could eat easily in one sitting. I decided it was the perfect food for cyclists: full of sugar and fat, does not dehydrate you, costs less than £1, tastes delicious. After my ice-cream lunches, my speed increased markedly and I was propelled onwards through whatever landscape I was in for the rest of the afternoon.

The day I left Cairns, my host warned me not to go because there was a storm building up 200 miles offshore. After Papua New Guinea, I was overly used to shrugging off warnings of danger, so I paid no attention and set off anyway. After an easy day's ride through lush, green fields, I spent my first night on the road in Australia staying with Nikki, Tim and their three children, about 20 miles south of Cairns. Nikki was the sister of a friend of my sister. She lived in a large bungalow beside the main road with a fenced garden and a small swimming pool outside.

After dinner, we turned on the television to learn that the storm had been officially upgraded to cyclone status and named Larry.

Larry was still out at sea, but winds were gusting at 150 miles per hour and he was moving rapidly towards land.

The next day I had been intending to camp shortly before the town of Innisfail, 50 miles south, so that the day following I could give my first paid slideshow at the Innisfail primary school. However, the television weather forecast predicted that Innisfail would be the precise point at which Larry would hit land. Stern warnings were given for us to tie down any loose objects in the garden, to stock up on food and to fill the bath with water. As a small child Nikki had survived Cyclone Tracy when she destroyed Darwin in 1974. Nikki told me of how families had been forced to take their children and lie in the empty bathtubs as the roofs of their houses were ripped off and debris flew in all directions. Nikki was insistent that I should not set off for Innisfail until Larry had passed, and I agreed reluctantly that the next day did not sound like ideal camping weather.

I was woken at six the next morning by a loud bang. I lay in bed for a moment and listened to the noise of blasting wind outside. The whole house was groaning. I walked through to the kitchen and found Nikki and her children staring out of the window. The cyclone was ripping branches off trees and massive pieces of debris were rolling across the lawn. The swimming pool was filling up with wreckage, and the house electricity line had been brought down by a fallen tree. Emergency radio reports warned us not to go outside. They reported that, in the worst part of the cyclone, now over Innisfail, there were gusts of over 200 miles an hour. I thanked God that I hadn't been camping there as originally planned.

By mid-morning the storm had passed and the ferocious winds died down. In the afternoon the radio reported that the cyclone had dissipated, though heavy rains were now falling further inland. It reported extensive damage to housing, forests and farmers' crops all along the coast, and that Innisfail had been particularly badly hit. We spent the rest of the day clearing debris from the garden. Several trees had come down entirely, and the side of the house was plastered with leaves.

The next morning, the road south was closed to cars. The radio announced that the rain now flowing out of the hills was likely to cause severe flooding later in the day. I decided that, as long as I found a safe place to sleep, I should be able to continue. I waved goodbye to the family, skirted past an unmanned police barrier, and set off once more, shaking my head at the fact that even sunny Australia was proving a little more complicated than I had anticipated.

The sky was grey, and the air felt cool; the empty road meandered to the horizon, covered in puddles and pieces of wood. The forests made me think of a defeated army, their broken branches hanging from decapitated trunks. Banana plantations were completely flattened and I had to keep my eye on the road to dodge the snakes which, disturbed from their usual habitats by the storm, slithered across in front of me. Billboards had been ripped off their stands, metal road signs were bent horizontal, and electricity pylons were snapped in two. I reached Innisfail at lunchtime though it was clear that my talk in the school was cancelled! Like a real-life disaster movie, people with traumatised faces were wandering around in front of smashed shop fronts and broken houses. The McDonald's sign hung limply off its stand, and the chimney of a factory stood bent over at 90 degrees. A motorboat had been thrown into a tree.

I pressed on and as evening approached it started raining heavily and the rivers began to burst their banks. I joined a queue of cars to cross a flooded bridge over the River Tully. The water was up to my thighs as I pushed and dragged the bike through the water with cars' bow waves slopping up to my waist.

In darkness I reached the town of Ingham, where emergency volunteers with big torches told me I could sleep in the village hall with other stranded motorists. Inside, we were given free food, and bedding. I talked with a man who was desperate to drive back to his farm, further north. He had cattle that would die if they did not receive water soon, but the route over the Tully River had now closed because of flooding and it was unlikely to open for several days. Some people were complaining that the government had not done enough to prepare people for the cyclone; that not enough relief was being given afterwards; that the bridges should have been made flood-proof. I felt grateful that I had a warm room to sleep in, and that I did not have to sleep in my tent that night. I was also grateful to hear on the radio that nobody had been killed in the disaster, though the people complaining had lost too much to notice.

The next day I made it to the next school I was scheduled to speak at. I was out of the cyclone zone now, so the electricity was back on and I was able to give the slideshow and earn my fees. The teacher was slightly shocked by my appearance when I arrived. I explained that I had just had to wade through a river. A few weeks later, a teacher tried to throw me out of a school when he saw me walking through his corridor in my dishevelled state (I had slept in a field the night before). I didn't mind, though. It made me feel more heroic.

39
Four months later

Distance to home = 18,322 miles

21 JULY 2006

It is four months later and I am sitting on Alanis and riding through the darkness towards Melbourne. An icy, blustering headwind blows against me, and cuts through my thin fleece. I knew it would be winter in the southern hemisphere, but I did not expect it to be below freezing and I do not have enough clothes. Car headlights flash past. I brace myself when I hear the rumble of big trucks approaching. I am wearing a dim head-torch under my helmet, and I have a flashing red light at the back, but I feel vulnerable and in danger. I tuck closer to the side of the road and keep pedalling.

My mind flits between keeping my wheels straight and a blur of memories from the past few months. At Easter, three months ago, Christine came to meet me in Brisbane. We had eight days together so we rented a car and drove up the coast. Our relationship began to feel much more light-hearted than the intense, emotional days of Hong Kong. One night we camped in a national park. As Christine had never slept in a tent before, she was very excited. The next morning, after we had cooked breakfast on a fire, she used her mum's scissors (which she had brought especially for the occasion) to cut the dreadlocks out of my hair. Back on the coast, we went for long walks along the waterfront, had kung-fu play fights in the sand and waltzed under the moonlight.

We also caught up on recent events in our lives: she had been busy negotiating with angry corporations and checking the minutiae of incomprehensible documents in the urban jungle of New York; I had been dodging rascals and carrying Alanis through rivers in the eco-jungle of Papua New Guinea. Our worlds could hardly be more different, yet a deep friendship was developing. I asked if she could come and meet me in Singapore in three months' time and she said she would try.

After she left I continued south 700 miles to Sydney, giving lots of talks along the way. Then my wheels spun 250 miles west to Canberra and now another 600 miles south-west to Melbourne. At least I am finally moving towards rather than away from England. It is 22 months since I flew to Magadan, and I hope to be home in 18 months' time. What other adventures might I have to face on the way back? I have found a passage on a freighter to take me from Perth to Singapore, but before that I must cross the empty plains of Western Australia. Once back in Asia it looks as though I will have to cross Tibet in the winter: –30°C passes and deep snow, but this time on my own. The thought unnerves me.

And what about tonight? I do not know where I will camp. There are plenty of trees around, so hopefully I can put the tent up behind some of these. Last night, as darkness arrived, it began to snow gently. My feet were numb, my SPD shoes were beginning to fall apart, and I was hungry. When I reached a town of neon-lit restaurants, I sat alone in a McDonald's drive-through eating a Big Mac meal to warm up while repairing my shoes with a piece of string. Riding out of the town, I felt fed up with always being in a hurry to reach the next school to speak at. I was annoyed with how massive the distances were between everything in Australia. Everything was too far apart. It would be far more sensible to drive than cycle around this country.

Too tired to ride further, I stopped where I was, and pitched my tent on the verge beside the road. I did not even look for a tree to hide behind. Putting on all my clothes, I climbed into my thin sleeping bag, and prepared to sleep.

A moment later I heard a car pull up beside me and saw flashing lights coming through the side of the tent. It was the police.

I climbed back into the cold to talk to the officer. He was several years younger than me, and asked what I was doing. I told him that I did not feel safe riding any more in the dark, so was sleeping by the road. I would move on as soon as it was daylight. Would that be okay?

'Well,' he said in a manly Australian drawl, 'if you move on tomorrow morning, you can stay here for tonight. But if you wanna know what I think, then I'd say you were a crazy bastard.'

40
An uncontrollable shivering

Distance to home = 18,074 miles

The trouble with always trying to preserve the health of the body is that it is so difficult to do without destroying the health of the mind

G. K. CHESTERTON

'It doesn't look like malaria,' said the doctor decisively, 'it looks like flu. Take a few days in bed and you should be fine. Come and see me again next week if you're not feeling better.'

I had gone to see the doctor in Melbourne because the previous day I had come down with a fever in the middle of a lecture I was giving at a school. I staggered through to the end of the presentation before, feeling nauseous, I ran from the room and threw up in a toilet.

The doctor's prognosis was reassuring, so I did as he ordered and went to bed for the rest of the afternoon. I felt better in the evening and was confident that I would soon recover.

But the next day the fever came back, worse than ever. My hosts were away for the weekend and I shivered uncontrollably in bed for an hour. Then I became boiling hot for an hour and sweated profusely for an hour. Christine phoned to see how I was. I was in the midst of a shivering fit at the time, but I tried to tell her, with chattering teeth, that I was fine; the doctor had said it was flu.

An hour later Christine rang back, sounding concerned. She had been in touch with a doctor friend who had advised that, in view of my symptoms and travel history, I should go to hospital for a malaria blood test. I reluctantly promised her that I would, and was touched that she cared so much. I caught the tram to a hospital and told the nurse at the casualty counter that I thought I might have malaria. She looked at my face for a fraction of a second and then said, 'It doesn't look like malaria,' and asked me to take a seat.

Six hours later, at a quarter to midnight, my name was called. I saw a young trainee doctor called Janet. She looked at me and took my pulse.

'It looks like the flu,' she said, 'but, just in case, we'll you give you a blood test.'

I gave some blood and then, because the trams had stopped running, I walked home. I arrived an hour later, at one in the morning. I had not eaten dinner and was very hungry. As I put some toast on, my mobile phone rang. It was Janet, the doctor.

'Rob,' she said, 'we've received the results back from your blood test. You've got malaria.'

'Oh dear,' I said, rather Britishly. 'Should I come back tomorrow?'

'We think you should come back immediately.'

I packed my bag again and walked for an hour back to the hospital.

My first night in hospital also marked one year since Christine and I had started going out. She was tearful when I phoned from my bed in the casualty ward to say she'd been right about the malaria. I spent the next three days on a drip and taking all the pills I was given. I had no visitors, but both Christine and my sister ordered hampers of fruit and biscuits to be delivered to me. Christine also sent me a little teddy bear, which I named Christine and tied to the back of the bike for the remainder of the ride home. The fever did not return, and after the doctors gave me the all-clear I walked 'home' again. When I got back, I weighed myself and found that I had lost 11 kilograms during the illness. At 63 kg I was the lightest I'd been since the age of 17.

41
The Nullarbor Plain

Distance to home = 17,069 miles

If there is a road that has not been travelled,
then that is the one I must take
EDWARD JOHN EYRE

After ten days' rest I had regained some strength, so I set out once again. Over the next few weeks I rode 700 miles to Adelaide and from there a further 300 miles to Port Augusta. As I left the port behind me, the road narrowed, the earth turned red and an empty scrubland stretched away to the horizon like a giant's blanket. I was now encroaching onto the edge of the formidable Nullarbor Plain.

The name 'Nullarbor' comes from the Latin for 'no trees', and its 800 miles of arid saltbush scrub is uninhabited apart from some scattered Aboriginal settlements and the occasional petrol station. The barren land acts as a divide between the western coastal city of Perth and the rest of Australia. Edward John Eyre became the first European to cross the Nullarbor Plain in 1841. He described it as 'a hideous anomaly, a blot on the face of Nature, the sort of place one gets into in bad dreams'.* Although, after Eyre, the plain was spanned by a telegraph line and then a railway, it was not until 1976 that a proper bitumen road was completed across it. In preparation for the long crossing, which I expected to take about ten days, I had marked the petrol stations on my map. They were spaced up to three days'

*During his crossing, Eyre frequently ran desperately short of water and was saved only by using Aboriginal techniques for digging in sand hills. In the tradition of all great English explorers, Eyre often used the hard-earned water to brew a cup of tea.

ride apart, but I had been told that each of them should allow me to fill my water bottles. Otherwise I would have to be self-sufficient.

Lilwall, I said as I clicked into a higher gear and forced my legs to rotate faster, *this is one of those places where you have to just put your head down and have a motto of 'miles not smiles'*. The 'miles not smiles' phrase had originally been coined by an old school friend during a rafting trip down the River Severn. We had just completed our A levels, and were time-rich, money-poor. We scrounged two barrels from a local factory, tied them to a door from the local dump, borrowed a paddle, and then set off for Bristol. The raft floated so low in the water that, however hard we paddled, we went at the same speed as the river, about one mile per hour. I grew frustrated, but my friend told me that our motto should be 'smiles not miles'. The phrase stuck, and Al and I had often since adapted it to describe the contrasting types of progress on bicycles.

As I pressed on across it, the balance between smiles and miles on the Nullarbor Plain was largely dictated by the wind direction. Some days the wind was behind me, and I was swept along at 20 miles an hour, with minimal effort. Other days, the wind was against me and I was down to five miles per hour with maximum effort. I pedalled for eight hours each day and, as the time dragged past, the terrain altered slowly, like the seasons. The hues of red earth merged to brown; the large, parched bushes became small, parched bushes; the dead-flat gradient rose into a cacophony of rolling hills for 50 miles, before flattening out once more. The stillness of the land was broken only by the occasional troop of kangaroos, which bounced past, strong, elegant and utterly implausible, with their long tails trailing behind them.

Although the battle I waged with the distance was a solo one, there were also other human crossers of the plain. It felt as though we were almost a sub-culture. My least favourite fellow travellers were the titanic articulated lorries known as road trains, which thundered past me at high speed. More amenable were the grey-nomads: grey-haired couples who were spending their retirement circumnavigating the country in caravans. They sometimes stopped to offer me water and, one night, when I camped beside a caravan, I was given a glass of sherry.

There were also some crazy characters. One afternoon I reached the Bunda cliffs, which dropped down into the sea like a colossal pack of pillars. I rode up to a viewing point and at that moment a carload of photographers also pulled in. Three men climbed out of the car, took a bag of golf clubs out of their boot and then, while two of them took photographs, the third walked to the cliff edge, teed up, and started hitting balls into the sea. They let me have a go, though with my poor swing the ball shot off at right angles and nearly hit one of the photographers in the face!

Every few days I met other cyclists coming in the opposite direction. They looked haggard, and it reminded me of what I must look like. My favourite was an older man, in his sixties. He told me that, as a widower, it was his children who were worrying about him rather than his parents. He had a broad grin on his face and said he had loved every minute of his ride.

But if we cyclists thought we were tough for pedalling the Nullarbor, then we were mistaken. One day, I met a solitary man approaching *on foot* on my side of the road. It was a young Japanese man. We exchanged greetings as if it were normal for a cyclist and a walker to meet in such a place. In front of him he was pushing a baby buggy, which was loaded up with bottles of water and bags of biscuits.

I also began to anticipate an encounter with someone more unusual still: a Welshman on a skateboard. I had been hearing about Dave Cornthwaite for months, by word of mouth and on the radio. He was attempting to break the world record for distance-skateboarding, by pushing his way 4,000 miles from Perth to Sydney. Some motorists coming from the other direction told me he was still crossing the plain from the opposite direction. Because there was only one road, I knew we could not miss each other. Each day I asked the cyclists and motorists I met how far away he was: three hundred miles, two hundred miles, a hundred miles . . .

But the following day I did not meet him. I wondered why not. That evening, I camped in a lay-by, where I met a pair of Dutch travellers. They had overtaken me an hour beforehand in their beaten-up saloon. As we ate dinner around a campfire I mentioned that I was looking forward to meeting the skateboarder soon.

They told me they had seen him earlier that day.

They were travelling in the same direction as me, which meant I should have seen him too.

'Are you sure?' I asked.

'Yes,' they said.

I realised that at lunchtime, while I sat eating a sandwich in a rest area obscured from the road by a big bush, he must have skated right on past without me noticing.

The next day, I set off before the Dutch travellers, but in the mid-morning they caught me up. Before I left Melbourne I had bought a video camera to film the rest of the ride. However, because I had no support crew to film me, to get footage I often had to balance the camera on a rock and ride past it and then pedal back to pick it up. When the travellers stopped to see how I was, I asked if they could take my camera and drive past while filming. They got some great footage, and even stopped to give me the camera back.*

After ten days of hard riding, I cycled down '90-mile straight', Australia's longest straight road. After that I was at last approaching the end. I saw from my notes that there was a dirt track shortcut I could take. It even had a derelict farmhouse on it where passing travellers were welcome to stay. I needed a rest day, so I took the turnoff and bounced through some potholes for an afternoon until, as it grew dark, the silhouette of the stone homestead came into view. I felt I was in the *Blair Witch Project* as I held my video camera in one hand and pushed open the door with the other.

Inside, there were two dusty beds, a fireplace, and a desk covered with papers. I laid out my sleeping bag, lit a fire and enjoyed having a real chair to sit on. Before bed, I looked through the pile of papers on the desk. On the top was a typed sheet which explained the history of the homestead. It had been built in 1922 by a pioneering farming family, who had eked a living from the land for 33 years before abandoning it.

*To watch some movie shorts made from this video footage, please see www.cyclinghomefromsiberia.com

The inheritor of the homestead had renovated it in the 1980s, and now welcomed weary travellers to make use of it. There was even a guestbook for us to sign. Before I went to bed a final scrap of paper caught my attention.

It was undated, and said: 'Be careful, there is a tiger snake living in the hole above the door.'

For the rest of the night I wished I had not read it. Every creak and groan from the old house sounded, to my ears, like a hiss or a slither.

42
What ships are built for

Distance to home = 15,496 miles

A ship in port is safe, but that's not what ships are built for
GRACE MURRAY COOPER

After five days of peaceful sheep country, I descended into the pleasant city of Perth. My 6,000-mile ride through Australia was finally over. I stayed with a lovely British family for two weeks and gave more talks. Then I cycled the coastal path to Freemantle Port and pushed the bike up a ramp and onto the enormous freighter that would be my home for the next week. I had found the boat through a Swiss travel agent. The agent had a network of captains who were prepared to take paying guests to get around the difficult paperwork. It was not cheap, and the £600 I paid was twice as much as a flight to Asia, but I had earned good money in Australia and did not want to spend months waiting around for a boat again.

Six hours later, I stood on the bridge as a tug pulled us out of the harbour. Two hundred metres of hull stretched out in front of me, loaded with 2,500 containers, bolted together in neat stacks. With our massive engines rumbling, the tugboat cut us loose. We pulled away from the coast and chugged off on our way to Singapore. After Australia had slipped out of sight, I went back down to my cabin. It was a luxurious suite including a lounge with a DVD player, a set of sofas, and an en-suite bathroom. I looked forward to a week of reading, watching films, writing my diary and gazing out to sea. I was so excited to have a chance to do some serious relaxing.

Forty-eight hours before we reached Singapore, we passed between a group of Indonesian islands. The captain handed me a folder and asked me to read it. It was titled: 'Security precautions for passing through waters where there is a pirate threat.'

There had been an increase in pirate activity in Indonesian waters since the end of the Cold War when the superpower navies reduced their patrols. The route leading to Singapore was ideal for pirates. There were plenty of islands nearby on which they could base their operations. Two years previously, 40 per cent of global pirate attacks had occurred in Indonesian waters, sometimes resulting in the kidnapping or murder of the crew.

I was told that one of the pirates' favourite techniques was to use two motorboats with a long rope held between them. When the targeted ship came past, it would catch on the rope and the two motorboats would be drawn alongside so they could board. The captain told me that he had given the crew a strict order that they were not to fight the pirates if they came on board, unless 'they start killing us'. There were various precautions we would take nonetheless. First, all but the essential lights would be turned off. Second, there would be extra men on watch. Third, the radar would be carefully monitored – an officer showed me how they could put a tracker on any ship that appeared, to see which way it was moving. Finally, metal gates were lowered onto the outside steps that led up to the cabins and fire hoses were positioned so that they could be turned on to deter anyone from trying to climb up the banisters. If the pirates made it past all of these deterrents, the captain said he would simply give them all the money on the ship and hope that they did not kidnap us.

I felt quite excited that night as we ploughed onwards across the dark sea. When I woke up the next morning and realised we had not been hijacked after all, I was almost disappointed. The following evening there was no more pirate threat and the sky ahead lit up with the lights of a huge city. Singapore. While giant dockside cranes unloaded our cargo methodically and rapidly, a mini on-board crane lowered Alanis down to the quayside.

I walked down a ramp and back onto solid ground. It was almost exactly a year since I had left Hong Kong on my island-hopping detour. I was back on the Asian mainland, and now all that remained was to ride 10,000 miles to get home.

Statistics for Part 5 (Australia)

Dates:	March– October 2006
Total distance covered from start:	22,729 miles
Distance left to reach home:	12,449 miles
Distance covered by bicycle:	8,047 miles
Distance covered by boat:	625 miles
Age:	29
Nights in hospital:	3
Most consecutive days without a shower:	9
Maximum wind speed outside:	Over 100 mph
Total tubs of ice cream eaten:	26
Dead emus seen on road:	4
Dead kangaroos seen on road:	Over 30

Part Six

Singapore–India

October 2006–April 2007

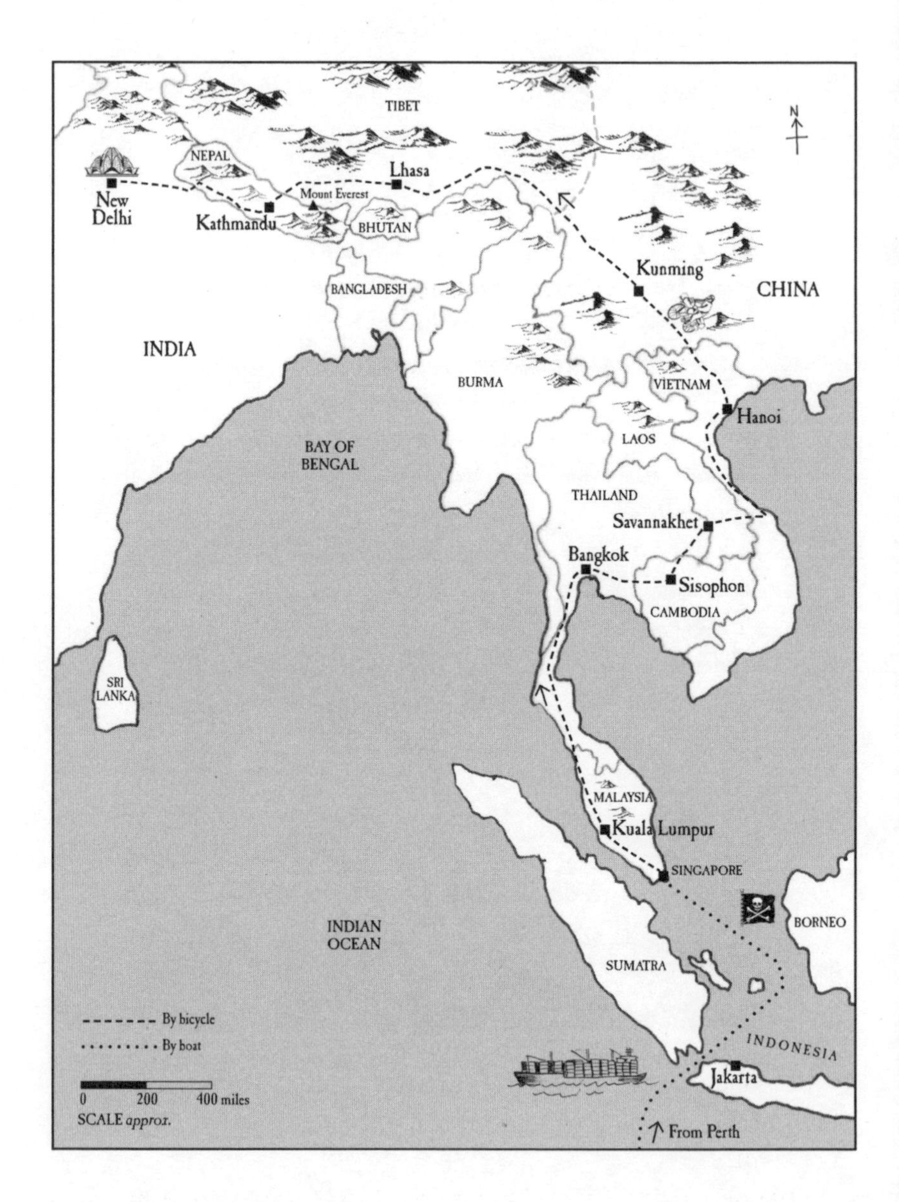
TIBET
NEPAL
Lhasa
New Delhi
Mount Everest
Kathmandu
BHUTAN
Kunming
CHINA
BANGLADESH
INDIA
BURMA
VIETNAM
Hanoi
LAOS
BAY OF BENGAL
THAILAND
Savannakhet
Bangkok
Sisophon
CAMBODIA
SRI LANKA
MALAYSIA
Kuala Lumpur
SINGAPORE
BORNEO
INDIAN OCEAN
SUMATRA
By bicycle
By boat
INDONESIA
Jakarta
0 200 400 miles
SCALE approx.
From Perth

43
A date in Singapore

Distance to home = 12,449 miles

Isn't there something in living dangerously?
ALDOUS HUXLEY

'Rob!'

Christine called out to me as I ran straight past where she was sitting. Somehow, although I had travelled thousands of miles in order to be there in time, I had managed to get lost at the airport and miss being at the gate when she arrived. Fortunately she had spotted me, and a moment later she was in my arms again.

'I can't believe that you're real,' I said to her. We had been staying in touch with letters, emails, and occasional phone calls, but sometimes I wondered whether I had gone mad and was imagining this amazing girl on the other side of the world.

'You look so thin,' she said, scanning my face and frame.

I was so happy to see her again and corrected her that I was actually looking very lean and muscular. The week that followed was full of laughing, eating and resting. Christine had been to high school in Singapore, so she knew it well. The buildings were clean, tall and dazzling. The people were smart, serious and hard-working. There were lots of vast shopping malls. Located almost exactly on the equator, the humidity was stifling outside, but inside there was plenty of air-conditioning. I was glad that my first country back in Asia was so safe, but the sanitisation made me think of Huxley's *Brave New World*.

We took a three-day break from the city on the Indonesian island of Bintan. One day I insisted on renting a Laser dinghy on the beach so I could teach Christine to sail. Standing on the front and holding the mast I yelled expert instructions to her: 'Okay, now pull the tiller towards you . . . no, urmm, sorry, I mean push it awwwwwaaa . . .'

We capsized five times and I think she wondered how I had made it so far on the bike.

We had survived a whole year of 'long-distance relationship', and somehow it was beginning to feel 'normal'. It amazed me how we were getting used to it. If before I set off someone had told me that I would find a girlfriend along the way, I would not have believed them. Christine joked that when she tried to explain me to her friends in London, some were convinced that I was a mythical, made-up boyfriend, as they had not met me. It would still be another year before I was home. I often thought of her and missed her while I was riding, but I knew it must be even more difficult for her – stuck in a stressful office job while I was off on a high adventure. Sometimes I felt guilty for being such an ever-distant, unconventional boyfriend and sometimes I felt insecure and worried that she would meet someone else while I was so far away. However, although I could not really put my finger on why, I just really trusted her.

Before she left, I asked Christine if she would visit again when I reached India and she said she would if she could. India felt a very long way away. I knew that it would take me many months to get there and that I would have to negotiate several daunting new obstacles on the way.

We caught the clean, smooth metro back to the airport and said goodbye yet again. I watched her walk through the security check, and just managed to catch her eye and give a wave before she disappeared out of sight.

I went back to my host's flat, picked up Alanis, and cycled over the Causeway Bridge to Malaysia.

I rode a thousand miles north through Malaysia and Thailand, passing sweltering palm oil plantations and sprawling industrial cities. Almost every day the skies cracked and I was drenched by a terrific, cooling thunderstorm. Four days before I reached Bangkok, the metal rim of my front wheel started to split. It was the original wheel I had started with in Siberia. It had served me well but this was definitely the beginning of the end. I unclipped my front brakes so that the wheel could still rotate, but each day it worsened until 10 cm of the metal had torn off, causing regular punctures. I wrapped an old piece of rubber around the tube to protect it before eventually limping into the capital at nightfall.

I took several days off to give some talks, rest and get Alanis fixed. Throughout the journey so far I had tried to take Alanis for a check-up at a good bike shop every six months. I carried only basic spares and was not a proficient mechanic, so I hoped that these occasional services would stop me from having a severe breakdown in the middle of nowhere. I bought a new wheel at a bike shop in the city centre, and also asked the mechanic to 'please replace anything that is likely to break in the next four thousand miles, because I am about to ride through Tibet in winter'. The mechanic nodded indifferently and turned back to his work. I don't think he was very impressed.

44
The man who forgave

Distance to home = 10,983 miles

Does not the most enlightened philosophy teach us to mistrust man: the optimal being, the supreme creature, the natural aristocrat of the living world? Man who – when, exceptionally, he becomes his true self – can bring about excellence, yet also bring about the worst. A slayer of monsters and forever a monster himself

FRANÇOIS BIZOT*

I left Bangkok on my thirtieth birthday, setting off at dawn to beat the rush-hour traffic. In the afternoon I was cheered up considerably when I saw an elephant ambling down the road carrying a farmer home from work. That night I stayed in a dingy truckers' hostel 50 miles along the road to Cambodia. To celebrate the start of my fourth decade of life, I treated myself to ice cream for dinner and then sat on my bed and opened a package that Christine had given me in Singapore. The parcel was full of cards from friends and family in England. I read each one several times, before placing them back in my pannier. I was touched that people still remembered me.

I had been away from home for over two years now, but apart from a brief rendezvous with my parents in China and the occasional old friend I stayed with, the vast majority of people I met had been entirely new acquaintances. Despite this, it had been rare for me to feel really lonely or homesick. I think this was partly because my hosts made me feel so welcome; partly because I had

*Bizot was the only Westerner to survive being interrogated by the Khmer Rouge.

a fortunate propensity for losing myself in a good book; and partly because of my faith in a God who watched over me.

But that birthday night in Thailand was a lonely moment. I began to wonder whether, as a 30-year-old, I was too old to be still exploring the world. Was my trip just an over-elongated, tenuously glorified, late-in-life-gap-year by an insecure man who was still trying to prove to himself that he was not afraid? That night I did not feel like a 30-year-old adult at all. I felt like I was a frightened child.

The next day, I cycled to the Poipet border. There was a large stone gateway over the road with a sign emblazoned over the top that said 'the Kingdom of Cambodia'. It looked like a portal to another world and framed the scene of motorbikes, money-changers and animals that scurried through to the other side. I queued up and paid 30 dollars in cash for a visa and then cycled on through myself.

In Cambodia, the tarmac road quickly disappeared and was replaced by a dusty, pale-brown track full of tyre ruts and potholes. Cars and trucks veered and bounced past me, honking their horns furiously and throwing up clouds of dust. I was sweating a lot, so the dust stuck to my forehead, infused my beard and clogged the corners of my eyes. On two occasions, the verge of the road was so sandy that my tyres slipped out from under me and I tumbled in a heap to the ground.

On both sides of the road, fields of grassy crops stretched out like a green sea to a skyline of shimmering mountains. Lines of people were strewn out across the fields, working in the burning sun to harvest the rice. They wore long-sleeved shirts and various types of headgear, ranging from sunhats, to baseball caps, to bowler hats. In the straw-roofed villages there were lots of children. They waved excitedly at me as I rode past and leapt in the air with delight when I waved back. They were mostly thin, with bare feet, and they drastically outnumbered the adults. It was normal for children to outnumber adults in the developing world but it seemed even more pronounced here. I realised with a chill this was probably because a huge proportion of the older generation had been killed in the genocide.

A teacher in Bangkok had given me two books about Cambodia's recent history. I had read of how, after being destabilised by the war in Vietnam and many years of civil war, the Cambodian government had been toppled by the communist Khmer Rouge in 1975. The army of teenage soldiers in red bandanas had initially been welcomed into the capital city as liberators by cheering crowds. Everyone hoped that, at last, peace might return to the country.

But the smiles and celebrations were short-lived, for Pol Pot, the Khmer Rouge's infamous leader, subscribed to a deranged, fundamentalist vision of agrarian utopia, based on a fusion of eleventh-century agricultural models and the distorted, Maoist ideals of communism. Pol Pot believed that, in order to create his utopia, the population of the country had to be reduced. To achieve this, rather than a birth control campaign, or expelling people, he instigated a programme of mass execution. High up on the list of those to be eliminated was anybody from an ethnic minority, and anyone who had an education or connection with foreigners (if you wore glasses, that was evidence enough). First of all, you would be tortured and forced to give the names of friends and family (who would therefore also be arrested). After that came your execution, probably at the hands of a brain-washed child soldier. The land was filled with screams, tears and blood for three terrible years, and it is estimated that over two million people (a quarter of the population) died from execution, disease, exhaustion or starvation during this time.

After their recent humiliating withdrawal from Vietnam, the Americans were unwilling to become involved. The Chinese government were supporting the Khmer Rouge. Eventually, in 1979, the now-victorious communist army of Vietnam intervened and drove the Khmer Rouge into some isolated corners of the country, where the fighting did not cease entirely until the mid-1990s.

At nightfall on my first day in Cambodia, I reached the town of Sisophon. I did not know where I was going to sleep that night. Spotting a large blue building with a cross painted on it, I wheeled Alanis through the gate and asked a huddle of teenagers if I could see the pastor. A man appeared, wearing a clean, flowery Hawaiian shirt, dark trousers and black sandals. He spoke English and said his name was Pastor Navi. After I had explained my journey to him, he said I could sleep in the church. He gave me a bucket of cold water and, after I had washed, he invited me to join him for dinner.

'I was nine years old when the Khmer Rouge took power,' said Navi. We were sitting at plastic tables, outside a glass-fronted restaurant. The night was warm and insects buzzed around the street light above us. 'I lived in a village with my parents and I had seven brothers and sisters. I did not go to school, but I helped my parents around the house. One day the Khmer Rouge soldiers came to the village. They ordered me to go with them to work on a farm 23 kilometres from my home.'

I asked if his brothers and sisters were sent with him.

'No, we were separated and I did not know anyone else,' he said. 'They forced us to work very hard, all day, and they beat us if we did not work hard enough. I worked there for three years and I was very unhappy. But then the Vietnamese invaded and I thought that we were liberated. But I still wasn't allowed to return to my family. Instead, they sent me to work in the forest, cutting down trees. I was a teenager now and this was very dangerous work. There were many land-mines and, every month, someone from the work camp was killed or injured. There was also a lot of malaria. The Vietnamese soldiers did not care and I knew that if I stayed there I would die,' he paused and looked out into the night, 'so me and a group of friends decided to escape.'

I leant forward in my chair as Navi continued.

'We left the camp in the middle of the night and started to head for the Thai border. There were 12 of us at the beginning, me and my closest friends. But it was very dangerous. We had to crawl through the grass and the mud and often we had to travel at night. Several of my friends were killed by stepping on land-mines. When one friend was injured by a land-mine, we had to leave him behind because we could not take him with us. The Vietnamese soldiers were also trying to kill us. They shot at us if they saw us. Eight of my friends were killed. I was sure that I would die too.' His face was tired and expressionless as he spoke.

'At night, we climbed trees because it was safer to sleep up there. One night, we were sleeping in a tree on the edge of a field. In the middle of the night, I heard a voice speaking to me. The voice said that I would not die. I thought it was one of my friends and told him to be quiet. But he said it wasn't him. Then I heard the voice again, saying that I would not die. I didn't believe in God. We had been told there was no God in the camps. But, later on, I realised it was God telling me this.'

Navi wiped his brow and the waitress brought our food. We started eating.

'Eventually we crossed the Thai border and reached a refugee camp. I lived there for seven years. It was like a town; there were so many Cambodians. There were Christians running a school and they gave out Bibles. I accepted a Bible because the pages were good for rolling cigarettes. Gradually I started to take an interest in what they were saying. After a number of years, I became a Christian.' Navi smiled for the first time, but there was still sadness in his face.

'When the war finished, I came back to Cambodia and went to my village to look for my family. I found my neighbour, an old man, and asked if he knew where my parents and brothers and sisters were. The neighbour said that, shortly after I had been taken away to the farm, the Khmer Rouge had killed my parents and all of my brothers and sisters. They killed them by making them kneel down and then they broke their necks by hitting them.' Navi indicated a chopping motion to his neck with his hand. Then he said quietly, 'So I was the only one who had survived. I was all alone.'

The tragedy that befell Navi's family was not the exception in Cambodia; for many it was probably the norm. The majority of people of my age and above would all have unbearable stories to tell. Before we went back to the church Navi took me to his house to meet his wife and three young children. 'My life is still full of sadness. I do not think I will ever be truly happy,' he said, taking his daughter onto his lap, 'but I believe that God is good. He has helped me to forgive and to love. I even forgive the people who killed my family. Cambodia still has many troubles but I believe God has called me to start a church here so that I can teach the people how to forgive.'

45
Chinese intestines

Distance to home = 9,492 miles

By perseverance the snail reached the ark
CHARLES SPURGEON

'Those look like intestines,' I said in English, raising my eyebrows.

Having spent the last month cycling north through Laos and Vietnam, I was now back in China. Since crossing the border 48 hours previously I had been drenched by rain; got lost on a muddy, unmarked road; been fed and hosted by a village family; and listened to Brazilian funk music on my iPod as I climbed an enormous hill. It felt great to be back.

The middle-aged Chinese woman standing behind the street barbeque laughed and again gestured that I should try eating the stringy, slimy-looking pieces of meat.

'Okay, okay,' I smiled, 'I'll give them a try.' I handed her some money, and she dolloped two onto my plate. I sat down with a crowd of townsfolk behind me. They had briefly stopped chattering to watch our exchange, but now their excited conversations resumed once more. The 'intestines' were chewy, if tasteless, but they were another interesting thing to add to my list of 'things tried once'.

The next day, however, my stomach was churning and nauseous and I regretted being so bold. I did not want to lie in bed, so I started cycling. I was weak, with no appetite, and gave myself energy by eating sweets. Almost every hour I had to drop the bike and run into a field to squat. I managed to cycle 60 miles before, totally exhausted, I reached a village hotel at nightfall.

Throughout the night, I was up regularly going to the loo. My room had an en-suite bathroom, but it was very dirty and the squat toilet was placed directly beneath a cold, dripping showerhead. The next day I felt too ill to ride and did not leave the room all morning. I just slept, went to the loo and drank soft drinks.

In mid-morning, I was having yet another one of my squatting sessions. Halfway through, I was surprised to look up and see that the hotel owner, a Chinese man in his fifties, had entered my room, without knocking, and was standing in the toilet with me. I gasped at him, and then he started shouting something at me in Chinese. He seemed to be demanding that right there and then I pay for my extra night in the hotel.

I had a sudden flush of anger. 'I will happily pay you for tonight,' I yelled in English, 'but in case you hadn't noticed, I am currently taking a crap!' I then ushered him out of my room, shouting and waddling after him with my boxer shorts around my ankles. I must have made quite a fearsome sight.

Feeling ill was always a time when I imagined the worst-case scenarios for the road ahead. Now that I was nearing Tibet, as well as famously colossal mountains and notoriously ferocious dogs, I was also fearful about the fact that it would be winter in Tibet. Why did I always get my seasons wrong?

I was expecting temperatures to be in the –30s, but unlike Siberia, Al would not be there to save the day if things went wrong. However, I was better prepared. I'd had the best of my Siberian gear sent back to me and also, via mail order, purchased a sturdy new tent, some thick Baffin boots and a pair of spiked tyres to give me better grip on the ice.

The other main concern was the politically sensitive nature of Tibet. The Chinese government mandated that foreigners needed a special permit to travel in most of Tibet, but they gave such permits only to tourists partaking in special tour groups (in special tour vehicles, with special tour guides). The permits were not given to independent English adventurers such as me. This meant that I would have to cross the region without a permit, and therefore also somehow needed to avoid the military checkpoints on the way. I had read the websites of other cyclists who had attempted this in the past. The tactic they suggested sounded ludicrous, but it looked like my only option.

So as I lay in bed, ill, in the unfriendly hotel, I reminded myself that I had survived other difficult adventures, such as Papua New Guinea, even though I had felt just as frightened, if not more so. I pledged to myself that after Tibet I would take all the easy options to get home. I would go through only the most peaceful and mild of the Central Asian and Middle Eastern countries. I would take no more silly risks. I would have no more silly worries.

However, I did still need to get well. Before I left London, the Hospital for Tropical Diseases had sold me three special antibiotic pills.* The instructions said that each pill should be enough to clear basic bacteria-based stomach upsets. I had taken one pill shortly before leaving Papua New Guinea when my poo had turned green, and I had almost instantly recovered. After that I called them 'my magic pills'. I had two left and decided that I could now justify taking another one. I swallowed the magic pill and fell asleep. Waking an hour later, I felt better. By the evening I was able to eat a proper meal. The following day I hit the road.

Reaching Kunming, the provincial capital of Yunnan province, I checked into a backpacker hostel and took three days off to enjoy some final hot showers, pizzas and emailing before Tibet. While online my morale received a significant and unexpected boost. I was looking at the Lonely Planet Thorntree website† and came across a message from a French Canadian couple who were also in China and about to ride through Tibet. I quickly sent them an email. They happened to be online at the time and sent me an instant reply, saying that they were one week's ride, or about 400 miles, ahead of me. If I could catch them up, they said, I would be welcome to ride with them.

The thought of having some company appealed strongly, especially for wintery Tibet, so I climbed back on the bike and set off in hot pursuit.

*Ciroflaxin.

†www.lonelyplanet.com/thorntree is a travellers' chat room. In my experience it was the best place for finding information about the route ahead.

46
Tyre tracks in the snow

Distance to home = 9,053 miles

Man's greatest step is between the warm bed and the cold floor
ANONYMOUS

I chased the Canadians hard all day every day, riding for several hours each night. The warm onshore winds of Vietnam were now being replaced by the cold winds of the Himalayas, and the mountains around me began to look truly majestic. From the summit of each successive climb I could see row after row of them rolling towards me, like waves from an approaching storm. Some of them were capped with a menacing mantle of snow and ice. Like a surfer paddling out from the beach, I spent my days struggling up the front and then down the back of the next, only to see some even higher peaks coming at me on the other side.

I was finding the climbs hard work because I was once more so heavy with winter gear. As the passes rose to over 3,500 metres, I began to gasp for oxygen because of the thinner air. I knew that once I reached Tibet proper the passes would be much higher and I hoped my body would acclimatise in time. As the land gradually became less populated, I started camping in the hillside forests. During one long climb a big mongrel suddenly appeared on the road ahead of me and started barking and running towards me. I pulled out the Dazer II and pressed the button. The dog shook its head and backed off.

I stopped in the last town before the border to stock up with food. That night it started to snow. I asked the hotel manager if there would be much snow on the roads ahead. He nodded at me solemnly and gestured that the snow would be up to his thighs on the passes.

*

'Man's greatest step is between the warm bed and the cold floor,' I said to myself as I climbed out of bed the next morning. I looked out of the window and saw that it was still snowing. I put on my winter clothes and wheeled the bike out into the cold.

I was sweating profusely by the time I reached the next pass. Near the top, the road was covered in a layer of slippery, compressed snow and a slope dropped away precariously to my left. However, the new tyres, with their 2-millimetre metal studs, gripped perfectly. I even overtook a short queue of cars that were stuck. Looking across to the opposite valley wall, I saw a half-built ski resort, complete with chair lifts. I had not heard that skiing was taking off in China but with the growing middle class I suppose it was only a matter of time.

As I began the descent I could not see the valley floor, it was so far below me. Over the next hour of coasting around hairpin bends, I lost over 2,000 metres of altitude. I had always known that Tibet included many of the highest mountains and roads in the world. What I had found out only recently was that it also boasted many of Asia's great rivers. I was now about to cross the Yangtze River (for the first time since Shanghai), but later in Tibet I would also cross the Yellow, Mekong, Salween and Brahmaputra.* This meant that I would not have just one long climb onto a high plateau, but, rather, I would have to cross more than a dozen colossal passes, while descending into deep valleys between them. Nine of the passes would be over 4,000 metres high and four would be over 5,000 metres. By the time I reached Nepal, I would have climbed over 20,000 metres, the equivalent of scaling Everest almost two and a half times.

I stayed in a village by the river and the next morning left at dawn, hoping, optimistically, to be able to climb and descend the next 4,000-metre pass by the end of the day. A zigzag of switchbacks meandered up a near-vertical valley side and I felt like an ant climbing

*At one point, the Yangtze, the Mekong, and the Salween converge in gorges just 50 miles apart.

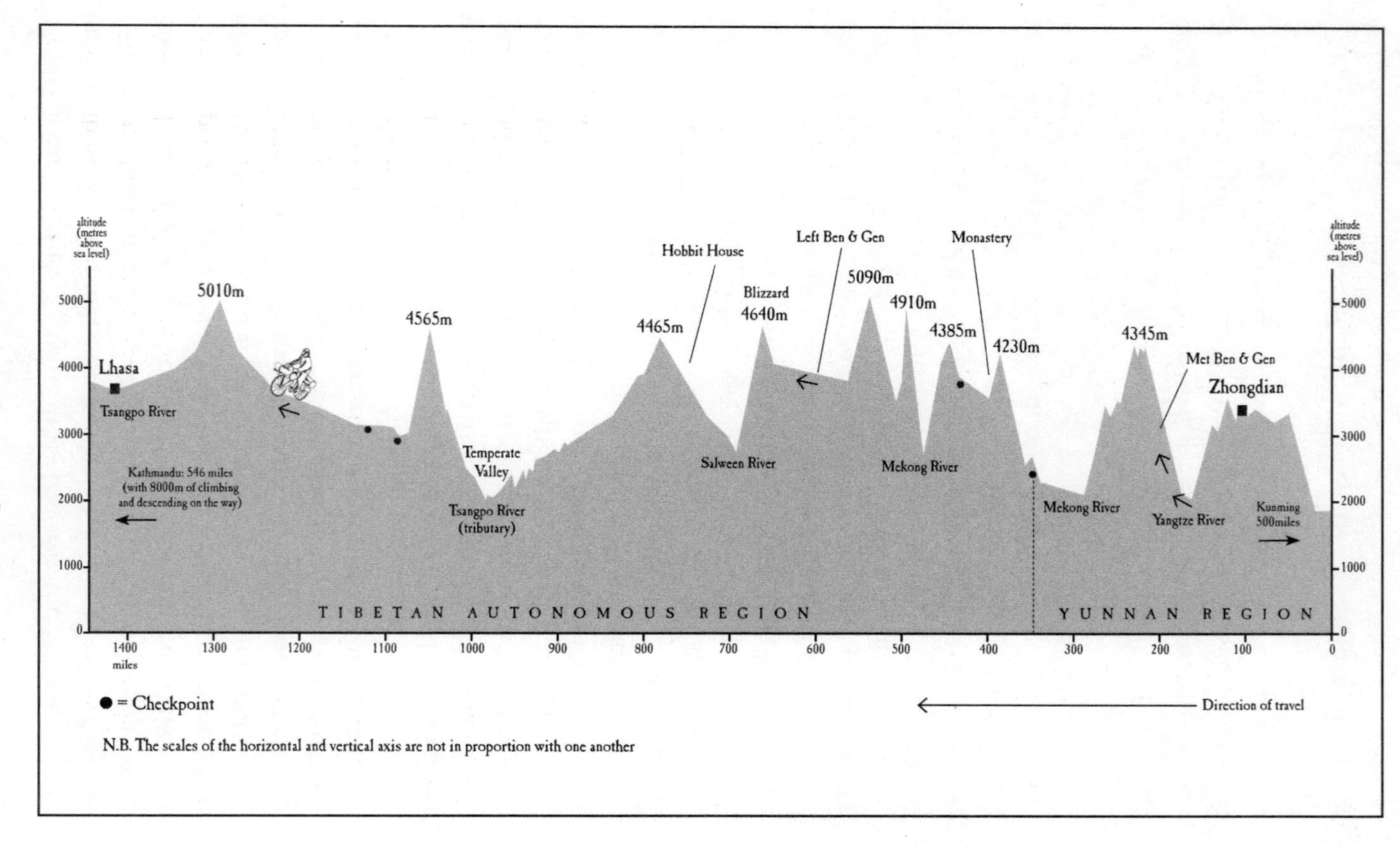
altitude (metres above sea level)
5000
4000
3000
2000
1000
0
Lhasa
Tsangpo River
5010m
4565m
Temperate Valley
Tsangpo River (tributary)
Kathmandu: 546 miles (with 8000m of climbing and descending on the way)
4465m
Hobbit House
Blizzard
4640m
Salween River
Left Ben & Gen
5090m
4910m
4385m
Mekong River
Monastery
4230m
Mekong River
4345m
Met Ben & Gen
Yangtze River
Zhongdian
Kunming 500miles
TIBETAN AUTONOMOUS REGION
YUNNAN REGION
1400
miles
1300
1200
1100
1000
900
800
700
600
500
400
300
200
100
0
● = Checkpoint
Direction of travel
N.B. The scales of the horizontal and vertical axis are not in proportion with one another

a garden wall. I clicked into my lowest gear and, though barely moving above walking pace, just focused on keeping my legs turning.

In the mid-afternoon, I noticed a pair of tyre tracks in the snow. They still looked fresh, but they were too thin to be motorbike tyres. I had hoped that I was gaining on the Canadians but expected they were still at least two days ahead. Over the next hour I spotted the tracks in the snow several more times. I felt like Robinson Crusoe who, after years on his own, all of a sudden discovers mysterious footprints in the sand, but does not know whom they belong to. My heartbeat quickened as I increased my pace.

At four in the afternoon, I rounded another bend and saw two Caucasians, wearing Nepalese hats, sitting beside the road. Two heavily laden bicycles leant against the verge. Attached to the back of one bike there was a red and white maple leaf flag fluttering in the wind.

47
No longer alone

Distance to home = 8,864 miles

Without thought or knowledge, one could have guessed that this bleak world was mountain high and the mountains rising from it were mountains on top of mountains. A range of them gleamed on the far horizon like a row of dog's teeth

JAMES HILTON

Ben and Gen sat in the warm Himalayan sunshine, having their lunch. They both wore smart, bright lycra outfits. Ben resembled an action man with a blond beard and Gen had long brown hair and a little silver stud in her nose.

'Ooh la la,' said Gen in a French accent, looking up at me, 'you 'ave ridden very fast to catch us.'

'Well, I wanted to catch you guys before Tibet,' I said, gasping for breath.

'But it is 'ard work cycling up these 'ills,' said Ben.

I sat down and joined them for some lunch. They were eating *tsampa*, a flour-like powder made from roasted barley. When mixed with water it made an edible (though in my opinion not entirely delicious) snack, popular with Tibetans. As we talked, I discovered that Ben and Gen were from Quebec and had been on the road for almost a year now. They had started their journey in New Zealand and then cycled through Australia and South-East Asia. It turned out I had only narrowly missed bumping into them in Brisbane.

'We are 'aving such a good time,' said Gen, 'and I am so 'appy to be going to Tibet.'

'You would be welcome to ride to Lhasa with us,' said Ben.

'he day after Cyclone Larry
.ustralia

apanese student on his gap year,
ie Nullarbor Plain
.ustralia

Fixing a puncture on the Nullarbor Plain.
I averaged about one puncture a week
throughout the ride
Australia

This guy makes my ride seem simple
Vietnam

Braving the streets of Hanoi
Vietnam

Meeting Tibetan villagers with Ben and Gen (two nights after the first checkpoint)
Tibet

Across the Tibetan Plateau

Climbing the switchbacks to a 5,200m pass
Tibet

Everest!
Tibet

Me, Christine and the Taj Mahal
India

Alanis on top of a taxi, about to enter Afghanista
Pakistan

Just beyond the Khyber Pass... gulp
Afghanistan

Tempted as I was to disguise myself, I didn't think I would get away with it. This is a friendly Afghan man I met by the roadside on my way to Charikar
Afghanistan

Afghan soldiers at a checkpoint
Afghanistan

fghan woman
full burka
fghanistan

Roadside
destroyed tank
Afghanistan

Climbing into the
Hindu Cush
Afghanistan

The children who witnessed me crash on my way down the north side of the Hindu Cush
Afghanistan

The Golden Journey ended here: Samarkan
Uzbekistan

The late President Turkmenbashi, with Superman cape
Turkmenistan

Two Ayatollahs on a wall
Iran

Broaching my first mountains
Iran

Breakfast with the Iranian Police
Iran

Donkeys laden with hay
Iran

Camping
Turkey

Me and Olly
Turkey

Me and Nate, Rome
Italy

Non-stop agony tours with Richard:
about to climb the Alps
Italy

Alanis finally breaks
Switzerland

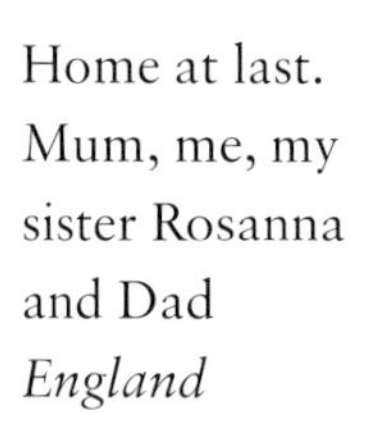

Home at last.
Mum, me, my
sister Rosanna
and Dad
England

'Thanks,' I said, feeling a surge of relief that I would not be riding on my own any more. For a little while in any case.

We set off again and snaked up the switchbacks in single file. I continued to feel elated. The previous two years of solo riding had been very difficult in many ways: I had been forced to make agonising decisions by myself and I had grown bored with my own company; I had sometimes felt very lonely, vulnerable or afraid. Even the really great moments, such as arriving in Australia, had been somewhat muted celebrations, because I had no one else to celebrate with. However, at the same time, I knew that riding alone had been an invaluable experience for me and that more people had invited me to stay because I was travelling by myself.

At five o'clock, the sun disappeared behind the wall of mountains and the temperature dropped rapidly. We still had some way to the top but, approaching a switchback, we saw an abandoned yak herders' hut and decided to sleep in it for the night. If I had been on my own I would probably not have felt comfortable sleeping there, but sharing it with fellow adventurers made it less of a big deal.

We collected some wood, Ben lit a fire and we sat on the floor cooking our dinner. We pooled our supplies. I provided my usual staple of instant noodles and ketchup, while Ben and Gen contributed some tasty yak cheese and processed sausage. The benefits of travelling in company seemed to be growing by the hour. We talked, ate and laughed and I almost forgot that we were in a stone hut on the side of a giant mountain. But there was no door on the entrance, so every now and then I took a glance outside. A full moon lit up the valley and, although we were almost 4,000 metres above sea level, the surrounding peaks still rose far above us. On the opposite wall of the valley, snowy slopes tumbled off a ridge and a scrubby rock face dropped out of sight into a valley far below.

After dinner, by the flickering light of the fire, we compared our maps and discussed the plan for the next few days. Like me, Ben and Gen did not have a travel permit for Tibet but had heard about the Chinese checkpoints. Gen had been reading the same cyclists' websites that I had. As we discussed the plan for getting past them,

I began to feel as if I had stumbled onto a scene in the *'Allo 'Allo* TV show.

'So 'ow do we get past the checkpoints?' asked Ben.

'Well,' said Gen, 'first we 'ave to stop before we reach the checkpoint. Then we 'ide somewhere until it is the middle of the night and when we think the guard at the checkpoint is asleep . . .' she paused dramatically, 'we cycle through it!'

'What!' exclaimed Ben. 'But 'ow do we know the guard is asleep?'

'We don't,' said Gen, 'we just 'ope that 'e is.'

As I had read the same thing, I reassured Ben that we would not be the first foreign cyclists to sneak through Tibet in this way. From the websites, it seemed that several foreign cyclists slipped through the Tibetan checkpoints in the middle of the night every year. Some websites even included tips about where the best hiding places were and the exact location of the road barriers. I admitted to Ben that virtually everyone had done it in the summer when it was much warmer. But surely in the winter the police were all the more likely to be inside and asleep, unsuspecting of multinational explorers slipping past their barriers outside.

''Ow many checkpoints are there?' asked Ben.

Gen passed him the map. 'There are four,' she said, looking up at me.

I nodded and said there were four checkpoint towns, but some of them had barriers at both the beginning and end of the town.

Gen turned back to Ben. 'They are 'ere, 'ere, 'ere and 'ere.'

'And where are we?' he enquired.

'We are . . .' she hesitated, ''ere . . . so we will reach the first checkpoint in three days.'

We smiled at each other bravely, though I think all three of us were afraid.

The next day we continued climbing towards the pass. I was riding in front of the others but as I neared the top I started to gasp, and so had to dismount. I looked behind and saw that Ben and Gen had climbed off to push too. Eventually we reached the 4,345-metre pass. A big mound of snow-covered stones marked the highest point and several lines of prayer flags flapped in the wind. The flags were red, yellow and blue and each had a prayer written on it in tiny characters which Tibetans believed would fly heavenwards when the flags fluttered. I was surprised to notice that even at this altitude there were tiny birds darting around. We stopped and congratulated each other, shared some cheap Chinese chocolate and took some photos.

But then we fell into silence as we looked out across the next valley. It opened like a chasm. On the far side a wall of jagged mountains rose into the clouds, as if it was a deliberate blockade to keep intruders out. Gen touched her head to the pile of stones and shouted, '*Om! Mani Padme Hum!*' into the wind. It was the Tibetans' favourite prayer, and was thought to bring good fortune. Translated literally, it meant, 'Hail! Jewel in the Lotus!'

We began the long descent again, this time freewheeling for 40 miles down to the Mekong. Halfway down, the tarmac road petered out to be replaced by a bumpy gravel track. We expected the road would be like this most of the way to Lhasa.

But, before that, there were nine more enormous passes to climb over.

And a lot of checkpoints to dodge.

48
Trespassers on the roof of the world

Distance to home = 8,739 miles

7 FEBRUARY 2007

It is three thirty in the morning on the Tibetan frontier, still five hours before the dawn. The light of a cold full moon gives glimpses of massive snow-capped mountains in the distance. On all sides shattered cliffs slip downwards into the dark, churning waters of the Mekong hidden in the darkness below. All of China sleeps.

Beyond the stillness of the night, three figures on heavily laden bicycles are weaving carefully up the dirt road on the north side of the valley.

Occasionally they draw together to hold urgent, hushed conferences. They point ahead with gloved hands to the glowing lights of the town. Then they continue: crunching and scraping forwards. Around a final corner and suddenly (just as they had expected) they see the bright, floodlit checkpoint: a red and white barrier across the road. It is half-raised and there is no sign of the guard. The three riders increase their pace, slip into single file and duck under the barrier.

They follow the dark road between a line of grey buildings and rubble-strewn side-streets. Their hearts are beating fast and their breaths are short. Last night they even re-oiled their chains to make them quieter, but now they fear that the noise of their wheels bumping through the potholes will give them away.

The town is first alerted to their presence by a lone bark. It is followed by a cacophony of other howls. The local dogs have picked up the foreigners' scent and decided that such people most certainly do not belong here. The three cyclists quicken their pace. The adrenaline is starting to rush through their blood. They dare not look behind to see if anyone is following. Halfway through the town they see a four-legged creature running towards them at speed. Two of the riders snarl and throw stones at it, until the third hisses in a French accent, 'Stop it, it is just a piig, you idiots.' The pig sprints past and up an alley, even more bewildered than the riders.

After two miles they reach the second checkpoint at the edge of the town. They duck under the barrier, and escape through into the emptiness beyond.

An hour of slow climbing later, the eastern dawn rises behind them. The three stop to smile, dig out the camping stove and boil up some porridge.

We were through the first two checkpoints and now officially trespassing on Tibetan soil.

49
The forbidden photo

Distance to home = 8,663 miles

In the practice of tolerance, one's enemy is the best teacher
THE DALAI LAMA

We climbed all day, passing a succession of Tibetans walking up the road with their pack-horses and goats. The people's faces were weather-beaten and smudged with dirt. I had been expecting them to be wearing traditional or home-made clothes, but they mostly wore mass-produced Chinese coats and trousers. Some had red ribbons in their hair. On the opposite side of the valley I could make out figures walking along the narrow paths etched into the hillsides.

That night we camped above the snow line, hidden in a pine forest just above the road. The reading on my thermometer dropped to –20°C during dinner. I remembered how much I had struggled when it first reached this temperature in Siberia, and yet I did not seem to be minding the cold in Tibet. So far in any case.

The next day we reached the 4,230-metre pass. Once again, it was adorned with prayer flags and there was a freezing wind blowing. Without even bothering to take a photo we began our descent. We had over a dozen more passes to cross before Nepal and the novelty of struggling over each one was already wearing off. Down in the next valley, in the middle of the afternoon, we came across a group of several dozen Tibetans having a picnic beside a parked tractor. They gestured enthusiastically that we should join them. The people sat in two circles, one for men and the other for women, so we took our places in the respective circles.

They passed us a piece of dried meat and a knife, and a cup of yak butter tea each. I had heard about the famous Tibetan tea and wondered what it was like. I was almost disappointed when it tasted like tea with butter in it, but it was also warm and refreshing. We could not speak any Tibetan, but we smiled and chuckled at them and they smiled and chuckled back at us. They were clearly very poor, but on the outside they seemed very cheerful. This scene came to mind again when I later read Patrick French's landmark book *Tibet, Tibet*, where he wrote:

> *I remember a moment in a pristine shopping centre in southern England. There were clean metal elevators, themed shops, designed spaces, corporate brands and coffee bars. As I rose sleekly from one floor to another, looking down through the glass and light, I felt that few people in this shoppers' paradise seemed content. There was an air of anxiety, as if time was running out for all of them. It brought me back to a moment in Tibet, to a memory of a group of men and women sitting, laughing, on the edge of a field of barley after a morning's harvest, wearing wide-brimmed hats to keep off the strong sun, each one spinning wool on a spindle, or carving a wooden peg, telling a joke, passing the day. In the free world, the invented world, there is little time for being. Each step is managed, and you have to work ever harder to get the money to buy the things that will keep you from falling out of the system. The people in the shopping centre had everything, but all they wanted was more, because having everything did not make life easier for them; they had to run just to stand still.*

After we had sat with them for ten minutes, all at once the Tibetans stood up and piled into the trailer of the tractor. The wrinkled driver revved the engine, gave us a happy wave, and rattled off down the road.

As the evening drew near, we met our first Tibetan Buddhist monk. He had a young face and bristly hair, but rather than saffron robes he wore a baggy grey coat. He emerged out of a village shop to greet us and indicated that he wanted to try riding Alanis. I climbed off and let him take her. He giggled but almost fell off several times. He stopped and asked us a question while pointing up the hillside. We did not know what he was saying. Then, slightly to our surprise, he solved the communication impasse by pulling out a mobile phone. He dialled a number before handing the phone to me. I put it to my ear to hear a voice in English. It was his friend in Lhasa. He told me that most of the monks were on holiday for Chinese New Year, but we were invited to stay the night with the monk in his monastery if we wanted. Gen was delighted at the thought of staying in a monastery, so we followed the monk up the footpath, pushing our bikes behind him.

We reached the brow of the hill and saw the monastery. It was surrounded by a tall, white, fortress-like wall. The wall was inset with two rows of decorated windows. We walked through a large gateway into the courtyard. There was a balcony running around the inside of it and up a short flight of steps in the centre was the temple entrance, painted in gold, red, blue, white and green.*

The monk showed us into a small room with a wood-stove, two beds and a shrine. There were posters of spectacular forests, hills and lakes on the wall, as well as a large painting of the Potala Palace in Lhasa. The monk indicated that we could sleep on the beds and that he and the one other monk would sleep on the floor.

He gave us some bread for dinner. While we were eating, Gen looked at the photographs of lamas lined up along the shrine. She wondered out loud why there was no photo of the Dalai Lama himself. Gen was a big fan of the Dalai Lama, so she said to the monk, 'Dalai Lama,' and gave him the thumbs-up sign. 'Why do you not 'ave a photo of the Dalai Lama?'

The monk seemed to understand, but he looked back at her awkwardly.

Over the previous few months I had been reading up on the history of Tibet. A Dalai Lama had first taken on the role as the political and spiritual leader of the Tibetans in 1641. Since then, each time the Dalai Lama died, according to Tibetan belief, a group of monks

*The colours symbolise earth, fire, sky, air and water.

had to recognise his next reincarnation in an infant, and bring the child to Lhasa. He was then raised to act as a god-king for the local people, who revered and adored him.

At the same time, however, for most of the past thousand years, Tibet had been under the ultimate rule of the Chinese Empire.* In 1950, the new Communist government of China decided to bring Tibet's latest brief spell of autonomy to an end, and an army came to take control of the region once more. They argued that Tibet had always been a part of its historical empire and also that they were 'liberating' the Tibetans from the oppressive tyranny of the Dalai Lamas. The Dalai Lama remained in Lhasa for nine years after this invasion/liberation, though he had no real power, was barely an adult, and was mostly confined to his palaces. Despite Chinese attempts to discourage it, many Tibetan people continued to revere him. As the decade wore on, the Tibetans also began to express this resentment against their Chinese rulers in increasingly violent protests. The protests culminated in 1959 with an 'uprising' in Lhasa, sparked by a rumour that the Dalai Lama was about to be kidnapped by the Chinese. In response, an angry crowd of 30,000 surrounded his residence and vowed to defend him to the point of death. The Dalai Lama urged calm, but tensions grew to boiling point until he was forced to flee secretly to India. The next day the Chinese army attacked the lightly armed protesters with artillery and shells. At least a thousand were killed, and many more were taken prisoner. There followed more crackdowns, with indiscriminate arrests, torture and executions. The Dalai Lama, meanwhile, was now maligned and the people were from then on forbidden even to own a photo of him.

As well as the brutal Chinese crackdown on any aspirations for autonomy, resistance or escape, the Tibetans also suffered from more general Communist Party blunders. In the mid-1960s Mao's

*There is a distinction between what the Chinese government has defined as 'the Tibetan Autonomous Region', and a much wider 'cultural' area where the Tibetan people live. While approximately 2.7 million Tibetans live in the autonomous region, up to 4 million live in the areas outside it.

disastrous 'Great Leap Forward' agricultural policies resulted in at least 200,000 Tibetans starving to death. A few years later, the Cultural Revolution brought massive destruction on the monasteries. Out of a total of almost three thousand, fewer than ten are said to have survived intact. A further, more recent, imposition from China has been the mass immigration of Han Chinese into the region. As I cycled through the valleys I would often notice Chinese flags flying over smart, newly built houses – a telltale sign of immigrants who have been subsidised to move there from China's crowded east coast. Some commentators say that Tibetans will soon be outnumbered in their own land.

The Chinese, meanwhile, argue that life under the Dalai Lamas, which both Tibetans and foreigners are sometimes inclined to imagine as an idyllic and harmonious era, is a seriously romanticised distortion of what it was really like. Even until the mid-twentieth century, Tibet was a 'feudal' society without electricity, schools or proper roads. The land teemed with brigands and wolves, disease was rife, and the life expectancy of the average Tibetan was the mid-thirties.* The Dalai Lamas and other Tibetan rulers did very little to improve things. In contrast, the Chinese point out the billions of yuan they have invested in the region since their arrival. They have built schools, roads, airports, hospitals and even an extraordinary high-altitude railway line. They have also largely rid the land of bandits. I certainly never heard of robbery being a problem while I was in Tibet.

But, despite these improvements, many Tibetans continue to resent the Chinese presence. They argue that China's modernisation programme has been more motivated by a desire to heighten Beijing's

*The Austrian climber Heinrich Harrer's book, *Seven Years in Tibet*, recounting his escape from a British prisoner-of-war camp in India and subsequent journey to Lhasa in the 1940s, depicts just how untamed a land Tibet was even then. The book was made into a film starring Brad Pitt in 1998. Shortly before his death, I heard Harrer give a lecture in London. He joked that if his journey from India to Tibet had been as easy as it looked in the film, he would have escaped from the prison camp and strolled up to Tibet in broad daylight, without any difficulty whatsoever.

control than to help them. I met many Tibetans who longed for a return to life under the Dalai Lama. Although the monk we were staying with did not have the forbidden photo, in Tibetan towns I stayed in later on, I did meet people who expressed both their dislike towards the Chinese and their reverence for the Dalai Lama. On two such occasions, I was shown photos of him, which they kept hidden in their houses. The consequences of possessing the photo could be severe, but they seemed to think it was worth the risk. Protests and demonstrations continue to break out, despite the severe response that they will inevitably provoke from the Chinese army.

While in Tibet, I wrote a short piece on my website, outlining the complexity of the problems, and trying to be fair to both sides of the debate. I admitted that then, as now, I was no expert and had been in the country for only a short time and so my understanding was tentative. In response, I received an email from a highly educated and well-travelled Chinese surgeon friend whom I had met in Shanghai two years beforehand:

Dear Rob,

Very glad to hear from you and get your recent information.

Firstly, welcome to China again. Having known our Tibetan [people] had given you help, I feel so proud and happy. As you know, Chinese people are warm-hearted and simple to foreign guests.

Secondly, I have to tell you seriously that I don't agree with you about your points on Tibet and Tibetan in last letter. In Chinese history, Tibet has been indisputable part of Chinese territory. In the people's revolution of whole country against the old social system, the people's liberation army (PLA) had helped the villains of Tibet to have changed their misery life. Their good lives own to our government. Maybe you were affected by few people's views which is not right. At least, you don't have a complete comprehension about that.

I think you need more investigation about that.

Wish you good trip!

Chinese friend from Shanghai

50
The hobbit house

Distance to home = 8,475 miles

Until the Chinese invasion, their Spartan way of life had hardly changed since the Middle Ages. They had no electricity, no wireless, no clocks or watches, no sewing machines, no modern medicines, no cars or bicycles, nor even the simplest wheeled transport . . . most Tibetans had no idea such things even existed

PETER HOPKIRK

I rode with Ben and Gen for another week. Together we grew used to living in two vastly different worlds. There was the world up high, on the passes, where the wind blew cold, the air grew thin and flags fluttered quietly all year round. And there was the world down below, in the valleys, where children waved, dogs barked and the villages sang with life. We sneaked past one more checkpoint in the night, camped in numerous beautiful valleys, and climbed over three more gigantic passes. We were happy with the steady progress we were making, though we were also beginning to feel weak from all the exertion.

In general, Ben and Gen had a more relaxed philosophy towards making progress than me, and most days we stopped several times for long food breaks. It was pleasant to ride more slowly. Why did I always put pressure on myself to ride hard and fast? But after ten days my impatience began to return and I decided that it was time for me to pick up my pace and press on to Lhasa by myself. On my final night with Ben and Gen we camped on a beach beside a gentle river, in a dry, deserted valley lined with grey cliffs. We pooled our food supplies one last time and cooked up a parting feast.

One of the things I had enjoyed the most on my journey was the chance I'd had to meet so many new people. However, being constantly on the move, it was rare for me to spend more than a few days with anyone. More times than I could count I had stayed with my hosts just long enough to answer all their questions and begin a friendship, before saying goodbye and cycling to the next place – where the process was repeated. With Ben and Gen, we shared enough time and adventures to develop deeper friendships. It made me realise how much I was looking forward to getting home and staying in one place again.

The next morning was Chinese New Year, so before leaving I dug out three small Chinese fireworks which I had been saving for the occasion. We lit one each and stood well back. As they exploded the boom echoed down the valley and off the mountain walls. We cheered, embraced and said that we hoped to meet again in Lhasa or Kathmandu. And then I set off, alone once more.

It had been good, clear weather for the past week, but as I began climbing the next pass the sky clouded over and it began to snow. The valley behind disappeared in a white haze. A brutal wind howled off the mountainsides and numbed my cheeks. It was late afternoon by the time I spotted colourful flags and gasping for breath, reached the pass once again. I pulled out my video camera and filmed myself with an ice beard, commenting on the bleakness of the scene. I reflected on how desolate it was up there, hundreds of miles from the nearest city and thousands of metres above sea level. Humans had tried to tame this landscape but, when the weather turned, it still belonged entirely to nature.

At that moment, a large car full of mainland Chinese tourists rounded the corner. There were no travel restrictions in Tibet for Chinese citizens, and it was an increasingly popular 'exotic' place to go on holiday. Their car slowed slightly as it passed by and the warm faces inside stared out at me. I smiled at them, and raised my hand. One of their windows began to wind down and a hand appeared holding something. I thought they might stop to give me some food. But then the hand dropped an empty fruit-juice carton out of the window and the car accelerated. The carton looked obtrusive as it sat there on top of the icy road, and fresh snowflakes slowly began to cover it. I guessed it would not decompose for years.

I rattled downwards through a gloom of snow and potholes, clinging to my brakes. An hour later, I was still halfway up the mountain, and it was virtually dark. I opened my bar bag to put my head-torch on, but was dismayed to find that it was not there. It must have fallen out somewhere behind. I dug out my temperamental spare torch from the bottom of a pannier. It took me 20 minutes of wheeling the bike down through complete darkness until I spotted a small patch of flat land on a cliff top beside the road. I put the tent up and climbed inside. My body was aching and I was too tired to cook so, in a bad mood, I ate cold oats with water and lay down to sleep. I missed Ben and Gẹn and wondered whether I had been foolish to press on without them.

The next morning, I looked outside to discover, with a shock, that I had pitched my tent right next to a yak skeleton.

Two days later I reached another icy pass at nightfall. This time, rather than being alone, I was surprised to see lots of Tibetans walking along the road, even up here at over 4,000 metres. Some walked on their own and some in groups. Some were accompanying their yaks, goats, donkeys, dogs and pigs. Two young men drove past on a motorbike. Although it was −20°C they wore no gloves. I had seen very few houses all afternoon and could not work out where everybody lived.

As the sun dropped below the snow-mantled ridges I saw a place beside the road where I could camp. I put Alanis down to take a closer look, but at that moment a man with a wrinkled face and a balaclava appeared. He gestured that I should come and stay in his house. I accepted gratefully. We walked further up the road, crossed a frozen river and pushed the bike up a hidden path. I could still see no houses, but when we reached the top of the small hill I saw why. Rather than being built out of bricks, these houses were dug into the ground, and their roofs were covered in soil and bushes. They reminded me of hobbit houses.

I left the bike leaning against a wall and a ten-year-old boy took me by the hand and led me inside. As I stooped through the low doorway and into the darkness I saw with a shock that I was being stared at by a dozen pairs of huge eyes. I froze for a moment until, as my eyes adjusted, I saw that the room was full of yaks and goats. The child led me towards a flickering light. We rounded a corner and entered another room. A wood fire glowed in the centre of the floor, with a middle-aged woman, a baby, and two girls sitting beside it.

They looked up at me, and the boy encouraged me to take a seat by the fire. Between two wooden beams in the roof there was a square hole for the smoke to escape from. The room flickered in the firelight and I could make out objects stacked against the walls: some small baskets of food; two cooking pots; a Chinese thermos; a pile of blankets. There was a little shrine with some photos of lamas, and a car battery which powered a single light bulb hanging from the wall. For now, though, at least, the worst instrument of cultural genocide had not yet arrived: the television.*

The man I had met by the road, the father of the house, walked in carrying my panniers. He gestured that I should make myself comfortable for the night. The room evidently acted as the living room, the kitchen and the bedroom for the entire family. The man sat down and began throwing rice and vegetables into the cooking pots. I gave him some instant noodles as my contribution, and he put these to one side. The father enquired with various gestures about where I was going. I tried to explain that I was cycling to India and eventually to England. But when I mentioned the names of the cities I would go through, apart from Lhasa, his face was blank and uncomprehending.

The boy came over and sat beside me and for the next five minutes asked me a continual stream of questions which I did not understand. I showed him my torch, my diary and my video camera. I was often unsure about bringing the camera because it had a tendency to make people feel awkward as well as reminding us all how much

*I had seen satellite dishes in the larger Tibetan settlements by the road, so perhaps it would not be long until TV arrived.

richer I was. At the same time, though, I wanted to get some footage. I started to teach the boy to count to ten, and he taught me to count to ten in Tibetan.

The rest of the family watched us and murmured to each other. The older woman started kneading some dough in a bowl, and put it in a pot on the fire to make bread. The older girl began combing the hair of the young girl, who looked about five years old. She grimaced as the comb pulled out the tangles, but when I smiled and made faces at her she smiled shyly back at me. I wished I could understand what they were saying. I wanted to ask them about their lives up there. Apart from a few basic pieces of technology, how had the lifestyle changed in the last thousand years?

I tried to ask the man how many goats and yaks he had. We managed to communicate the word for yak by using our fingers to indicate big horns and saying a deep 'moo', and for goats by indicating little horns and saying a high-pitched 'meer'. The man could write numbers, so we worked out that he had 25 yaks and 57 goats.* He said that, as well as the three children in the room, he had two older sons who were out goat herding. It was hard for me to tell the age of the older man and woman. They looked quite old, in their late forties or even early fifties, but they might have been a lot younger than this, especially as they had a young daughter. Living on top of a 4,500-metre-high pass where the air was cold, dry and sunny probably did not do much for their skin. The warm, smoky air in the room explained their slightly grubby faces and clothes. Earlier in the day, I had cycled past a woman who was washing clothes in a small, icy roadside stream. She had no soap, but was pummelling them with a stick to clean them.

After eating the vegetables and rice, the man produced some dried fruit for pudding. He then started to make some yak butter tea. I had not seen it being made before. From what I could make out through the darkness, the ingredients were boiling water, tea leaves, and some large lumps of butter. Then I noticed that it was not real yak butter, but Chinese manufactured margarine from a plastic tub.

*I later discovered that the word for 'yak' in Tibetan was, in fact, 'yak'.

He poured all the ingredients into a long, wooden didgeridoo-like contraption, shook it around for a while so that it made a sloshing noise and poured it into the kettle on the fire.

We were all exhausted from trying to communicate without language, so we just sat quietly, watching the embers on the fire. The man pulled out a needle and thread and started to sew up a hole in his son's trousers. He then stood up, and dug out a cloth. He dipped it into a pot of white paste, and began marking white symbols onto the walls and ceilings. '*Tashi delek*,' he said to me. '*Tashi delek*' were the only words I knew in Tibetan. It was a versatile greeting and meant 'good luck'. I understood that these marks were a way of welcoming me to the house for the night and wishing good luck on my onward journey.

I rolled out my sleeping bag and lay down. A gentle smattering of snow began to fall in through the hole in the roof and land with a sizzle on the fire. As I fell asleep, I realised that my pile of bags, which I was lugging across the world, contained considerably more possessions than they had in their entire household.

51
The highest capital in the world

Distance to home = 8,042 miles

Edward Conze, the great scholar of Buddhism, recalled that he 'once read through a collection of the lives of Roman Catholic saints and there was not one of whom a Buddhist could fully approve . . . They were bad Buddhists though good Christians'

ALASTAIR MCGRATH

After saying goodbye the following morning, I descended the other side of the pass. Near the bottom, I passed a Chinese military camp of green and black cabins. I had noticed several such camps. They were evidently there to remind the Tibetans who was in charge. As I passed the camp, a dog came running out and barked at me. In shock, I braked hard and my back wheel slid out from under me. I crashed to the ground and slid for several metres down the icy surface. It was the first time I had fallen off in Tibet. I was so angry that I forgot all about the Dazer II and instead stood up and yelled at the dog. It was clearly confused about me falling off, and was frightened by my shouting, so it ran timidly back down the side of the track where it had come from.

Over the next week the valleys and passes crept past. Some of the valleys were so low that I rode through deciduous forests where I could smell spring arriving. I also began to see small groups of Tibetan pilgrims on the road. They were travelling by foot to Lhasa, having started in their home villages off the main road. For every pace they took they knelt down on both knees and touched their forehead to the road in front of them. They wore pads on their hands and knees to prevent blistering, though I could see their foreheads were calloused. They were doing the pilgrimage because of the Lama Buddhist belief that it would improve their *karma* and thus their chances of a favourable reincarnation in their next life. I heard that for some pilgrims it would take the best part of a year to complete.

Occasionally I saw police cars passing me on the road. Although I tensed up, they never bothered to stop. I think they either assumed that I must have a permit to have made it this far, or else they thought that I wasn't their problem. Three days before Lhasa I rose once more in the middle of the night in order to sneak past checkpoints in two consecutive towns. Once I was past them, although extremely tired, I was increasingly excited to be nearing the fabled city at last.

At dawn on my final day, I toiled over a final pass under a blue sky. At the top there were even more prayer flags than usual, but here they were strung from a huge China telecom sign which straddled the road. I descended onto the home straight and, a few hours later, night arrived. My head was filled with images of hot showers and greasy food, so I pressed on into the darkness. The moon gave enough light to see the road and I followed the Tsangpo River upstream. Three hours later, I rounded the side of a cliff and suddenly saw the floodlit, white walls of the Potala Palace rising awesomely out of the night.

At 3,200 metres above sea level, Lhasa is the highest capital in the world. It was one of the few places in Tibet that travellers could visit without a permit. The night I arrived, I found a backpackers' hostel and spent the next week taking hot showers, eating yak steaks and meeting other travellers. Some of them were suffering from altitude sickness because they had come up by plane or train and their bodies had not yet adjusted to the thin air.

On the meandering streets outside the hostel, native Tibetan buildings and people mingled awkwardly with more recent Chinese architecture and immigrants. On a street corner opposite my hostel, a cluster of Tibetan women sat with their sewing machines, making a living. One of them happily sewed up the holes in my clothes and panniers. Most of the shops were full of Chinese goods: sweets, soft drinks and cheap electronics. There were internet cafés, fast-food restaurants and Chinese night clubs. A large sign outside the Bank of China stated emphatically in English that the bank was 'always with you'.

Lines of bicycle rickshaws heckled for tourist passengers. I figured I had earned a rickshaw ride so I paid 50p to be taken to the foot of the Potala Palace. The palace is built on top of a rugged hill and in places its white walls rise from the foot of the hill itself. This gives it the impression of being considerably larger than it actually is. Standing head and shoulders above all the other buildings in the city, even today its size is impressive. To Tibetans of bygone days it must have been overwhelming.

At the entrance, I reluctantly paid the hefty admission fee (which would go directly to the Chinese authorities, not to the Tibetans), and spent several hours walking through the intricately adorned burial chambers and bedrooms, the resting places of previous Dalai Lamas. I am not sure it occurred to me at the time, but, thinking back now, it seems intrusive for tourists to walk around a place that for generations had been viewed by Tibetans as the holy home of their god-kings. After all, it had not been the Tibetans who invited me to come inside the Potala Palace as a tourist, but the Chinese.

A few days later, I found my way to the Jokhang Temple in the city centre. This was one of the most important Buddhist temples in Tibet and the endpoint for many of the hardy pilgrims I had seen on the road. A huge crowd gathered in front of the main entrance, continually prostrating themselves. They raised their arms above their heads, then bowed to their knees and slid their bodies flat onto the ground. In the late afternoon, I joined a line of Tibetans entering the temple. As we passed through the gates, I looked up at the big paintings of the various deities on the walls. Some of them appeared sinister, with angry red grimaces on their faces. Inside the candlelit main temple chamber, we circled a central group of monks. They wore robes and were chanting deeply. Our line shuffled silently around them.

As a person devoted to a faith myself, I could understand the Tibetans' commitment. It gave their lives meaning and purpose. But as I read more about Buddhism, I saw that Buddhists' understanding of life was very different from mine. Buddhism and Christianity not only gave different answers to life's big questions, they were asking different questions in the first place. Buddha himself was uninterested in the question of God, and far more concerned with finding escape from a life of suffering. He taught and lived a life in which the highest ideal was complete detachment from desire, thus enabling tranquillity and liberation from a cycle of rebirths. The ultimate goal was escape from bodily existence.* Jesus, meanwhile, was a man of passion and frequently showed his emotions with tears, anger, love and anguish. He affirmed that God originally created the world as a good place and that it was to be engaged with, not escaped from. Jesus even chose to embrace suffering in his own life, in the form of a horrific Roman execution.

Over the coming months I would be passing through the heartlands of several other great world religions and so would have a chance to reflect on such differences more deeply.

*Over the centuries that followed, the Buddha's original teaching split into many different schools. Mahayana Buddhism, in particular, began to see Buddha as a divine figure, while also coming to accept the existence of other divine beings. When Buddhism reached Tibet, these ideas combined with vestiges of the region's ancient Bon religion, resulting in Lama Buddhism's own unique form. Lama Buddhists believe that the Dalai Lamas are manifestations, or *Boddhisattvas*, of the deity of compassion.

52
The scary thought

Distance to home = 8,042 miles

I asked him how he came to be a painter. He said,
'I liked the smell of paint'
ANNIE DILLARD

Besides my touristy visits, I spent a lot of time in Lhasa resting in my room. The previous month of riding had worn me out, though I was pleased that my plans had worked and that I'd made it to the city safely. Looking at my world map, I could see the tangible, definite progress that I was making towards England. But I also felt a sense of anticlimax. It had been tough to make it here, but not as tough as some of the other legs of the journey. During my final days of cycling to Lhasa I had come up with a ranking for the most difficult parts of the journey so far. I decided that Siberia had still been the most difficult. That had been 8½ out of 10. Next was Papua New Guinea, which was 7½ out of 10. I had been expecting Tibet to be at least as hard as Siberia, but in the end I decided to register it as only 6½. Whether this was because I had toughened up during the ride, or because the roads were genuinely easier, I did not know. I suspected it was a little of both.

Now, as I considered my map and thought about the places I still had to ride through, most of it looked rather tame. Even the exotic sounding ex-Soviet Stans of Central Asia did not really excite me. I ticked off the landmark cities that still lay ahead: Kathmandu . . . Delhi . . . Islamabad. From Pakistan, I had to make a significant choice about whether I should go under or over Afghanistan for, of course, going through it would be out of the question.

Then, all of a sudden, the thought came: 'Maybe I should go through Afghanistan after all?'

The idea exploded into my mind like a smart bomb.

Afghanistan! Was I mad?

Hadn't I pledged to myself that Tibet would be the final difficult option I would take?

But once the thought of Afghanistan had arrived, I could not get it out of my head.

Maybe this would be the concluding challenge before Europe, a grand finale to the ride. But it would not be such a grand finale if I ended up getting into trouble. I still did not know why I always seemed to be pushing myself to take on tougher challenges. I think it was because it made me feel more alive. Or perhaps I had just become an adrenaline junkie, addicted to taking bigger and bigger risks to achieve the same thrill.

I decided not to make a final decision until I got nearer and until I had done a lot more research.

A few days before I left Lhasa, Ben and Gen arrived. They had big grins on their sunburnt faces, and I treated them to a meal at my favourite yak-steak restaurant while we caught up on our various adventures. We started to discuss our different plans for what lay ahead. Gen and Ben were trying to ride all the way to Europe too, and planned to go through Pakistan and directly into Iran. I confessed to them that, rather than heading north into Kyrgyzstan, I had recently been thinking about Afghanistan.

I quickly went on to try and justify my new idea, saying that I had not fully made up my mind yet, but that I would get opinions from people on the ground first; after all, surely the headlines that we saw on the news were probably not representative of the whole country, but rather just focused on the riskiest parts; and so perhaps it was not the whole country that was dangerous; so perhaps I might be okay if I stuck only to the more stable regions; and, of course, it was such a fascinating country with such an extraordinary history . . .

Ben and Gen looked unconvinced.

'Oo la, la,' said Gen. 'But you are English.' She drew her hand across her neck and added with a concerned smile, 'They will chop your 'ead off.'

We all burst out laughing.

53
The Headwind Highway

Distance to home = 7,415 miles

Can't wait (to get to somewhere where I can) relax, speak English, stop worrying about stupid police. I haven't spoken to anyone (properly, apart from shouting hello at kids) for eight days. Have only had one proper shower in three weeks

DIARY ENTRY, TIBET

15 MARCH 2007

Two weeks later, I am riding along the Friendship Highway, the road that crosses the Tibetan Plateau for 600 miles westwards from Lhasa before descending to Nepal. The terrain here is different from eastern Tibet. Gone is the jagged rollercoaster of high passes and deep gorges. I now run through a high-altitude desert. Enclosing me on either side are lines of barren, crumpled hills. The skies are huge and the air is sharp, dry and clear. There is a cold, blue glacial stream trickling beside the road and behind the ridge line I occasionally glimpse a lofty white summit.

Although the bumpy roads that I endured before Lhasa are now behind me and my wheels can slip noiselessly over a smooth tarmac surface, the new challenge is the incessant, blasting headwind. From mid-morning until dusk, every day, it rages in my face like a malicious boxing opponent, pushing the bike sideways and making my mouth dry out. I shout at it in anger, but that only tires me out more. I put on loud music, but I can barely hear it above the roar in my ears. Sometimes, even riding downhill, the gusts are so strong that I have to pedal hard or I will stop moving altogether. I decide to rename the Friendship Highway with the more appropriate name of 'the Headwind Highway'.

At least it is easy camping here and I can pitch my tent in any number of dry irrigation channels or gentle hollows beside the road. I still try to make sure I am out of sight, and the occasional shepherd who stumbles upon me is not a worry. For dinner, I am cooking up huge pots of potatoes with yak butter stew. Before I sleep I write another page of a letter to Christine, which I will post when I reach Nepal. Each morning, I rise early, if possible before dawn, in the hope of covering a fair distance before the winds pick up again.

There are still occasional villages around too, a jumble of old and new houses. I see young boys and old women herding their goats and yaks on the hillsides. Sometimes I wave at them, because I feel so alone. Occasionally, I stop to talk, though I know we will not understand each other. However, they do offer me yak butter tea, or lead me through a maze of courtyards, past an array of bored-looking yaks and angry-looking dogs, to fill up my water bottles in their simple kitchens.

There are now more tourists on this road, who speed past me in their four-by-fours without stopping. Occasionally I see them handing out sweets and money to people in villages. This has made the peasants in some areas less kindly towards me. One afternoon, several groups of Tibetan peasant women pick up their skirts and run across the plains towards me, as if I am a life-raft passing their desert island. As they get closer, they outstretch their palms and shout eagerly the only word they seem to know in my language: 'Money'.

A few nights ago, halfway up a snowy pass, I was invited to spend the night with some goat herders in their wigwam-shaped tent. There was a hole in the top to allow the smoke to escape from a yak-dung-fuelled stove. The nomads had red-string plaits in their hair and wore shabby clothes and corduroy jackets. We smiled at each other through the gloom and I slept squashed against the leaky yak-skin canvas. The next morning I gave the main herder my trainers to replace his rotting shoes. It was a gift to thank him for his hospitality and worth a lot more than the cost of a night in a Chinese hotel. I thought he would be happy with them. As I prepared to leave, though, he began to tug at my coat, indicating that he would like me to give him that as well.

After my months on the road in poor countries, I have grown used to the unashamed begging that is directed at me. I reason that it is a natural response to the unimaginably hard lives that these people live. The Tibetans have suffered so much, both from living up here on a cold, dry, infertile plateau, and from the oppression of the Chinese. But now I feel offended. Perhaps they only invited me to stay because they wanted my things?

I pedal ever onwards each day, for pedalling, I feel, is the only thing I am good at these days. I press on like a fighter, with clenched teeth, into the wind; my eyes fill with grit; my lips start to crack; my body is covered in grime; my beard is long. I have also developed a 'high-altitude cough'. It rasps out of my lungs and shakes my body every time I speak, though, apart from while taking video footage, I do not speak often. And I realise that perhaps I am beginning to become jaded from my years on the road. The novelty of encountering exotic cultures and sleeping alone under the cold starry nights is wearing off. I'm bored with always being on my best behaviour among people who are still forming their first impressions of me. I'm fed up with always being an object of special fascination before the people whose lives I am bypassing all too briefly. I've had enough of chilly Himalayan nights, feeling not quite warm enough in my sleeping bag as the cold sun goes down and then waking to yet another morning with no idea where I will sleep the next night.

Today, however, my spirits receive an unexpected boost. I reach a junction and decide to take a detour up a gigantic ridge because there is something I want to see on the other side. I leave the tarmac and climb a gravel track for the next six hours. Two hours before the top I clamber off and push, hoping continually that this detour will be worth the effort and that the sky will not be cloudy. At the last switchback, I lean heavily into the lion-like wind and wheel Alanis between two boulders to reach the viewing point at last. In the distance, the mountains fold back before me . . . and there she stands, a sight that makes me howl with exhilaration.

Everest.

She is 50 miles away, beyond a sea of brown hills, like a goddess rising from of the deep. Crags and glaciers toss like broken waves around her foundations before spilling carelessly into the valleys below. Occasionally a cloud dances across her face, but mostly the peak remains clear. I am at 5,200 metres, barely two-thirds her height, and yet I am completely worn out. But, weak and exhausted though my body may be, by seeing her, my mind, once again, is fired.

54
The story of the healed heart

Distance to home = 7,496 miles

There are now more slaves on this planet than at any time in human history
FOREIGN POLICY MAGAZINE, 2008

Two days of bumpy downhill brought me off the Tibetan Plateau and into the lush valleys of Nepal. For the first few hours, my senses sprang to life with the Eden-like cacophony of sounds, smells and colours. The valley sides rising above me were painted with rich greenery. The air was thick with the smell of fresh leaves, sizzling food and raw human sewage. Insects buzzed around my head and I batted them away with a hand as I rode. The people in the villages looked more Indian than Chinese now. The houses were built from large brick blocks and hens scurried about looking for food. The women wore colourful saris; there were Hindu temples at the roadsides; wide Indiana Jones-style bridges swung across the rivers.

After the high-altitude training, my red blood cell count was high, meaning the 1,000-metre climb up from the valley floor the next day was almost effortless. I crested the ridge and joined the busy highway of cars, buses and taxis into the capital. I had made it to Kathmandu.

In Kathmandu I met up with a Nepali and his wife who ran Viva's national partner, Carnet Nepal, to help children at risk in the country. Dhan Raj invited me to come to his church, and after the service we went back to his house for lunch.

'My wife and I used to be very hostile to Christianity,' he explained, 'but then we experienced a miracle.'

He described to me how his wife had once suffered from a dangerous and incurable heart condition. They lived in a village at the time, and were both working at a local mission hospital run by Christians from Korea, Dhan Raj as a teacher and his wife as a nurse. They liked working at the hospital, but clashed with the missionaries because they did not share or like the Koreans' Christian beliefs. Dhan Raj even complained to the local authorities and, as a result, the Koreans were gradually forced to leave the country as their visas were not renewed. But his wife's condition was now deteriorating.

'One night, while my wife was on duty at the hospital and there were no other staff around, her heartbeat suddenly became irregular, and she felt very sick. She came back to our house in a terrible state. I made her lie down. She was crying and screaming. I tried to help her, but there was nothing I could do. There were no doctors at the hospital and I was sure that she was going to die. Then she asked me to "go and get the Bible". The missionaries had given us a Bible, though we had never read it. I didn't know why she wanted it, but I was desperate so I gave it to her. She held it to her chest. All of a sudden, I don't know why, I cried out a prayer.'

Dhan Raj paused and then spoke in a soft, urgent whisper: 'Jesus, help us.'

I asked what happened next.

'Well, I could not believe it. My wife's condition immediately started to improve. Her heart started to beat more regularly. Within ten minutes it was back to normal and she felt better. The next day, she was well enough to travel, so we caught the bus back to Kathmandu to see the specialist. He did some tests and said that her heart was completely healed. He could not explain it at all; it was a miracle.'

I had heard and read about 'miracles' before, but it was thrilling to talk with people who had experienced something so dramatic first-hand. The experience of the healed heart had changed their lives. They began going to church, and not long after moved to Kathmandu to work with the capital's street children. After several years they started to focus on a different sort of problem.

'We learnt about the Nepalese girls who were being taken from their villages and into India where they were forced to work as prostitutes,' said Dhan Raj. 'The conditions are atrocious and the girls are often very young, barely even teenagers, and of course many of them never return home.'

I had heard about trafficking of girls across the Nepali–Indian border. It has been estimated that over two thousand girls a year are lured away from their villages by promises of well-paid and glamorous work in the cities to the south. Sometimes they are taken on a 'holiday' by relatives and then sold. Once they are in a brothel they are treated like slaves, having to 'service' up to ten men a day. In return they are paid less than £1.*

'This society often looks down on these girls, or blames them,' he explained, 'but we need to understand that the girls are the victims. It is the men who use them who are guilty.'

He said that the best way to stop this happening was to educate people in their communities, so they knew how to protect their girls. Dhan Raj is now mobilising the network so that technical agencies and churches know the dangers of abuse and trafficking and are able to do something about it and make a difference to vulnerable children.

*

Before leaving Kathmandu I posted home a large box of my winter clothes, making the bike much lighter again. Delhi was 800 miles away and I had only ten days to get there. I did not want to be late: I had a date to keep.

*This is substantiated in Louise Brown's book, *Sex Slaves: The Trafficking of Women in Asia* (Virago Press, 2001).

55
The land where might is right

Distance to home = 7,027 miles

> Although during my first year in Delhi, I remember thinking that the traffic had seemed both anarchic and alarming, by my second visit I had come to realise that it was in fact governed by very strict rules. Right of way belongs to the driver of the largest vehicle. Buses give way to heavy trucks, ambassadors give way to buses and bicyclists give way to everything, except pedestrians. On the road, as in other aspects of Indian life, might is right
>
> WILLIAM DALRYMPLE

Dalrymple was right. Bicyclists did have to give way to everything except pedestrians in India. I learnt this within a few hours of crossing the border from Nepal and joining the highway to Delhi. I was astounded the first time a truck ostensibly tried to hit me. It was coming in the opposite direction and overtaking the car in front of it. The truck pulled into my lane and did not waver as he accelerated towards me. He was confident that I would plough off the road and into the sandy verge before we collided, which is exactly what I did.* The only exception I would add to Dalrymple's rule was that cows, the holy animal of India, trumped everything. They wandered around wherever they pleased, happily holding up traffic, nibbling at the piles of rubbish left by the roadsides and depositing steaming cowpats everywhere.

As I rode towards Delhi, there were occasional moments of tranquillity: the quiet road lined with shady poplars; the meadows where

*This was very different from the driving in China, which seemed dangerous but was actually quite safe because of the excellent Chinese swerving and braking techniques.

youths played cricket with home-made stumps and cheered as I rode on by. But mostly the volume of cars, trucks, buses, people, noise, rubbish and cows just kept on increasing exponentially.

A box room with a fan and a cold shower in the backpacker district of Delhi cost me £1 for the night. Outside, I mingled with the other backpackers, young and old. Some were obviously veteran travellers and, with their henna tattoos and misty eyes, looked as though they had never left India since the first wave of hippies arrived here in the 1960s. I sat outside a café and had breakfast with a Canadian with long grey hair and white marks painted on his forehead. He told me he led tour groups for spiritual seekers from Canada. He had spent ten years searching for enlightenment in India while he was a young man though eventually he had returned to Canada because his dysentery became so serious. When I told him I was a Christian and that Hinduism was difficult for me to understand, he told me knowingly that Jesus believed in reincarnation too. He said that he had survived the crucifixion and afterwards walked to India and set up a community in Kashmir.

As I explored the streets the prevalence of poverty and the scramble for survival was all the more evident. Frantic markets sold products from around the world; street vendors sold samosas, boiled up in large pots of oil. Beggars sat in the gutters, and rickshaw drivers rode frantically past calling out 'brother' and 'friend'. Like me, they spent their lives pedalling, but they did not have a choice. They carried sweaty foreign and Indian tourists through the scorching Indian sun and were paid a pittance, and at night I saw them sleeping under the streetlights in the back of their rickshaws.

After being late to meet Christine in Singapore, I made sure I arrived at the airport in plenty of time in Delhi. I felt slightly nervous while I was waiting. Staying in touch for the last few months had been difficult. We had continued to write letters and emails. When I was staying in cheap roadside hotels, Christine had sometimes been able to call me on the hotel landline. Her voice on the phone sounded sweeter than ever, especially as I had often not had a conversation in English for several days. At times, though, the conversations were difficult. We had had brief disagreements during our 'holidays' together, but now our arguments were becoming more emotional. This was all exacerbated when the phone line was crackly and we could not hear each other properly. We'd often had very different days. Maybe I had had an exhilarating and fast day's riding, while Christine had had a long day at work. Or maybe I had had a lonely day, while Christine had been meeting friends. Sometimes a comment was completely misinterpreted. Once, Christine had asked me, as a joke, what time her flight was arriving in Delhi. I was exhausted, and thought she was expecting me to be late again, and I felt upset that she was teasing me like this.

But now, in Delhi airport, I saw her walking out of the arrival gate and grinned at her.

'Look at your beard!' she said, amused.

'Errr . . .' I had forgotten how wild I must have looked. 'I'll shave it off soon.'

'I don't mind.'

The next day, after I had shaved the beard off, she confessed that, to her surprise, I looked better now that she could see my face.

We spent the next week visiting the Red Fort in Delhi, the Taj Mahal in Agra, and the tranquil lakes of Udaipur. It was now very hot and it was a relief to escape from the hectic streets and into air-conditioned restaurants to relax. At the same time, though, the difference in our lifestyles became a point of contention. Naturally, Christine wanted to enjoy herself after working so ridiculously hard, and she wanted to treat me. But for me, after living on £2 a day for the past few months, I felt very uncomfortable eating and staying in smart places. It was a shock for her to be in India, seeing the abject poverty and the begging children. I realised that over the previous six months of riding through Asia, I had started to become desensitised.

Before she left, we talked about how things might be between us when I got home, hopefully in less than eight months' time. We knew that, although it would be brilliant to be in the same city, there might be new challenges as we would no longer be in romantic holiday mode the whole time. I also told Christine that I was contemplating Afghanistan. She was alarmed, but said she would try to trust my judgement and to trust God for both our lives. When we hugged goodbye I did not want to let go of her, and I was holding back the tears yet again. When she had gone I missed her instantly. I wondered when I would see her again.

56
Tragic news

You don't choose your family. They are God's gift to you,
as you are to them
ARCHBISHOP DESMOND TUTU

Before I left England, I had said to myself there were only two reasons why I would fly home in the middle of the trip. The first would be if my sister got married. The second, though I hardly dared think it, would be if there was a tragedy in my family.

After Christine left, I was not going to depart for Pakistan straightaway because I was waiting for another visitor. My sister, Rosanna, had recently got engaged and I had never met her fiancé, Mark. They were coming out to India on holiday a week later so this was the perfect opportunity to meet him before they got married in several months' time. I had also promised Rosanna that, come what might, I would make it to their wedding even it meant I had to fly home from wherever I had reached and then fly back to the bike to finish the journey.

But, as it turned out, I would not meet them in India, because the following week something unthinkable happened. Something that changed everything.

Five days before Rosanna and Mark were due to arrive, while I was staying in the backpacker hostel, the manager came and knocked on my door. He said I had a phone call. I went downstairs, sat on an old sofa and picked up the handset. It was my father. I wondered why he was calling.

'Rob, I have some sad news about Aunt Elizabeth.' He spoke quietly and he sounded tired. 'This morning she died in a bus accident in London. Sarah and Pollyanna were injured and they are now in hospital, which is where I am calling you from.'

I froze as I tried to take in the news. Sarah was my cousin, and Pollyanna was her little two-year-old daughter, who had been born while I was away. It sounded very serious, but the doctors were still not sure about anything. I spoke to my father for ten minutes and he said he would call again the next morning. I put the phone down. I could not believe it. My family were all so far away. I had not seen them for years. My ride suddenly seemed frivolous. I walked up to my room in a daze and sat on my bed. And then the tears came.

I lay awake for much of the night. Thinking. Praying. Crying. I thought about my dear Aunt Elizabeth. She had not been taking any great risks when she died. She had just been walking along a pavement to a bus stop in London with her daughter and granddaughter when a bus had lost control and hit them. How fragile life suddenly seemed, how suddenly it could end. I thought about my cousins in hospital, and I prayed they would be okay. I thought about the rest of Aunt Elizabeth's close family. I also thought about my mother and how she must be feeling. Aunt Elizabeth was her only sister. I realised that, if it were me losing a sibling, I would want those people nearest to me to be there.

I drifted in and out of sleep. By the time I got up the next morning, I had decided that family was far more important than my bicycle ride. I booked an air ticket, caught a taxi to the airport and boarded a plane. After an eight-hour flight, and two years seven months away, I was back on English soil.

Statistics for Part 6 (Singapore–India)

Dates:	October 2006–April 2007
Total distance covered from start:	28,151 miles
Distance left to reach home:	7,027 miles
Distance covered by bicycle:	5,422 miles
Distance covered by boat:	0 miles
Age:	30
Most times to the loo in one day:	11 (Yunnan, China)
Highest pass:	5,200 metres (Pang-La Pass, Tibet)
Coldest temperature:	-21 (Tibet)
Police checkpoints dodged at night:	4 (Tibet)
Cumulative altitude climbed and descended:	over 23,000 metres
Number of days without speaking to anyone who understood me:	5 (Tibet)
Number of elephants seen:	3
Cups of yak butter tea drunk:	38

Part Seven

India–England

May–October 2007

N
UK
Home: London
Brussels
BELGIUM
FRANCE
SWITZERLAND
Geneva
ITALY
Rome
TYRRHENIAN SEA
GREECE
MEDITERRANEAN SEA
BLACK SEA
Istanbul
TURKEY
Tabriz
CASPIAN SEA
IRAQ
IRAN
Mashhad
TURKMENISTAN
UZBEKISTAN
Samarkand
Mazar-e-Sharif
Kabul
AFGHANISTAN
Peshawar
Islamabad
Lahore
PAKISTAN
New Delhi
INDIA
By bicycle
By boat
By vehicle
0
500
1000 miles
SCALE approx.

57
The Golden Temple

Distance to home = 7,027 miles

The question the atheist asks is: 'who turned on the lights?'
The question the person of faith asks is: 'whatever for?'
ANNIE DILLARD

I stayed in England for three weeks. I visited Sarah and Pollyanna in hospital. They had both sustained serious leg injuries, but were stable. Tragically, little Pollyanna's leg had been amputated below the knee. I also spent time with my family and saw Christine. Two days after Aunt Elizabeth's funeral, I boarded a plane and flew back to Delhi.

I caught a *tuk-tuk* from the airport to the city centre. After the relative cool and orderliness of London, the sudden blast of Indian heat and noise was bewildering. The *tuk-tuk* arrived at the house where I had left Alanis. My trip home had made me feel very different. For the past two-and-a-half years, as I had pushed and pedalled my way around the various obstacles in my path, I had been building up great momentum and making steady progress towards home. But now I had been home, all the momentum was gone. I did not have any regrets about flying to London – it had been an important gesture of love towards my family at an incredibly sad time, and important for my own grieving – but flying back to India again in order to cycle home seemed pointless. In London I had considered abandoning the rest of the journey altogether. I felt I had learnt the main lessons that I could learn from the saddle of a bicycle. But when I thought about it I knew that I had to finish what I'd started. I knew that I would never be able to get on with whatever was next in life unless I did.

But the road home looked stupid and dangerous. Before going to sleep on that first night back in India, I wrote in my diary:

I feel trapped. I feel crazy. I feel frightened. I have come back here – to the midst of chaos. To a hellish journey . . . what lies ahead looks so hard to me . . . often on this trip people have said to me that 'I couldn't do what you are doing'. Usually I just shrug this comment off, telling them most of the time things are pretty easy – just pedalling the bike down long roads and meeting lots of people (with an occasional tough bit thrown in). However, now I have to say it feels very hard. I am frightened of the road ahead – both the dangerous parts (Afghanistan) and the tiresome parts (slogging down a road at 45°C) . . . It's strange to be alone again . . . Turkey feels unbearably and impossibly far away . . . I am nervous about so many things . . . even where to stay, etc., which I haven't really worried about for years. I am missing Christine desperately. I am missing home and missing family. Just one day at a time, that's all I need to do. O Lord, out of the depths I cry to you.

The next day I set out from Delhi. It was now late May and I started sweating heavily as soon as I left the air-conditioned apartment. There were people everywhere and I swerved out of the way of *tuk-tuks* and rickshaw drivers who, in turn, were swerving out of the way of buses. I dodged cows and cowpats, and bumped through unexpected potholes. But then the road opened out into a wide highway lined with poplars and a good hard shoulder. Signs on the verge stated that 'Life is precious', to remind us road-users to travel with care. And then my legs found their old, familiar rhythm of pushing and turning and gradually, as the miles began to click by, the ride home started to feel possible once more.

Four days later I reached Amritsar, near the border with Pakistan. I visited the Golden Temple of the Sikhs, floating like a heavenly dwelling in the middle of their sacred lake. Little ripples on the lake reflected the temple's shiny cupolas and the whole place seemed to be murmuring with the enchantment of the exotic East. A gentle tide of pilgrims walked ponderously around the outside and an old man bathed in the lake, holding his young grandson to his chest. A Sikh told me that if you washed in the water it would wash away your sins. I stayed a night in the free accommodation provided for all visitors (whether Sikh or not), and the next day rode to the border.

58
The five pillars of Islam

Distance to home = 6,705 miles

I love the youths who hunt the stars
IQBAL THE POET

When I finally entered it, my first few minutes in Pakistan were filled with frightened thoughts about dangerous Muslims, although I knew that this was an unfair perception which I must have picked up from sensationalist news coverage. The men wore baggy shalwar-kameez clothing and the women headscarves. There were lots of mosques. I stopped to buy some bananas from a street stall and ask for directions. The man behind the stall looked a little perplexed at my appearance and crouched down behind his counter. A moment later he reappeared bearing a cup of sweet milky tea. He beamed and refused to take any money for the bananas. A small crowd gathered. They smiled shyly and, as I rode off, I felt their genuine good wishes go with me.

After two hours I arrived at my host's house in Lahore. Anwar lived with his wife, parents, sister and brother in a new suburb of the city – it was normal for entire families to live together in Pakistan. Anwar was my age and had a PhD in mathematics from Cambridge and a post-doctorate from Harvard. He now worked as a lecturer at a university in Lahore. He was also a devout Muslim and, over the course of my stay, we both enjoyed being able to talk and ask each other questions about our respective religions.

The five pillars of Islam, said Anwar, were very simple. You had to: acknowledge that Allah was one God and Muhammad was his prophet; pray five times a day; give to the poor; fast during daylight in the month of Ramadan; and, if possible, make the pilgrimage to Mecca (the haj) once during your lifetime.

To me it still sounded like a burdensome list of requirements. I wondered whether Muslims carried out these pillars more out of fear than any real sense of love for God. But, as I talked more with Anwar, I began to look at each of the five pillars in a different way. I could see that, for all the many disagreements among Muslims, the first pillar (acknowledging Allah and Muhammad) at least gave them a point of unity and reminded them how they were distinct from other religions. The second pillar (praying) was not necessarily a burden, but more a chance to share moments of peace with other followers of Allah in the midst of the tensions of the day. During my stay Anwar would regularly excuse himself to go to the mosque. 'I actually quite enjoy going to prayers,' he said.

The third (tax) was a way to fund the expansion of the religion and help the poor. The fourth and fifth (fasting and pilgrimage) were excellent ways to foster a sense of community. Anwar showed me a video in which a Westerner spoke of his own conversion to Islam, prompted by the desire to join the amazing communal feasts that happened at the end of each day during Ramadan.

It was an important conversation for me to have and some of my distorted caricatures of Islam began to slip away. Rather than oppressive rules, I began to see the pillars as deeply insightful and effective ways to foster community and devotion.

We also spoke about Muhammad. I realised that previously I had always pictured him as an angry figure, but now I tried to see him through Muslim eyes. For Muslims, he was not vicious, but rather someone who sincerely wanted to help people to follow God. Through my imagined Muslim eyes, I saw a bearded man with huge charisma who could put his hand on your shoulder and encourage you to submit to Allah – for the meaning of the word 'Islam' is 'submission'. And if God had chosen this great man as his messenger, how dare anyone insult him? No wonder Muslims got angry when the materialistic Westerners were disrespectful.

We also managed to find some common ground. We both knew what it was like to aspire to a way of life based on the worship of one God. However, it was clear that our views of what this one God was like were very different, especially with regard to how he related to Jesus of Nazareth.

'Muslims believe Jesus was a great prophet and we believe in the virgin birth and in Mary,'* said Anwar, 'it is just that we do not believe he was God.'

He seemed to think it would be but a small step for me to agree that Jesus was only a great prophet. He implied that Muslims were meeting Christians halfway – so could we not simply agree that Jesus was a great prophet instead of God?

I said that, for me, it was critically important that Jesus was God, because it showed that God loved his creation enough to become part of it in order to make it whole again.

'And I have heard that Muslims think that Jesus did not die at the crucifixion,' I queried.

Anwar said that this was true – the Qur'an said that God had rescued Jesus before he was crucified and someone else (possibly Judas) was crucified in his place.† I explained that this was actually another major divergence between the two faiths. For Christians, the cross was central to the whole faith. It was through suffering and dying that God, out of love, took humankind's wrongdoing onto himself, allowing forgiveness and the world's eventual healing. Moreover, if there was no crucifixion, then there would also be no resurrection, without which the notion of Christianity as a religion of hope would crumble.

It was a vital difference, though I was not sure I was making myself clear to Anwar. We belonged to different worlds, and it was hard to see through each other's eyes. And yet the conversations were important. They allowed us to acknowledge each other's opinion, conclude the other to be categorically wrong, and yet still maintain and even deepen our friendship.

*

*The longest Sura in the Qur'an is about Mary.

†This is based on Sura 4:157, which says that 'They did not kill Jesus, nor did they crucify him, but they thought they did . . . they knew nothing about him that was not sheer conjecture.'

As I lay on my bed later that night, reading a book about Islam, I pondered afresh the big question of how the world's great religions related to each other. Did the differences between Anwar's beliefs and mine actually matter?

In Delhi I had spent some time with a young and articulate philosophy-graduate-cyclist called Tim. Tim was an atheist and, as he did not believe in God anyway, he said that the different religions' varying 'mythologies' did not matter. Why not instead focus on the common mandate that we should live good lives? I thought that this made good sense for an atheist. However, I did believe in God, so I needed a different way to understand the world religions.*

I thought about what other approach I could take to make sense of all this. Many people I'd met during my journey though, especially Western travellers, shared my belief in some kind of spiritual world, but they still argued that the differences between the religions did not really matter. Again, why not focus on the similarities in ethics? I thought back to an evening in Kathmandu, having dinner in an outdoor restaurant with a mixture of European and Japanese backpackers and also some local Nepalis. One girl said that she thought all religions were just equally valid but different paths up the same mountain, and that the great religious leaders had differed in their teaching because 'God' was just so much bigger than any of them could grasp. All the religions had insights into the meaning of life, but none of them had got it quite right.

*There had been times in my life when I had seriously doubted God. When I contemplated suffering; or how tiny the world was in a vast universe; or the disunity and hypocrisy of the church; or when I just wanted an excuse to live my own way. However, most of the time, I found it hard to believe that there was no God. The wonder of the human experience of life – with its intensity of thought and feeling, the yearning for justice, the longing for friendship, the dazzling beauty of nature (not to mention occasional heart-shaking 'religious' experiences) – convinced me that life was far more than a freak accident in an indifferent universe. The atheists' explanations for these things simply did not convince me (just as my explanations did not convince them).

I appreciated the appeal and sincere intention behind this approach. I had also read a little about the serious attempts to find common ground such as concern for afterlife, concern for other humans and humility before some sort of God/higher power. However, although I still had my L-plates in my understanding of other religions, the more I learnt, the more I felt that the 'different paths up the same mountain' approach did not really work.

The main problem for me was that, although adherents to this approach claimed to respect all religions, in actual fact they failed to engage with any on its own terms. They argued that the things that each religion itself said were central – the need to escape desire in Buddhism, or the five pillars in Islam, or the resurrection of Jesus in Christianity – were actually not so central. Far more important was the 'common ground' that *they* deemed central.

I wondered on what basis they could be so selective. Wasn't it rather presumptuous for them to claim that they understood the heart of all the religions better than both the founders and the followers of the religions themselves?*

On a more personal level, I decided that I could really accept the 'different paths up the same mountain approach' only if I was at the same time willing to accept that many of my deeply held Christian beliefs, which I believed were important and true, were peripheral or false. With many of my core beliefs dismissed because they were too 'exclusive', what motivation would I have to follow the more challenging aspects of my faith? Why should I give to the poor; why should Christine and I refrain from sleeping together (because we were not married); why should I try to love and forgive

*I had been learning that the founders of the great religions were certainly aware that there were other options available, but they chose to make their own teachings markedly distinct. When Muhammad preached the message of Islam, he said it was putting right what the Jews and Christians had got wrong. Buddha propounded Buddhism only after concluding that the Buddhist way was better than the Hindu way which he had tried up until then. Christianity came into being amid a melting pot of Judaism and Greco-Roman polytheism.

my enemies – if I was free to just choose whichever beliefs were most appealing to me?

Although I thought, and still do think, that the 'different paths up the same mountain' approach is very inadequate, my mind continues to be full of questions, contradictions, uncertainties and provisional answers. While I do not believe that other faiths are completely invalid, I do not think that all can be equally valid. As time goes on I believe more strongly that I need to work hard, as a Christian, to respect and genuinely listen to people of other faiths, while also having the integrity to articulate and live by my own beliefs.

59
Persecution in Islamabad

Distance to home = 6,460 miles

Blessed are you when people say bad things about you because of me
JESUS OF NAZARETH

BEEEEEEEEEEEEEEEEEEEEEP (taxi mini-bus).

SMACK (Alanis being hit).

ARRGGGHHH (me leaping from Alanis).

I had said goodbye to Anwar and was on my way out of Lahore. Before I reached the outskirts, as I wove across a lane of traffic to make a turn, a taxi mini-bus drove into my front wheel and knocked Alanis from underneath me. In a rare display of coordin-ation I landed on my feet as she crashed to the ground. The mini-bus did not stop and I saw the passengers inside staring at me from the back window as it disappeared into the flurry of other vehicles.

I picked Alanis up and saw that she was not damaged. I looked around. There was no one for me to grumble to so I climbed back on and continued riding north to Islamabad.

On the way to the capital I was invited to stay with a family of Pakistani Christians. Their house was on a back street in the midst of the small church community. It was safer for them to live together. They welcomed me into their big house, which was full of aunts, uncles, brothers, sisters and children. I never worked out how many people lived there. We sat on old sofas in the living room and, while the children watched cartoons on an old television, we ate curry from plates on our laps. They were well educated and spoke good English, but over dinner they told me that, because they were Christians, it was hard to find jobs.

'I can speak six languages,' said a man, 'but when I apply to a company, or an international aid organisation or an embassy, it is usually a Muslim who is in charge of making the shortlist of applicants. They can tell from our names that we are Christians. My name is James, so I am automatically excluded. If my name were Muhammad, then I would get a job far more easily.'

It was not only in finding employment that the Pakistani Christians felt oppressed.

'My uncle is a priest,' said one woman. 'Recently he got permission from the high court to build a church on some land he owned. But about a hundred mullahs got together and protested against it. They caused such a fuss that the police told my uncle that he could not build it.'

The next day I met Pastor Tom, who was in charge of their parish. He was German and in his fifties, and had a round, earnest face, and grey hair. His eyes rippled with genuine care for his flock.

'Well, Pakistan is currently going through a crisis,' he said in a German accent. 'I've been in Pakistan for 33 years, and one thing I've noticed is that Pakistan is always going through a crisis. It seems to go from one crisis . . . to the next. The current crisis is to do with the Taliban, but there will be another crisis coming along after this.'

He sat back in the armchair. 'In Islamabad, Taliban supporters have been blowing up CD stores because they do not allow music. They have been trying to force the girls' schools to close. They have even blown up some barber shops because they cut beards. It was even more terrifying last year when the Danish cartoon incident sparked riots. We thought they might burn down our houses.'

I had heard about the Danish cartoons incident while I was in Papua New Guinea. It had seemed a distant problem at the time, but for the Christians in Islamabad it was deadly serious.

'It is much better near Islamabad than in the North-West Frontier Province, though,' said a man called John. 'Earlier this year two Christian villages were threatened that if they did not convert to Islam then they would all be murdered. The Taliban are so strong there that the police would not dare intervene even if they wanted to.'

*

There were other reasons why it was a frightening time to be a Christian in Pakistan. An armed gang had recently forced their way into a Bible school and held a gun to the head of a junior member of staff, threatening him and saying, 'We hear that you are converting Muslims.' At the same time, Pakistan's National Assembly was considering a draft apostasy bill which would impose a death penalty on any adult men who left Islam and imprisonment for adult women. More recently, I read about two Christian girls in a village who had been kidnapped and forced to marry Muslim men and convert – it took weeks before the police intervened and reunited them with their own families.*

Anwar had told me outright that Muslims who persecuted Christians had a wrong understanding of Islam, but evidently this view was not shared by all. I also thought again about the 'different paths up the same mountain' approach. If the differences between the religions did not matter, then why should these Pakistani Christians continue to hold on to their beliefs in the face of such hardship?

Pastor Tom stood up to leave. 'Please tell people in England that the Christians in Pakistan are going through a tough time,' he said as he shook my hand goodbye. Then he smiled, 'and please give my *salaams* to any other Christians you meet on your way home.'

*These stories are all substantiated by the Barnabus Fund charity, www.barnabusfund.com

60
To the point of tears

Distance to home = 6,460 miles

People don't take trips . . . trips take people
JOHN STEINBECK

Live to the point of tears
ALBERT CAMUS

'Mum,' I said into the receiver, 'I have decided that, after Pakistan, I'll be going through Afghanistan.'

After months of fretting, I had finally chosen my route to Europe.

It had been a tough decision. On the one hand, I had heard the news reports of the Taliban's resurgence and knew that, as an Englishman on a bicycle, I would be an easy target. On the other hand, I knew not to base my decision about Afghanistan solely upon a few scary reports on TV. Friends in Kabul told me that while parts of Afghanistan were extremely risky, even when travelling in a convoy, other parts were not quite so bad. Provided, they said, you avoid the south, the east and the west and you ride only in the north, and you ride only in daylight, you might be okay.

I was slightly encouraged but at the same time I reminded myself that just because I had survived a few dangerous places in the past, this did not make me immune from harm in Afghanistan; it had been the fate of many an adventurer to have survived several tough challenges only to become over-confident and get themselves killed the next time. I emailed Al (who had now made it back to England) to ask what he thought. Instead of his usual 'go for it' attitude, he wrote, 'If it was me, I wouldn't go.'* This freaked me out. There were also some horror stories for me to think about. I remembered a teacher in Australia who told me about his friend who had cycled into Afghanistan in the 1990s. He had been shot dead at a checkpoint in his first week.

I wrestled with the dilemma almost every night in my diary. One night I wrote: '*My heart says yes, my mind says fine, my emotions tangle both ways . . . my sense of responsibility says no . . .*' Another night I wrote: '*In my darker moments I am seriously terrified – almost to the point of tears.*' I felt a responsibility towards my family, especially having recently seen the pain they had been experiencing in England. I prayed about it, but was not sure what to think. Was I wanting to go through Afghanistan to prove myself? Was it that I was bored with going through safe places? Was I just very curious about Afghanistan and its amazing history? I still do not know the reason – it was just a definite draw.

All the advice seemed to agree that the road I would use to enter Afghanistan and reach Kabul would be extremely risky. With a conscious effort to remember my loved ones, I decided that, for this initial stretch of 250 miles, I would be prepared, for the first time on the expedition, to compromise on my 'cycling the whole route' rule, and instead catch a bus or taxi. Once in Kabul, I would climb back on the bike and ride northwards through the Hindu Kush, before crossing into Uzbekistan. It would therefore be a calculated risk, not a completely reckless one.

I explained my decision on the phone to my parents, emphasising that I had done plenty of research in reaching my compromise. I asked them to trust my judgement. I was very grateful that, although it must have been difficult for them, they said they would.

From Islamabad, I cycled through Taxila and across the Indus River. There was a big fort on the eastern bank. I neared the outskirts of Peshawar and a wall of arid, inhospitable mountains rose up ahead

*He later added that 'if you get your head chopped off you will feel like a real idiot (though it would be great publicity)'.

of me. On the other side of the mountains was Afghanistan. Riding into the city I saw for the first time women wearing full burqas, covered in a white cloth from head to foot. Some of the billboard advertisements above the road had been vandalised because they showed women's faces. There were more armed police and soldiers on the street.

I had been invited to stay by a British NGO worker called Amy. Tall and short-haired, with an air of calm and a welcoming smile, she had been working in Pakistan for years. Over dinner she told me of her work in the North-West Frontier Province villages. She had some heartrending stories about the women who, from the age of 12, were trapped in their houses.

'It's not just oppression, it's boredom that they have to struggle with,' she said. 'The worst is for the women from the wealthier families, because they are not needed to do any household chores. At least the poorer women, if they cover themselves, can go to the well to wash clothes. There they can meet their friends and talk. The richer ones are trapped inside for their whole lives.'

She told me about one very intelligent girl she knew who had pleaded for a way to escape. But it was impossible. The villagers would kill her if she tried to leave. Even the ten-minute bus ride to the local school was seen as undignified.

I asked Amy if she ever felt in danger.

'Well, I have occasionally had stones thrown at me in the villages. There is roughly a bomb a week here in Peshawar, but I know that it is more dangerous just crossing the road. You would be unlucky to be there when the bomb went off.'

I found it hard to get to sleep that night. I was thinking about where I would be going the next day.

61
Fear and compromise on the Khyber Pass

Distance to home = 6,383 miles

Do one thing every day that scares you
ELEANOR ROOSEVELT

Should another 9/11 type attack happen in the US, it will likely have its origins in this area
US STATE DEPARTMENT REPORT ABOUT PAKISTAN'S NORTH-WEST FRONTIER PROVINCE, 2008

At seven o'clock the next morning, with Alanis strapped to the roof and the compulsory Pakistani policeman with his Kalashnikov in the passenger seat, my taxi set off for the Khyber Pass. The adrenaline was already beginning to flow.

We drove through several checkpoints and wound up into the rugged hills. The roadside villages were simple and without colour. Many were enclosed in defensive walls. Amy had told me that the walls were not just to keep the invaders out, but also to keep the women in. Just below the road, I caught sight of the defunct Khyber railway which had been built by the British in the early twentieth century. We passed several military barracks and medieval-looking forts with slits for firing from in their walls. The land alongside the road was untamed and severe.

We reached the border, where I was stamped out of Pakistan and into Afghanistan. I wheeled Alanis (with the British flag now removed) into the fenced, one-mile corridor of no-man's-land, and a river of people jostled past in both directions. Most men wore shalwar-kameez, though their headgear varied. Some wore the loosely wrapped turbans, while others wore Chitrali caps, and occasionally

I spotted a baseball cap. The majority of the women were wearing full burqa, but from now on it would always be a sky-blue colour.

Lightly armed guards stood at intervals, watching us walk past. I saw one guard holding onto a man by the sleeve and slapping him repeatedly on the head, apparently demanding he hand something over. Behind a wall, I caught a glimpse of an armoured personnel carrier and several NATO soldiers in full combat gear. A line of World Health Organisation workers gave a polio-vaccination sweet to every child that passed. This was one of the busiest borders I had crossed and I remembered Amy telling me that there were still almost three million Afghan refugees in Pakistan.

I reached the end of no-man's-land and, as if in a dream, stepped into Afghanistan. Just ahead was a bus park, crammed with people and vehicles. As I drew nearer I was all of a sudden engulfed by a crowd of enthusiastic taxi-drivers eager for business. I had been advised to take a mini-bus, as the odd, rogue taxi-driver might be tempted to sell me to kidnappers. The drivers shouted at me, and several tussles broke out. One took me by the hand and pulled me towards his taxi. I pulled in the direction of a mini-bus.

A smart man who spoke English came to my side. He asked if he could help. I said I wanted to catch the bus. The man joined in the shouting match and I was gradually pushed towards a mini-bus, where a man with a ginger beard and a freckled face appeared. He reminded me of a Celt from olden times, but he was Afghan.* He smiled at me before roaring and leaping noisily into the crowd. He punched one man, thumped another and then pushed the taxi-drivers away from me. He helped me lift the bike up onto the roof of a mini-bus and encouraged me to climb aboard.

*There is a huge variety of different racial appearances native to Afghanistan. It has sometimes been suggested that the green eyes and ginger or blond hair are a result of Alexander the Great's army, which came through 2,300 years ago. It is now generally believed that the mixed racial influences come from many different invading armies and migrating peoples. I was reassured that, while I was on the bus in any case, perhaps people might not recognise that I was English.

Child vendors walked around the bus windows selling cigarettes and sweets and gradually the bus filled up. The men on board were very varied, both racially and in dress. The man sitting next to me had green eyes and wore a white skullcap. The driver had brown hair and a huge forehead. The women all looked identical – wearing their blue burqas. The Celt continued ushering people onto buses and hitting taxi-drivers. Before we left he bought me a packet of sweets and handed them to me with a grin.

A minute later, the bus bumped out of the dusty bus park, and accelerated down the smooth tarmac and past a 'Welcome to Afghanistan' sign. A shiver went down my spine. I had crossed the Khyber Pass.

We entered a world that was just as I had imagined Afghanistan to be: brown, with deserted hills, twisting gullies, rocky crags. Occasionally we swept through lush green valleys, with gentle streams. I saw more mud-brick villages. There was a collapsed wire bridge across one of the rivers with the wire still dangling in the water. Had it collapsed from old age, I wondered, or had it been destroyed in one of the wars? In the afternoon, we climbed a series of gorges. The road veered through crumbling tunnels and sheer cliffs fell away from the roadside, but this did not stop us overtaking other vehicles, already two abreast, on blind hairpin bends going uphill. As we reached a small mountain stream I glimpsed two men perched on slabs of rock in the middle of the water bowing Mecca-wards.

The people on the bus ignored me. As we swerved from side to side, the woman behind me started throwing up underneath her burqa. I could hear that she had a bag to vomit into, but it was obviously unthinkable for her to expose her face for fresh air. Everyone else on the bus pretended not to notice. A few minutes later she had recovered and I heard her chatting noisily into her mobile phone.

As I looked out at the beautiful gorges and rugged mountains, I started to rue the fact that I was in a mini-bus. It all looked very peaceful. '*This would have been fine for cycling,*' I thought to myself. But then I reminded myself that whether a place 'feels' safe or 'feels' dangerous does not really mean anything. Danger was not dependent on my perception of it. Indeed, I had recently been reading that this part of Afghanistan had a history strewn with the corpses of those outsiders who, down the centuries, had underestimated the danger. The most chilling recent examples occurred during the NATO invasion. Six years beforehand, in November 2001, a car full of international journalists, eager to get a scoop by being the first to drive to Kabul, had been ambushed on this very road. They were pulled from their car and forced to march up onto a hillside. Their Afghan driver who witnessed the event described afterwards how 'they took the journalists and when the journalists turned to look at them, the gunmen shot'. The four bodies, an Italian, a Spaniard, an Afghan and an Australian, were dragged back to the verge and left for other cars to see.

Things had calmed once NATO were established, but tensions were on the rise again. Just a month previously an American patrol had opened fire on a crowd of civilians in Jalalabad after being attacked by an ineffective bomb. Eight civilians were killed and 35 injured. Although compensation and apologies had been made, emails from Kabul had told me that resentment towards foreigners was brewing yet again.

Two hours before dark, the bus climbed out of a final gorge and came onto a dusty plain, surrounded on all sides by snow-capped mountains. The bus drew into a big, potholed car park and, to my surprise, everybody started to disembark. I had thought that we were going all the way to Kabul, but now the bus was stopping in the middle of nowhere.

Someone passed me Alanis from the roof of the bus. The other passengers zoomed off in taxis. A small crowd of men gathered to watch me. I could not speak a word of either Pashtun or Dari, so I just said, 'Kabul?' and gestured a cycling motion with my hands.

The four men looked at me for a moment and then pointed casually towards some dimly lit buildings on the horizon. It would be dark soon, so I set off, pedalling hard.

'This was not part of the plan,' I said to myself. But, actually, more than fearful, I felt excited. I felt alive.

After a few minutes, I was among the buildings. They were mostly mud-brick and one or two storeys high. A few minutes later I started to pass concrete blocks. The traffic was increasing. I later discovered that this stretch of road was popular for roadside bombings, so I was not the only person keen to get into the city quickly that day.

All of a sudden, a van, with a large, upside-down table strapped to its roof, screeched to a halt beside me. The window wound down and I was hit by a gush of American rap music. A teenager leaned out and shouted at me in English.

'Hey, man, what are you f***ing doing?'

'I am riding to my friends' house in Kabul.'

The boy jumped out. He was about 17. 'Why don't we give you a lift? It's f***ing crazy!' he said.

Two other teenagers were sitting in the front of the van grinning at me. 'We have some room in the back.'

'Well, I was supposed to catch a bus to the city centre anyway,' I thought, and these guys didn't exactly look like the Taliban. We shoved the bike into the back, and I squeezed into the front seat with the other three. The driver turned the volume up, hit the accelerator and swerved back into the line of traffic.

I asked them what they did.

'We are DVD salesmen,' they yelled back cheerfully. 'We supply DVDs to the NATO troops. Here, you want a DVD?'

The dashboard of the van was strewn with DVDs. The boy grabbed one at random and offered it to me. It was a horror film I had never heard of.

'No thanks,' I said. 'Do you get a lot of business around here?'

'Yes, yes, we get so much. The American colonel lets us visit the troops in the barracks. They give us orders and then we find them the DVDs. We can get them anything.'

He pulled out a certificate from the colonel which said that they were good and reliable DVD providers. I did not think the copyright lawyers would be very pleased but, hey, this was a war zone.

As we drew into the city centre, I felt I was in a Hollywood movie myself. Soldiers patrolled the streets, helicopters flew overhead, and the high walls of the NATO bases with their watchtowers lined the roadsides. I had my video camera out and pointed it out of the window.

'Hey, man, f***ing put that away,' said one of the boys. 'You can be shot for filming the barracks.'

I apologised. They said they would drop me at my friends' house, but without warning there were suddenly Afghan soldiers on the road ahead waving all the traffic on a diversion.

'F***ing, there is a convoy coming through,' yelled the driver, slamming on the brakes.

They said I would have to continue on my own and pulled the bike out of the back. I shouted a genuine thank you to them as they roared off, hollering directions back at me as they went.

I started cycling straight up the street, though I had no idea where I was going. I had scribbled a rough map in the back of my diary but I had yet to find any landmarks. There were all of a sudden no more cars on the road. I came to three Afghan soldiers with Kalashnikovs. I drew up next to one of them, smiled and asked if they knew where the street I needed was.

The soldier scowled at me and started to wave me on. I could not understand what he was saying. He waved more frantically and when I hesitated he levelled his gun at me.

'Okay, okay,' I said, suddenly afraid and starting to pedal again.

A second soldier yelled at me and waved me the opposite way. I spun round and followed his directions, wheeling Alanis up to a wall he indicated. In the midst of this confusion, a stream of motorbikes and Toyota trucks appeared and sped past.

When the convoy had gone, I saw that the two soldiers had started laughing at me. 'Tourist, tourist!' the second soldier was shouting at the first. They apologised, and pointed me in the right direction. As I rode off, I realised that, with my shaggy beard, my grey shalwar-kameez, and my grimy bicycle strapped with suspicious-looking bags, I had initially appeared to them as an unusual-looking suicide bomber. I made a mental note, in future, to always identify myself as an English tourist before I asked directions from Afghan soldiers.

62
Kabul

Distance to home = 6,207 miles

He goes because he must, as Galahad went towards the Grail:
knowing that for those who can live it, this alone is life
EVELYN UNDERHILL

Successive invading forces have come and gone from Kabul, but it has rarely been tamed for long. In 1840 a British regiment marched in from India to place an inept puppet king on the Afghan throne. After a few years of watching the British camp throw tea parties and play polo, the local population had had enough. A small-scale disturbance escalated into an all-out uprising. The British force, plus their families and servants, decided to abandon the capital and retreat along the road on which I had travelled by bus. But they were betrayed by a local leader and the mountain tribesmen attacked them mercilessly. The result was a wholesale massacre. Apart from a handful of captives, there was only one British survivor: Dr Brydon. He stumbled out of the blood-bath on the back of a half-dead pony and into the safety of the British fort in Jalalabad. Sixteen thousand men, women and children had died on the passes in those few days.

One hundred and sixty years later, after the Russians had had their go, yet another foreign force had arrived: NGOs and diplomats; adventurers and journalists; officers, analysts and spies. I had been invited to stay in Kabul with Arabella and Nick, a hospitable, high-flying, diplomat couple. Arabella worked for the UN and Nick for the Foreign Office. They lived in a walled compound which was guarded by ex-Gurkha security guards. After I had taken a shower, Arabella told me over a cup of tea that it was not unknown for suicide bombers to use bicycles in Kabul, and this explained the soldiers' reaction to me earlier. She said that suicide bombers were usually recruited abroad, trained in Pakistan and given missions in Afghanistan. Invariably they ended up missing their high-profile target and killed lots of civilians instead.

That night Nick and Arabella had a party. The guests were made up of various other diplomats and people who worked at the UN. Their servant prepared an impressive array of dishes which we ate outside in the warm air on a pretty veranda. I felt relieved to have made it safely to Kabul, but I was worn out from a day of thick adrenaline. I had a scruffy beard, and even scruffier hair. My shirt had holes in it and my trousers – my 'clean' pair – were stained with oil. In contrast, all the other guests were bright and smart. Some spoke to each other off to the side in hushed voices, while sipping their wine. I wished I could listen in on their conversations.

One man gave me advice: 'The trouble is, the people here can be quite devious, and they might welcome you in and then turn nasty. If you do not speak any Dari, you will not find out that you are in trouble until it is too late.'

Another told me a story of the Taliban days: 'If a girl was raped and the case subsequently came to trial, then there were two possible outcomes for her. The first was that the judge might order that she marry the man who raped her. The second was that she would be forced to climb to the top board of the old Kabul swimming pool, and jump to her death on the empty, concrete floor below her. They have a very different way of understanding things. Honour, and the honour of the family, are of supreme importance.'

I spoke to a European girl who was working on a project to eliminate poppy growing. She said it was stressful and she was thinking of pursuing a different career, or perhaps even going travelling for a while. I asked why it was not possible for the international agencies to buy up all the opium crops and use them for morphine. It was an argument I had read in a newspaper.

'If we licensed the growing of opium, then people would happily sell their quota of opium to us,' she said, 'but at the same time they would also grow some extra opium to sell to the drug dealers. In order to prevent this, we would need a good police presence which could monitor and control the opium farms. But the police force is not at that level yet.'

I asked what sort of strategies they were using to eliminate the opium.

She said there were a number of strategies, but ended the conversation by admitting that 'Basically, my job is telling the army which people to kill'. I began to understand why she might want a change of career.

In the middle of the party, Christine phoned me on the landline. We spoke for half an hour and I told her honestly that I was staying somewhere safe now though perhaps I gave her a slightly censored version of what had happened earlier that day. After I had finished talking to her, people at the party found it extraordinary that, doing what I did, I had a girlfriend, but I was too tired to explain the story. The night drew to a close and everyone went home.

The next day I went out into the city again. I realised that my slightly dramatic experiences upon arriving the day before were not the norm. Apart from military-compound areas, Kabul was mostly full of typical city scenes: shops, restaurants, houses and markets. It felt tense, but people here were keen simply to get on with their lives in peace, making a living, talking and laughing with friends, and bringing up their children well. I went to the Embassy of Turkmenistan and was delighted to succeed in collecting my Turkmen visa. Arranging visas for this leg had been the most complicated of the entire journey because most of the countries were either ex-Soviet (and thus imbued with paranoid bureaucracy) – Uzbekistan and Turkmenistan – or had bad diplomatic relations with Britain (and thus were reluctant to let me in at all) – Iran. After hours of delving through travellers' websites for up-to-date advice, I had finally worked out a plan. I had picked up my Iranian and Pakistani visas in Delhi, my Uzbek visa in Islamabad, and my Afghan visa in Peshawar. Now, with Turkmenistan's obtained, I had a clear run all the way through to Turkey, assuming that I did not have any trouble with temperamental border guards.

My other main task in Kabul was to meet the people I had been put in touch with and so gain more first-hand advice for the road ahead. That afternoon I went to visit the Kabul stadium. During the Taliban era, the stadium had been used as the site of public executions. Law breakers were forced to stand in holes on the playing pitch to be publicly stoned while the crowds watched. When I arrived, there was a team of students having a football match on the pitch. I had been given a contact at the stadium who turned out to be the Head of the Afghan Olympics Committee. He was a busy man in a suit and he had greying hair. As a sportsman, he liked what I was doing and gave me the phone number of his friend in the first town where I would be staying.

That night, I arranged to have dinner with the next person on my list, an ex-diplomat Scot called Rory Stewart. In a bookshop in Islamabad I had stumbled upon Rory's book, *The Places In Between*. The book recounted how, in the cold January weather of 2002, shortly after the Taliban had been toppled, he had walked from Herat to Kabul. It took him six weeks. Along the way, he was shot at by a local commander, crossed frozen passes and talked his way out of a tight spot with the Taliban by pretending he was an Indonesian historian.

Rory sauntered into the compound wearing a smart shirt and jacket and looking as though he had walked straight off the pages of a Kipling novel. He was shorter and younger than I had expected, only a few years older than me. In the car on the way to the restaurant, he explained that he had now set up a charity in Kabul which worked to revitalise traditional Afghan arts-and-crafts skills. Rather than speaking in a Scottish accent, he had a clipped English public-school accent. His driver dropped us at Flashman's Restaurant. During the Taliban era the property had been rented by Osama Bin Laden's third wife.

As we sat down to eat, Rory explained that his walk through Afghanistan had been part of a longer walk of almost two years from Turkey to Nepal. He said that when he set off across Afghanistan, he had expected to die before he reached Kabul. It was an extraordinary thought. I had sometimes feared I might die, but

I never outright expected it. He said that he thought it would be all right for me to ride the western road to Herat, the way he went. I said I wasn't as brave as he was so I planned on taking the northern road. I admitted that I had already ended up catching the bus from Peshawar. Rory said that he had not walked the Khyber Pass road either. He had caught a taxi, but because he thought that bandits would be looking out for Westerners in the passenger seat, he had driven it while the taxi-driver and his wife sat in the back.

'Two things I want to advise you,' he said, as our food arrived. 'The first is: do not camp. There were two Germans who were driving across Afghanistan last year. They were in the north of the country, near the route you are taking, but they camped on the outskirts of a village without asking permission, which was really not a good idea. In the night they were both shot dead.'

I agreed and explained that I was busy making contact with various people along my route so I would have safe places to sleep.

'The second thing,' Rory continued, 'is to buy yourself a mobile phone here in Kabul. If you ever get into trouble, call me, and I will speak to whoever you are with.' Rory spoke fluent Dari. It was a generous offer, which I gladly accepted. He also offered to write a letter for me, to act as a kind of magic letter for Afghanistan.

As we left, we saw the owner of the restaurant, Peter Jouvenal, sitting at a table behind us with his Afghan wife. Rory said that Jouvenal was one of the very few Westerners who had filmed Osama Bin Laden and Mullah Omar.* We went over to say hello. Peter smiled when I said I was about to cycle up north, and said that I was a crazy bugger.

'Being called crazy by Peter', said Rory as we walked out to the car, 'is a great compliment.'

*Joevenal later described Bin Laden as 'rather like a bank manager'.

63
A short ride in the Hindu Kush

Distance to home = 6,207 miles

10–13 JUNE 2007

I look absurd the morning I leave Kabul. I am wearing my old sunglasses (held together with safety pins) and my bushy beard pokes out from beneath my lop-sided bicycle helmet. With a true geography teacher's sense of fashion I have tucked my baggy trousers into my socks, which I wear under my sandals to stop my feet getting sunburnt.

The sky is blue and the sun is blazing as I climb away from the city. I pass over the brow of hills that nestle around Kabul and free-wheel into a wide valley. Flat fields spread far away from the road before rising abruptly into a rocky brown wall, crowned by snow-spattered peaks: the Hindu Kush. I ride fast through the fresh air that smells of countryside. The silence is broken every few minutes as a car overtakes.

I have about 400 miles of Afghanistan ahead of me. I expect it will take me about five days to ride. I have been worrying about what will happen for months. Now it's time to find out.

I stop for my first night in the town of Charikar, after covering just 40 miles. This is the last town before I cross the mountains. I am saving the big climb for tomorrow – I do not want to get stuck halfway up it in the dark.

I am not sure where I will stay in Charikar, but I call the number given to me by the Head of the Olympics Committee. My contact comes to meet me. His name is Abdul. He is partly bald, with a big moustache and a huge grin. He speaks barely a word of English. We have lunch in a kebab restaurant, and then, in order to find a safe place for me to sleep, he takes me around the town to meet various local leaders. We meet the police chief in the police station. He has a chiselled face and grey stubble, and wears a smart waistcoat. He too cannot speak English so tries to communicate with me in Russian. Exasperated that I cannot understand, he writes me a note, which is what Abdul was hoping for. After that we go to meet the hotel owner. He is a fat man in a suit and his office reminds me of Brando's study in the Godfather *films. The two photo portraits on the wall are the same as those that I had seen in the police station. One is of President Karzai and the other is of Massood, the leader of the Northern Alliance who was assassinated by Al-Qaeda a few days before 9/11.*

Having established that I can stay in the hotel that night, Abdul takes me to the local college. We enter a classroom full of middle-aged Afghan civil servants. They have grey beards and all wear suit jackets over the top of their shalwar-kameez. They are here for English lessons. I am invited to help them practise. The young, slightly camp Afghan English teacher opens the class by saying, 'First we will revise pronouns . . . there are seven types: personal, demonstrative, relative, reflexive . . .'

'Oh dear,' I think to myself, 'even I don't know what any of these are. How can you learn English like that?'

But it turns out that the teacher is very good at teaching and the civil servants are very good at learning. I am impressed by how well they can speak after just three months of lessons.

When the class is over, Abdul takes me and two friends up the side of a mountain to a mulberry orchard. Mulberries are a popular fruit in Afghanistan. One of the men climbs a tree and shakes it, and the other two hold a rug beneath it. We wash the berries in a stream and sit watching the dusk settle quietly over the mountains ahead of us. This is a place of real beauty and it is hard to imagine the armies that have raged up and down this valley over the centuries. Alexander, Genghis, Tamerlane, Babur . . . then more recently the Russians, the Taliban and NATO. As we pack up our picnic, there is a shuddering in the sky and a jet roars past on a mission from the American airbase at the end of the valley. My three new friends are so used to it that they do not seem to notice.

The next day I am up at 4.30 a.m. I get changed, eat a small bowl of oats and look out of the window at the pale-pink dawn lifting over the mountains in the distance. The ridgeline casts a long, looming shadow over the whole valley.

I set off, riding hard and fast. Within an hour the sun is above the ridge and scorching my back. Reaching the valley wall, the road now pitches headlong into the mountains and my short ride in the Hindu Kush begins. I follow a gurgling stream up a twirling V-shaped valley. Villages cascade precariously off mountain sides and steep rocky walls rise jaggedly to distant peaks. As I climb higher the sun intensifies and I sweat heavily. Sometimes I pass through the shade of a valley wall and the temperature drops markedly and my sweat feels icy. The adrenaline is giving me energy and I feel too impatient to stop for a proper lunch (the butterflies in my stomach have stolen my appetite), but I force myself to eat a pack of biscuits and drink water.

I start to gasp and slow down as the air thins. The altitude is mild compared to the Tibetan passes of February, but that was four months ago and I have lost my high haemoglobin count now. At last, around noon, I reach the Salang tunnel.

The Salang is an impressive feat of Soviet engineering. Several hundred metres below the actual pass, it burrows straight through the core of the mountains. I had been continually warned about the inadvisability of cycling this – three miles of potholes and water, big Pakistani trucks and thick smoke, unlit and crumbling walls and, according to one person in Kabul, the occasional flock of sheep. I had promised my mother that, as well as the Peshawar–Kabul road, this would be the other place I would refrain from riding. I wave at passing vehicles for 20 minutes before a small van stops and gives me and Alanis a lift. It is dark and cavernous inside the tunnel, and I am glad that I'm not riding as the trucks thunder past.

Three miles later, on the other side, I climb out and begin the massive 30-mile descent to the desert. I hurtle downwards, weaving around the hairpins and sweeping past the villages where children turn and look. Serrated ridges and rocky scree slopes are all around me. A stream rushes past below and I see a bullet-ridden, Soviet armoured personnel carrier that sits rusting in mid-stream. After half an hour of downhill, I take my eyes off the road to look for a possible photo opportunity. In the moment of lapsed concentration, Alanis skids off the road and onto the stony shoulder, and – at 30 miles per hour – my wheels skid out of control. I brake too hard and a moment later am flying over the handlebars, through the air, and landing with a crash on my side on the gravel.

I lie still for a moment before climbing to my feet with a groan. My gloves and trousers are ripped and I see blood on my knee. I look up to see that a group of village children have gathered around. They help me lift Alanis back on her wheels. She is not damaged. I thank the children and take a photo of them standing, looking concerned, beside her.

I am still trembling as I continue my descent, now at a much more cautious speed. As the sun goes down, after 12 hours of riding in the heat, I reach the town of Pul-i-Khomri. I have an invitation to stay the night in a compound owned by HALO, the land-mine-clearing charity.

I take a day off at the compound to let my cuts recover and rest from the sun before hitting the road again. As I move onwards the terrain changes hourly. Sometimes it is an array of lush, irrigated paddy-fields; at others, a pastureland of camels, donkeys, sheep and cows; at others, a barren desert where signs warn of land-mines. Over dinner last night, the HALO manager, Richard, explained to me that the people here know all about the danger of land-mines, so they do not need educating. The reason why they still try to work the uncleared land is that they are poor and they have no choice. Ninety thousand mines have been cleared so far and it is thought that there are about half a million left.

I stop in a small village to buy some snacks and drinks. A crowd gathers around, staring at me. I smile and say, 'As-salaam alaikum' *('Peace be with you', the traditional Muslim greeting). The crowd* returns my smile, mostly. They are all men and boys, wearing shalwar-kameez. They have weather-beaten faces with strong features. As I buy a two-litre bottle of Fanta, the crowd starts to gesture their enquiries. Who am I? Where am I from? What am I doing? I reply with my own gestures that I have cycled from Hindustan (India) and I am going to Uzbekistan. I mime out a few set routines about how high the mountains are and how hot the weather is. They nod and smile and laugh. They persist in wanting to know where I am from. I decide just to be honest so I say Inglestan (England). They still seem friendly. Then the crowd parts to let a man through. He is in his mid-fifties, with a long beard, a white skull cap, and hard eyes. He looks important. The important man is scowling at me so I say, 'As-salaam alaikum' and hold out my right hand to shake his hand while putting my other hand to my chest – I had been told that this was a way of showing respect. The man glowers, refuses my hand and says something to the crowd. Is it my imagination or is everybody starting to tense up? I offer him my hand and smile once more. He refuses my hand and his glower deepens. Feeling suddenly very uncomfortable, I decide it is time to leave. Keeping the smile fixed on my face, I wheel Alanis out of the crowd while throwing out lots of 'As-salaams', and then climb quickly back onto Alanis, and ride off at speed.

I feel shaky as I follow the road beyond the village and back into the fields. It had been very rude for that man to refuse my hand and I was alarmed to have no idea what anyone was saying. Hearing cars approaching behind me, I find myself wondering whether I am being pursued. A memory flits through my mind from a month beforehand, in Pakistan. I was staying in a cheap roadside hotel. Halfway through dinner I was approached by a Pakistani man. He was my age and I assumed he was from the local area, until he started speaking, to my surprise, in a broad Manchester accent. He was an English Pakistani, he said, and was back in Pakistan to bury his father. We chatted for a while about life in Pakistan compared to England, and he warned about some of the more dangerous characters in the town, adding 'but you'll be okay – with all your experience'. I now wonder again in what possible sense any of my *'experience' could help me if I did run into trouble. All I could think of was that perhaps I take scary situations in my stride a little more – things faze me less these days. However, being unfazed is unlikely to be of much help here in Afghanistan.*

The cars overtake me without stopping. It seems no one is going to pursue me after all. I am probably just being melodramatic. I thought I was coming to Afghanistan to learn about the country, but now I seem intent on just riding through it as fast as possible. I am annoyed that my fear is stronger than my curiosity.

In the afternoon my wheels spin from valley to valley and endless waves of arid hills rise, fall and disappear into the hinterland. Half-destroyed tanks litter the roadsides at regular intervals. Looking up at the rocky crags I see how easy it must be for ambushers to hide in this region. In mid-afternoon I see a military convoy coming towards me. It is a long line of tanks and armoured personnel carriers, complete with square-jawed, big-muscled soldiers whose torsos emerge from their gun turrets. It is a NATO convoy and I feel reassured to see them. I wave and smile at them as they pass. The soldiers continue looking straight ahead. They are blank-faced and completely ignore me.

Later, I come to a checkpoint of Afghan policemen with their Kalashnikovs. They sit beside huge towers of sandbags, near their home-made speed bumps (made from piles of gravel in the middle of the road). These young men look bored and fatigued. They are more pleased to see me than the NATO troops were. I seem to be a pleasant interlude from their daily routine of doing nothing. There has been relatively little fighting in the north in recent years, so it is an enviable place to be on guard compared to the south.

Two hours before dark I enter a canyon that will lead me through to the flat northern plains. The ruffled rockfaces tower over me, splurging green bushes from their cracks.

A taxi full of people overtakes me, beeping furiously, and I am alarmed when the driver leans out and shouts angrily at me: 'Ash-hadu anal elaha illa-Allah Wa ash-hadu anna Mohhamadan rasul-Allah.'

He scowls, waves his fist and roars off ahead. I cannot speak Arabic, but I recognise the phrase as the Shahada – the first pillar of Islam – which means 'I bear witness that there is no God but Allah and Muhammad is his servant and messenger'. It is also the phrase that you have to say to convert to Islam and it is said every time a Muslim goes to prayers. I wonder if the taxi-driver was trying to get me to convert or if he was just angry because I was a Westerner. If he was angry, was it an ideological hatred because I was an infidel? Or has he had bad experiences with the foreigners meddling in his country? I do not know.

After 20 miles, I emerge from the other end of the canyon.

The hazy plains of Mazar-e-Sharif roll out ahead of me. I can see a mud fort with a destroyed tank sitting symbolically beside it. Just beyond the fort there is a turnoff to the village where I have been invited to stay with another NGO. I notice my face is sunburnt. I have cycled the last three days on just adrenaline and a few packets of biscuits. My body is suddenly without energy as relief sweeps through me.

64
Alexander and Roxana

Distance to home = 5,918 miles

Outside there was no sound but the scraping of the pine trees in the wind. Danger was cumulative, of course, it crept up step by step, half-noticed as your journey took you deeper, farther. Until you woke up at night in a place beyond help

COLIN THUBRON

I had arrived at my hosts a day early so I decided to have a sight-seeing day before completing my journey to the Oxus and crossing the border 40 miles away. The next morning a young American from the NGO gave me a lift into Mazar-e-Sharif. He dropped me in the city centre, beside the famous Blue Mosque. Legend had it that the mosque was built over the tomb of Ali, cousin and son-in-law of Muhammad. The mosque had been destroyed and rebuilt many times over the centuries and in its latest version the blue tile-work stood out magnificently against the pure blue sky. One-legged men on crutches hobbled up to the entrance, and formless women flittered past in their waves of burqa.

I walked around the mosque for a while and then sat in a kebab shop and ate several plates of greasy chips for lunch. I was very hungry from the previous few days' effort. Mazar-e-Sharif had been the regional capital for only the previous 130 years. Before that, there had been a much grander capital. It was only a village and a ruin now, but in the afternoon I went to see it.

'This is Balkh,' said Ali, my English-speaking guide. He smiled, held his arm out and gestured at the circle of massive mud buttresses around us. It was impressive, even today. Thirty-five centuries ago,

Balkh had been known as 'mother of all cities'. Twenty-six centuries ago, according to many historians, it was the birthplace of Zarathustra, founder of Zoroastrianism. Three centuries after that, Alexander the Great had arrived and surprised his troops by marrying the beautiful local princess, Roxana.

At some point in Pakistan, I was not exactly sure where, I had begun criss-crossing the extraordinary route that Alexander took as he conquered his way beyond the known world. He had left his homeland in Macedonia in his early twenties and defeated the superpower's immense Persian army, aged 25. I pondered on whether the equivalent today might be a 25-year-old Mexican defeating the USA on home soil? In Taxila, in Pakistan, I had visited a museum displaying arrow-heads and swords from Alexander's era. He had probably come through the canyon I cycled down the previous day. Cycling through these places in the relatively ordered twenty-first century was a tough feat for me. Alexander had managed to bring an entire army.

We walked onto the huge concave field where the city used to be. Beneath our feet there were shards of pottery, though Ali said that the really old material was buried a lot deeper. A motorbike roared along the top of the ancient wall, spewing dust. From the edge of one wall we looked down on several streets of ramshackle houses. Balkh was little more than a village now. 'The people just take bricks from these walls when they want to build a new house,' Ali said. The beginning of the end for Balkh, like so many other great cities of the Islamic world, had been the passing hurricane of Genghis Khan. In 1220 he had destroyed every building of note and butchered its thousands of inhabitants. Timur had sacked it again about a century later. But in the end it was malaria and water-supply problems that sealed its abandonment and led to Mazar-e-Sharif becoming the new capital.

Lastly, Ali took me to the site of a French archaeological dig from a few years previously. Creeping down some earthen steps, we saw evidence of the changing civilisations: Islamic styles near the surface; Buddhist influences lower down; and Greek columns from Alexander's day at the bottom. They were still well preserved 10 metres below the ground. Ali told me that the archaeologists only came rarely because it was still perceived to be too dangerous for them. He said that he had worked out a theory for where to find the actual building where Alexander and Roxana had got married, and one day he hoped to organise a dig there.

For aspiring Indiana Joneses, there was still a lot to discover in Afghanistan.

I had been in Afghanistan for less than two weeks, but a sense of background fear that something bad might happen, and a need to keep on schedule for fixed visa dates on the route ahead, meant that, after my day off at Balkh, it was time to leave. A terrible head-wind picked up as I rode through the parched, desert-scrub towards the border. It took me three hours of hard effort to cover the first 20 miles. It felt as if the elements were conspiring to stop me leaving. Maybe I would not escape from Afghanistan after all. I reached a turnoff and the wind swung round. Sand dunes began to encroach onto the road. A taxi overtook and screeched to a halt in front of me. The driver jumped out and ran towards me. I was taken aback. But then I saw he had a huge grin on his face as he grabbed my hand and shook it enthusiastically. And then at last I saw a line of checkpoints and buildings.

I cycled onto the 'Friendship' Bridge, and across Amu Daryu River, previously the Oxus. It was half a mile wide, brown and fast-flowing. The Soviet tanks had spilled into Afghanistan over this bridge when they invaded in 1979. They had also retreated over it ten years later. Almost 2,500 years before that, somewhere in the hazy upstream, Alexander had ordered his troops to assemble makeshift rafts by sewing up their tents, so they could cross the river in pursuit of his (latest) arch-enemy, Bessus the pretender. I looked back at the Afghan side. There were big ugly docks and old, rusty boat carcasses. Ahead, on the Uzbek side, the bank was lined with green reeds.

I showed my passport five times to five different officials in five different offices to get through into Uzbekistan. I could hardly believe it when I was past the final one and riding out onto the smooth, unblocked tarmac. The contrast with Afghanistan was amazing. In place of the gasping deserts, deadly minefields and heavily armed soldiers, there was now a sea of unending, green cotton fields. Unbearded farmers sat casually on their tractors and unveiled women sat outside their quaint little houses. I felt a burst of euphoria. I had made it. I realised that perhaps I had been expecting to die in Afghanistan after all. I knew it was unfair for me to remember Afghanistan in such a negative way. It had been a land of awesome beauty and the vast majority of the people I'd met had been kind and helpful. But I had seen everything through the lenses of fear. Now I was through to the other side, all of a sudden, the rest of the journey seemed possible. I felt that I could, and maybe even that I would, make it home.

65
Golden journey

Distance to home = 5,699 miles

But who are ye in rags and rotten shoes,
You dirty-bearded, blocking up the way?
JAMES ELROY FLECKER

I meandered north in Uzbekistan, with a head full of possibilities. A land of gentle hills, green meadows and gurgling streams drifted past. I stopped in several sleepy villages to fill up with water. One man I asked led me down a back street and encouraged me to sit on a bed in his porch and eat tomatoes and cheese. As evening approached, I was riding through ideal camping territory, so I stopped in a village shop for supplies. I bought pasta, a tin of peas and a tin of beef with the face of a cow on the side of it.

A few miles later, I wheeled Alanis over a grassy knoll and pitched the tent beside a stream. The sound of cars on the road echoed off the side of a cliff across the valley, but, otherwise, all was calm. I felt very safe camping here. The feeling of euphoria of having escaped Afghanistan had still not left me. Under the moonlight, I boiled the pasta and poured the tins into the pot. In my tired state, it was a couple of seconds before I noticed that the contents of the second tin did not resemble beef. It was a whitish, creamy liquid. I looked at the side of the tin and saw that it said '*Malakoi*' in Cyrillic. This was Russian for 'milk' and I realised that I had bought condensed milk instead of beef. I am usually very tolerant of my unconventional cooking techniques, but this was inedible. I poured it on to the grass, and ate stale biscuits for dinner instead. I did not really mind, though. I still relished the state of no longer being afraid, and soon fell asleep.

I was woken the next morning by the sound of animals. A herd of goats was wandering past. Three teenaged shepherds smiled at me, and their dog ambled over to lick the pasta off the grass.

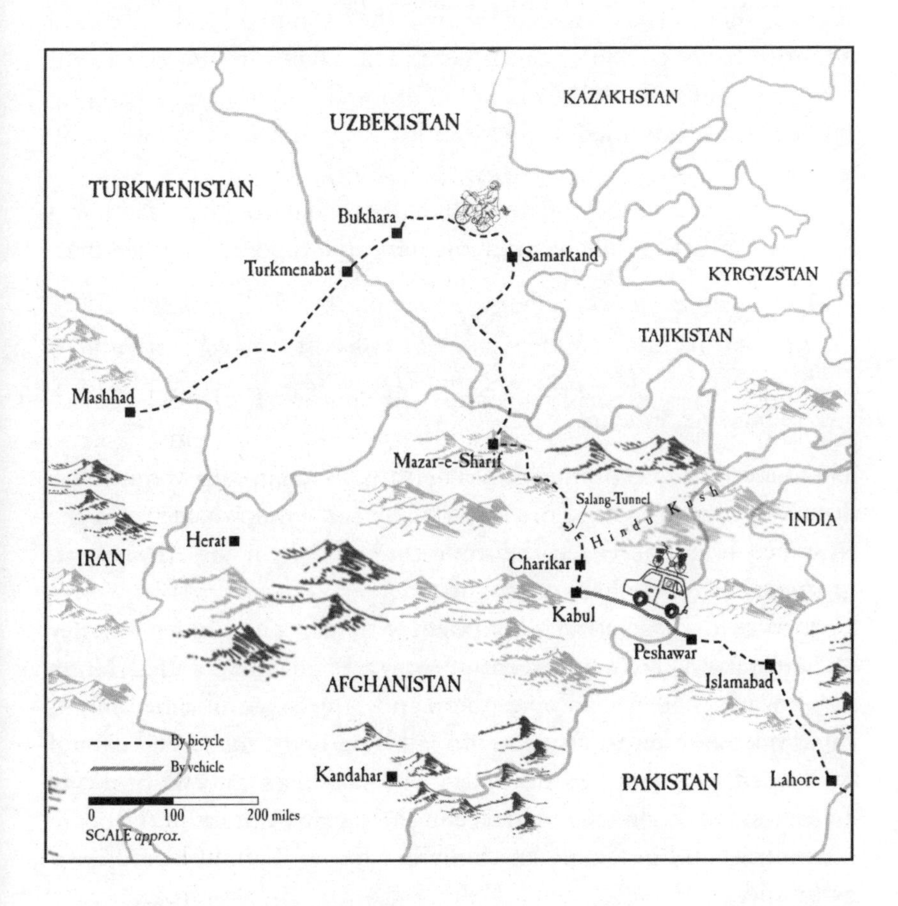

For the next three days I climbed through small, rounded foothills and saw the Pamir Mountains rising like a bank of clouds to the east. Old cars overtook me and occasionally I overtook people on donkeys and horses. The Uzbeks were boisterous and friendly. They all shouted at me to stop for a chat. With my basic Russian, I could just about explain that I had come from Afghanistan and, in a manner reminiscent of the coalminers of Siberia, they were suitably impressed. I wondered what horrific tales they had heard coming across the border during the Soviet war.

But, although charming at first, their friendliness gradually started to feel intrusive. At one roadside restaurant I was relentlessly questioned by an endless stream of adolescents. Like English people abroad, they seemed to think that if they shouted louder I would be more likely to understand them. The owner of the restaurant offered me a room for the night, but after half an hour of answering the teenagers I decided to press on for a few more miles and camp in the wild.

I put my tent up behind an embankment, but even here there was not much peace. While writing my diary that night, I recorded that:

> *As I write a guy on a horse has come over for a chat – the horse has just done a huge multi-litre pee. A herd of cows and its herder wanders past . . . and (I can see) someone else is coming to say hello.*

The persistent questioning continued the following day. From their donkeys, or their bikes, or out of their car windows, or from the roadside, everyone yelled the same three words at me: '*Strasvitya, ot kuda?*' (Hello, where are you from?]

Years before, Al had shared a poem with me: 'The Golden Journey to Samarkand', by a nineteenth-century Englishman called James Elroy Flecker. It was an epic poem and, ever since first reading it, I had been hoping to visit the old Silk Road city, the fabled capital of Tamerlane's empire and home of Ulag Beg's ground-breaking astronomical observatory. I had been carrying a printout of the poem for months and now taped it to my bar bag so I could memorise it as I cycled.

To stop myself growing too annoyed with the incessant inquiries, I decided to respond to the Uzbeks with a line from the poem.

'*Strasvitya, ot kuda?*' a man cried at me as he roared past in his battered old car.

'We make the golden journey to Samarkand,' I cried back with a huge grin on my face.

The man frowned, and then returned my smile.

'*Strasvitya, ot kuda?*' cried a boy on a donkey, which idled along above the road.

'We travel not for trafficking alone:
By hotter winds our fiery hearts are fanned:
For lust of knowing what should not be known
We make the golden journey to Samarkand'

I cried back, before adding as an aside to myself:

It was ever thus.
Men are unwise and curiously planned.

'*Strasvitya, ot kuda?*' cried a woman from the back of a motorbike, which her husband was driving with hunched shoulders.

And now for my favourite verse, though they were out of earshot and did not hear the majestic lines:

We are the Pilgrims, master; we shall go
Always a little further: it may be
Beyond the last blue mountain barred with snow,
Across that angry or that glimmering sea,
White on a throne or guarded in a cave
There lives a prophet who can understand
Why men were born: but surely we are brave,
Who take the Golden Road to Samarkand . . .

but surely we are brave, who take the Golden Road to Samarkand.

Three days later, at last, I completed the golden journey and arrived in Samarkand. Riding up the potholed street to the city centre, I saw that, sadly, the final approach of the Golden Road was lined by ugly, concrete, Soviet tenement blocks. But then I reached the main square; the concrete drew back and there before me boldly stood the great buildings of another age: Samarkand's famous trinity of madrassas. They were an exuberant cacophony of domes, minarets, archways and corridors, covered in an array of geometric shapes painted in shades of blue and brown. A splendid sight for travel-weary eyes.

Just as Samarkand had been a vital stopping point for the Silk Road caravans in olden times, nowadays it was a bottleneck for backpackers and cyclists travelling overland through Asia. I realised that this was in fact the first place (since near the start of China) that my route had crossed Al's. It was strange thinking of all that had passed in those two years. I even ended up staying in the same backpacker lodge that Al had stayed in. In his book, Al later recalled his first night in Samarkand:

> *In the backpacker hostel I sat in the vine-shaded courtyard and listened to the conversation bouncing around between the backpackers. An American . . . held forth at high volume about the epic nature of his backpacking trip and the dangers he had faced . . . people of five or six nations were sitting around comfortably . . . boasting gently about their escapades . . . I listened to the conversations but did not speak much . . . I had nothing to brag with these people about. I had been humbled by the road.*

I wish that I could have written a similar thing. I wish that I had achieved a similar sense of poise to not need to prove myself. However, that night, although I told myself not to, I found myself bragging incessantly.

'I faced such terrible headwinds in the deserts of Kazakhstan,' said a friendly German cyclist called Andrew.

'Oh, really?' I replied in a loud voice. 'Well, when I was in *Afghanistan . . .*'

'In Turkmenistan there are these amazing natural gas craters, which were set on fire as an experiment, but once they were alight no one could put them out again,' said a Swiss motorcyclist.

'Wow,' I said, pretending to be amazed. 'Well, when I was in *Afghanistan . . .*'

Despite my aspirations, I was as vain as ever.

'*Why am I such an idiot!*' I wondered to myself as I went to bed.

From Samarkand I rode west to Bukhara, and then south towards the border with Turkmenistan. Everyone I encountered seemed cheerful. But in Samarkand, a junior foreign diplomat I'd met in a bar had told me that the reality was somewhat different. The government were corrupt, inefficient and oppressive. A few years previously, they boiled two dissenters to death. Apparently this was not an isolated incident.

The government also forced the people to increase output to impossible levels. If you failed to meet the targets, there were even more absurd consequences. 'Recently,' he said, 'there was a local farmer who failed to meet the apple quota that he had been set. In response, the government came round and cut his whole orchard down. Now, I ask you, what were they trying to achieve by that?'

He went on to explain that Uzbekistan's president, Islam Karimov, had stifled democracy. In the last general election, his main opposition candidate had actually boasted of voting *for* Karimov.

'The people here are told this is a democracy,' the diplomat said, 'so this is what they think democracy is.'

66
Renaming the months

Distance to home = 5,397 miles

A country with more portraits of the President than road signs
has surely taken a wrong turn somewhere
A. J. HUMPHREYS

I felt like a windsurfer skimming through waves of sand as the powerful tailwind swept me south through the deserts of Turkmenistan. I had crossed the border the day before and, apart from skirting through a few towns, the landscape was nothing but a road and a desert. In the daytime, the temperature rose to +40°C, but I decided that +40°C was a lot more pleasant than –40°C provided there were occasional truck stops so I could fill up with water. At night I camped in the empty dunes. I felt relaxed in this wilderness. I lay down in my tent and was soon lulled to sleep by the sound of the cool Turkmen wind, whispering across the sand like gentle music.

For centuries Turkmenistan had not been such a safe place. Bandits had hidden in hollows beside the road and attacked the Silk Road caravans as they passed. It was eventually the Russians who had tamed the land and suppressed the people in the late nineteenth century. A hundred years later, when the Soviet Empire collapsed, the previous communist leader, Saparmurat Niyazov, had become president. As he took over the role, he announced that he was committed to making Turkmenistan a market economy and a full democracy. It therefore made outside observers raise a few eyebrows when, not long after, a parliament (which he had hand-picked himself) voted that he should become President for Life. He quickly accepted the title and went on to rename himself *Turkmenbashi*

(Turkmen the Great), and spend much of his country's huge natural gas wealth on shameless self-promotion. In the cities he built a plethora of luxury hotels that remained empty; he renamed one month after himself and another after his mother; he renamed September *Ruhnama*, the name of his book of wise sayings, which, like Mao's 'little red book' in China, was compulsory reading for everyone.

Perhaps most astonishing was his propensity for erecting statues of himself and filling towns with posters bearing his face. Travellers in Samarkand had told me about this and I was used to seeing portraits of austere, self-important leaders on the walls of government buildings across the world. Yet on reaching the first town I saw that *Turkmenbashi* had raised the bar to a new level. From the corner of a crossroads I could see five giant images. His portrait was emblazoned on the front of every shop. A poster by a bank depicted him with a big friendly smile with his hand to his chin. I thought he looked like a big friendly teddy bear. Most impressive of all, though, was the golden statue dominating the main street. He stood nobly, with a straight back and one foot slightly forward. In his right hand he held a copy of the *Ruhnama*, his hair had a neat side-parting and, best of all, he wore a golden cape, reminiscent of Superman.*

Amusing though it was to find out about his bizarre ideas, there was also a dark side to his dictatorship. The mention of AIDS was forbidden. In 2002 he arbitrarily cancelled the pensions of 200,000 elderly people, and even demanded they pay back the previous year's payments. In 2005 he shut all the hospitals outside the capital – after all, why shouldn't an ill person come to the capital to be treated? Furthermore, the charity Human Rights Watch had been banned from entering the country since 1999, and it is reported that dissidents are regularly arrested and tortured.

All the statues and portraits of *Turkmenbashi* reminded me of

*Though I never visited the capital, Ashgabat, I heard of its huge, golden *Turkmenbashi* statue which revolved continually so that he always faced the sun.

other self-obsessed leaders who had tried to immortalise themselves. In Beijing I had been to see Mao's Mausoleum. I queued up for hours with thousands of Chinese tourists in Tiananmen Square to see his preserved body in a glass case for just a few seconds. *Turkmenbashi*'s bid for immortality, like that of other rulers, had failed. He had died unexpectedly from a heart attack at the end of 2006, aged 66. His successor has promised 'full democracy' by 2010.

After two days the sand blended into rough green meadows and pastureland and, with one day to spare on my week-long transit visa, I reached the border with Iran. I had mistimed my arrival, so the immigration building was already closed for the night. I camped in a hollow beside the road. I was now two miles from the barbed wire, minefields and heavily armed soldiers. Tomorrow I would enter the axis of evil.

67
Two Ayatollahs (on a wall)

Distance to home = 5,035 miles

North Korea . . . Iran . . . Iraq . . . states like these, and their terrorist allies, constitute an axis of evil, arming to threaten the peace of the world
GEORGE W. BUSH, 2002 STATE OF UNION ADDRESS

Americans . . . are the great Satan, the wounded snake
AYATOLLAH KHOMEINI, 5 NOVEMBER 1979

'*Oww!*' I yelled at the young man who had reached out of the window of his car and given me a firm pinch on the bottom as he overtook. The man and his car full of friends roared with laughter and accelerated down the road towards a line of grey mountains on the horizon. I had entered Iran an hour beforehand and, among my varying expectations of what might happen there, having my bottom groped by an inanely grinning student was fairly low down on my list.

My wheels spun me onwards into a gritty desert of man-sized shrubs. After two hours the road rose upwards into a twisted chaos of contorted ridges and fragmented cliffs. The afternoon sun glanced off the rock walls and cast a shadow across the valley. I stood out of the saddle and pedalled hard. My lungs burned and my legs seared but I was so fit now that I could ride to the top without stopping. On the other side of the pass I descended into a cooler, grassier valley. Shepherds in T-shirts waved jovially as I passed.

I camped that night on a grassy hillside. I sat on my roll mat, eating spaghetti, and looked out at the sight before me. A pale full moon rose above the horizon and the flat pastures below spread into the distance and were lost in the haze of night time. The view was just what I had hoped for here in Iran: rugged, weather-beaten and unfathomably old. It occurred to me that, apart from the occasional pair of headlights flickering across the ridges, the scene before me had probably not changed for a thousand years.

The next day I reached Mashhad, the second-largest city in Iran, and its holiest. As I approached the city centre I saw a giant mural painted on a prominent wall. On the left of the mural was an image of the current supreme leader of Iran, Ayatollah Khamenei. On the right was an image of his more famous predecessor, the late Ayatollah Khomeini. Though they both wore black turbans, it was easy to distinguish them – Khomeini had a whiter beard, while Khamenei wore his thick-rimmed spectacles. Between them, as if they were holding it like a banner, a giant three-word slogan was painted in English: '*down with USA*.'

It was hardly the friendliest welcome I had received when arriving in a legendary city. I pulled my camera out and had just taken a photo when a teenager ran up and told me I could not take photos. A crowd of women clad in black chadors (cloaks and headscarves) swept by and the aggressive Iranian traffic revved and hooted as it swerved past. The negative connotations about Iran that I had picked up over the years galloped through my mind.

Despite my recent attempts to read up on the history of Iran and the West's complex and fractious relationship, it was hard to reach a balanced view. On the side of the West, among other things, America had helped engineer a coup to overthrow the democratically elected leader in 1953 in order to put the pro-America Shah in power. Later, after the Islamic Revolution of 1979, they provided weapons for Saddam Hussein during the Iran–Iraq war of the 1980s. On the Iranian side, meanwhile, after Khomeini had taken power in the revolution, he gave his blessing to the students who took the staff of Tehran's American embassy hostage and later backed support being given to Lebanese militant groups (who also took Western hostages).

Another incident that exacerbated Iran's bad reputation in the West was the fatwah issued against Salman Rushdie for his award-winning book *The Satanic Verses*, in 1989.* More recently, two years before my arrival, President Ahmadinejad had expressed his desire that Israel 'be wiped off the map'† while also continuing to pursue nuclear technology 'for Iran's energy needs'. And, all the while, America was leading the drive to impose ever tighter international sanctions. Iran was the first country where I was unable to use my bankcard in ATMs to access money from my UK account. I had to change some American dollars I was carrying with money-changers at the border.

A lot more uplifting had been reading up on Iran's older history. Through the centuries, the Persian civilisation had given the world so much in so many fields: science, mathematics, philosophy, art, medicine, poetry, architecture. In his book *Mirrors of the Unseen*, Jason Elliot's list of 'the westward-bound influence of things Persian' goes on for several pages and includes:

> *the earliest models of international administration; the banker's cheque; the world's first postal service . . . the first modern astronomical observatory . . . the decimal fraction . . . the foundations of algebra . . . the earliest electric batteries; the windmill and the waterwheel . . . the domesticated rose . . . the Taj Mahal . . . the cult of the Assassins . . . Persian cats; Persian blinds . . . chess . . . polo; and even Kipling's Paree Pestonji, whose cake crumbs so irritated the Red Sea rhinoceros . . .*

For much of the past few thousand years, in fact, most European cities were quiet backwaters compared to the great Persian

*There were several aspects of the book that many Muslims found offensive, including that Rushdie had given the prostitute characters in the story the same names as Muhammad's wives. 'Even if Salman Rushdie repents and becomes the most pious man of all time, it is incumbent on every Muslim to employ everything he has got, his life and wealth, to send him to hell,' said Khomeini. Rushdie was in hiding for ten years and survived, but the Japanese translator of the book was assassinated.

†Some translators have said that Ahmadinejad actually meant that Israel should 'be made to vanish from the pages of history'.

metropolises which far surpassed them in splendour, size and learning.

I hoped that by crossing the land under pedal power I might catch some glimpses of what lay beneath the surface to overturn, or at least challenge, my negative preconceptions. Even as I rode through Mashhad this process was beginning. Although the women did wear chadors, the men were wearing tight T-shirts and jeans. There were fast-food restaurants, which looked very similar to their Western counterparts, though with different names. Food shops sold Coca-Cola and Pepsi as well as the Iranian brand of cola, *Zamzam*.* There were satellite dishes strewn across the rooftops, even though these were illegal.†

I stayed for two nights in Mashhad with a friendly carpet merchant called Vali, whose phone number I'd been given by travellers in Samarkand. He had a huge pile of rugs which he rolled out on the floor for me to see. I had bought few gifts during the journey so far, but I liked the carpets and was impressed by his sales skills. I bought a beautiful blue rug for Christine and posted it to her in England.

I left Mashhad on a fast three-lane freeway. The traffic continued to whiz past, hooting, screeching and juddering. Taxis seemed to be continually overtaking me. They then slammed on their brakes and swerved to a halt immediately in front of me. It was infuriating, and after it had happened several times I drew up alongside one taxi-driver's open window and scowled at him. He beamed back at me. Exasperated, I continued riding. The very same taxi-driver overtook me a second time, hooting his horn and smiling before all of a sudden veering in front of me and braking yet again. I later discovered that the taxis behaved like this because, as they drove,

**Zamzam* cola was named after the sacred well in Mecca. From what I could see in the shops, though, it was not as popular as Coca-Cola and Pepsi. The American brands had found a loophole in the sanctions to allow them to still be sold in Iran.

†According to *The Times* there are 4 million homes with satellite television in Iran.

they shouted out of their windows where they were going with their existing passengers. Pedestrians on the sidewalk shouted back where they wanted to go. Irrespective of the traffic around them, the taxis halted immediately if their destinations matched. I learnt to keep both hands on the brakes whenever there was a taxi around.

As well as the taxis, every few minutes I spotted some death-defying pedestrians scurrying across the lanes to get to the other side. It was no less dangerous than running across a motorway in England but, regardless of their agility, people dashed across as if the danger was a joke. I stopped at the edge of town for a drink. As I gulped it down and looked at my map, I heard a screeching sound and a dull thud. I turned to see a car skidding to a halt and a brown sack flying through the air and landing in the fast lane. I guessed it had come off the roof of the car. The driver got out and several men ran across to the sack lying in the road. A sickening feeling came into my stomach as I took in that it was not a sack, but a human. The car had hit one of the pedestrians. I was sure he must be dead. I had hoped not to witness death again on this journey. I climbed back onto the bike, shaking, and started riding away. There was nothing I could do to help.

A far greater threat than the Iranian Ayatollahs, it seemed, was the Iranian traffic.

68

Iranian police

Distance to home = 4,962 miles

Be kind, for everyone you meet is facing a great battle
PHILO OF ALEXANDRIA

Not far from Mashhad, as I pedalled on down the dusty valley, a motorcyclist rode alongside me and shouted at me in Farsi. I gathered he was asking where I was from.

'Inglestan,' I shouted back

'Uhhh?'

'Inglestan,' I yelled over the whine of his motor.

'Uhhh?'

'*Innggileesstannn!*'

This time he understood.

'Thank you, thank you,' he replied with a toothy smile. Then he waved, drew back and did a U-turn. I carried on. A few minutes later he reappeared alongside and beckoned me to stop. I was making slow progress and felt suddenly irritated by this inquisitive stranger whose only phrase of English was 'thank you'. Nevertheless, I stopped to see what he wanted.

He produced a piece of paper and wrote down his address for me in Farsi. He indicated I should do the same. I wrote out my address in English and handed back the piece of paper, feeling impatient to get going again. But before I could set off the man held out his open palms towards me while raising his eyebrows. He seemed to be waiting for me to acknowledge they were empty. It made me think he was about to do a conjuring trick. I nodded wearily that they were indeed empty. He then put one hand deep into his pocket and, as if drawing a white rabbit from a top hat, produced a small bottle of *Zamzam* cola and presented it to me.

'That's very kind of you,' I said, pleasantly disarmed.

'Thank you, thank you,' the magician replied with a huge grin. He then showed me his palms once more before thrusting them back into his pockets and this time producing a small plastic-wrapped cake.

I felt guilty about my being impatient a moment before. With a final double 'thank you' the man shook my hand and rode off.

The landscape continued onwards through windswept meadows, ramshackle villages and walls of distant mountains. I was heading west to the Turkish border, 800 miles away, and I had three weeks to get there. After four days I began a long, winding descent from the plateau down to the fertile fruit fields which led to the Caspian Sea. The increasing humidity made my eyes sting with sweat and my sunglasses continually slipped off my nose. It was easy to camp in the roadside fields and forests, but my clothes and skin were becoming very grimy. Furthermore, Alanis' chain was starting to slip over her well-worn cogs. I had last replaced the chainset and cogs when I was in Sydney and now she clearly needed some replacements. I was therefore delighted when, a day before I reached the Caspian, I met someone who could help. Ramin had spotted me riding through his city, Gorgan, and pursued me on his motorbike in order to flag me down. He spoke basic English and invited me to stay the night.

He lived in a new, small, clean bungalow, with his wife and baby. They had many elaborate rugs on the floor, and prints of nature scenes on the walls. Ramin's wife served us kebab, yoghurt and rice for dinner. She was not wearing a headscarf, because we were inside, but she put it on when I took a photo of them. I was exhausted from the hot weather, so after they had shown me their family photograph album, I quickly fell asleep in my sleeping bag on the floor.

Ramin had told me that he was a bicycle mechanic, and the next morning, before I left, he insisted that I should bring Alanis to his shop. Once there, he proceeded to spend over two hours working on her. He took her apart, and he put her back together; he took old parts off and he put new parts on; at one point, because he did not have the correct spare parts in his shop, he started to take parts off his own mountain bike so that he could then put them onto mine. He replaced the chainset, the chain and some spokes and he tinkered with the gears. Just before lunchtime he finished. I went for a quick test ride and was delighted that she worked much better now. I dug out my wallet and, hoping it would not be too expensive, pulled out some notes and asked how much I owed.

'Money?' Ramin replied, confused. 'No, I do not want any money.'

I was shocked, and tried to offer some money again.

'No, it is free,' he said, adamantly. 'You are a guest in my country, and in Iran we like to look after our guests.'

Smiling and shaking my head gently, all I could think of to say was: 'Well, thank you very much.'

'No, don't thank me,' he said, nodding to the sky. 'Thank God'.

I reached the coast of the Caspian Sea, the largest completely inland sea in the world. I don't know why, but it surprised me to discover that it was heavily built up with hotels, restaurants and cafés. There were shops selling inflatable dinghies, and buckets and spades for building sandcastles. Young Iranian hunks pranced into the water in their tight swimming trunks, followed by women wading in fully clothed in their black chadors. Aside from the Persian hotel signs and chadors, it could easily have been a touristy seafront in Europe.

I had been riding for a week in Iran, so I decided to take a day off in a seaside town. The first two hotels I asked in were way beyond my budget, so I wondered whether I should ride back into the hills and camp. All of a sudden a smart car drew up and a young man called out to see if I needed help. An hour later, he had arranged for me to stay with one of his friends.

For the next two days I hung out with the driver of the car, who was an engineering undergraduate called Reza, and his posse of bright, young friends. They refused to let me pay for anything. We spent the first day at the beach, and in the evening they invited me to come and play football at their weekly five-a-side match. Inside the sports hall, I tried my hardest to play well. My most fail-proof tactic for eliciting smiles from strangers all over Asia in the past few years had been to announce 'England! David Beckham!', and then do my impersonation of his free-kick. However, tonight, as I sprinted around the pitch trying to prove my country's glory, my Iranian friends seemed surprised at how badly the man from Inglestan played. I also discovered that football used different muscles from cycling. The next day I could barely walk.

After the match we went back to their flat and, as Reza produced numerous bottles of wine and distilled spirits, we sat in a circle on the floor.

'Wow, where did you get all this from?' I asked Reza, knowing that alcohol was illegal in Iran.

'Oh, it's not hard to get hold of . . . many of my friends brew it at home. Do you like it?'

'Well, yes . . . Who brewed this red wine? It's actually quite good.'

'Oh', replied Reza, 'that was my aunt.'

'But as a Muslim, are you allowed to do this?'

One of the students leant down and drew a mark with his finger on the carpet. 'I don't believe any of it,' he said, his tongue loosening with the wine.

The others looked shocked, but one suggested that perhaps Muhammad had needed to ban alcohol only because Islam began in the hot desert where of course alcohol would be a bad idea.

'If Allah had ordained Islam to begin in Russia, where it is cold, alcohol would have been permitted,' he said.

Some of the students burst out laughing, others looked uncomfortable.

As night settled we chatted about Bush and Blair, Ahmadinejad and nuclear bombs, girls and music. These young men had an equally distorted caricature of life in the West as, perhaps, I had had of Iran before I came here. They gained most of their experience of America from Hollywood and some crude television shows on their (illegal) satellite dishes. They also seemed to think that all Westerners are Christians, and thus the television shows and films were portraying how normal Christians behaved.* I remembered that in, Pakistan, Anwar had told me that 'there is nothing sacred in the West now. Your banks are bigger than your cathedrals.'

The next night we went for a meal with the students' (illegal) girlfriends. Rather than the black chadors, they were wearing lighter headscarves. These had been tolerated a few years previously, but with Ahmadinejad, the rules about wearing the chadors were tightening again. The restaurant we went to resembled an upmarket version of McDonald's. During dinner, they asked me about my previous job as a geography teacher in England. I explained that in England many teachers, myself included, struggled to control the more wayward pupils.

'Can't you hit the pupils?' a girl asked.

'Well, no, that is illegal.'

'It is illegal here, too,' she replied, 'but the teachers hit us anyway!'

The boys went on to lament that they would soon be forced to do their obligatory two years' national service. Still, they agreed, much better to do it now than 20 years ago during the Iran–Iraq war, which had resulted in half a million dead on both sides.

We also talked about what life was like for women in Iran. The women in their black chadors always looked rather oppressed to me, especially in comparison to the men in their tight T-shirts. Reza

*I later found Philip Yancey's analysis of the complex issues of Islam–West relations illuminating:

In determining morality, American society tends to apply the bottom-line principle, 'does it hurt anyone else?' Thus pornography is legal, but not if it involves explicitly violence or child molestation. You can get legally drunk as long as you do not break a neighbour's window or drive a car, endangering others. Violence on television is okay, because everyone knows the characters are just acting. Whereas we define 'hurt' in the most physical terms, Islamic societies see it in more spiritual terms. In that deeper sense, what could be more harmful than divorce, say, or pornography, or violence-as-entertainment, or even the cynical depiction of banal evil on television soap operas? It is from this vantage point that the US has gained its reputation as 'the Great Satan'.

spoke up and said that although it seemed the women were subdued by men and religion, it was actually the women who were in charge. It was not unusual, when his father arrived home from a hard day's work, for his mother to immediately start ordering him around. 'Take me to my relatives . . . take me shopping . . . give me more money for jewellery . . . give me more money for the swimming pool.' I said that some people would say it was the same the world over. Everybody laughed.

As we left the restaurant to put the girls in taxis to go home, Reza scanned the street nervously. 'I am hoping there are no police around,' he said. 'Last year I was arrested and spent a night in a jail because the police caught me walking down the street with my girlfriend.' I had heard that spending time with a girl who was not your sister, mother, daughter or wife was not allowed in Iran, but I did not realise that just walking down the street together could land you in prison. Reza said his father had had to bribe him out of prison last time. He was not keen to repeat the experience.

The next day I said goodbye to my new friends and, feeling clean and refreshed, continued through the resorts on the Caspian shore for another week. Huge mountains, higher than the Alps, towered over me to the south. In the land beyond lay so many of Iran's great historic cities, rich with legend and architecture: Shiraz, Isfahan, Persepolis. But such sites would have to wait for another visit. My visa was running out and my sister's wedding was coming up. I was still determined to keep my promise that I would be there, though it would mean another flight home.

I climbed 30 miles of steep switchbacks through a dense forest, leaving the Caspian Sea (which was 200 metres below sea level) behind me. I rolled into some dry arid hills. There was less traffic now, and I sometimes saw farmers walking down the road with their donkeys bearing heavy loads of hay on their backs.

Two days later the road merged with a rocky canyon, which led towards the city of Tabriz. I camped on a hillside above the canyon. The next morning I awoke, packed and set off at dawn. After an hour, the sun began to tip over the craggy ridge and paint the canyon walls a cheerful brown. I was riding fast and, although hungry because I'd not bothered to cook breakfast, I was at peace.

The peace was abruptly broken as a police car appeared alongside me and waved at me to stop.

'Oh dear, here we go!' I thought to myself. I had not had any trouble from the police in Iran so far, though I expected that at some point I might be questioned about what I was doing. In Kabul, Rory had told me that he was regularly stopped and questioned by the police while walking across Iran.

The police car stopped and two young officers climbed out.

'*Salaam*,' said the first policeman.

'*Salaam*,' I replied.

I thought they would probably ask to see my passport. But I was wrong, for the next thing the policeman said was: 'Have you had breakfast?'

'No.'

'Well, there is a café in ten miles, you can eat there.'

'Great, thanks.'

'Okay, goodbye.'

I kept riding, relieved that nothing had happened. The sun blazed hotter. Five miles later the police car appeared again, and once more I was waved over. I thought that maybe they were toying with me, and this time there would be more of an interrogation.

The policeman waited, leaning against his car with a dead pan expression. I drew up to him and stopped.

He paused. Then he said: 'The café is now five miles.'

'Er, okay, great, thanks.' I set off once more.

Five miles later, there was a concrete café by the road. The police car was parked outside. I went in and saw the officers sitting down. They invited me to join them and within a few minutes I was enjoying a tasty omelette of my own. We chatted casually and I told the policemen how friendly Iran had been and that it was a real shame that our governments did not get on. They agreed. As I got up to pay, they too stood and quickly dashed over to the restaurant owner and paid for me. They were adamant: breakfast was on them.

Back on the road, with a heroic pilot's wave, they overtook and zoomed into the distance. *'Well, so much for the axis of evil,'* I thought. I could not imagine an Iranian cyclist being treated to breakfast by the police in England. It was yet another country of which I had only skimmed the surface. There was so much that I did not even begin to understand. It had been full of rules in public, yet defiance behind closed doors. There were certainly some sinister aspects to it, and crossing the law here was a severely bad idea but, in my experience, it was one of the friendliest places I had ever visited.

I passed through Tabriz and three days later overtook a huge queue of over-laden trucks and rolled Alanis up to the border. I was stamped through. I was in Turkey at last. This meant, at least in football terms, that I was back in Europe. A smooth, straight tarmac road ran through a series of huge fields. Towering above me to my right was majestic Mount Ararat (where Noah beached his ark), capped in snow, though the actual peak was hidden in the clouds. I spurred Alanis on towards the next town in a whir of giddy triumph.

Four days later, in the town of Ezerum, I left Alanis with a friendly air force engineer and caught the bus to Ankara. I was still 4,000 miles from home, and my sister's wedding was in four days' time. The only way I would get there in time would be to fly. In Ankara I boarded a plane, and five hours later I was in England once again.

69
Non-stop agony tours

Distance to home = 3,891 miles

My generation had grown up with our own individual little pile
of happiness at the top of our shopping list . . .
my generation wanted perfect lives
TONY PARSONS

After a wonderful wedding, I flew back to Turkey. It was time to finish the ride. Several friends had offered to come and join me on different stages of this homeward leg. The first, an old friend from university, Olly, was on the plane with me. Olly was a doctor and had two weeks free until he started a new job. We returned to Ezerum, repacked Alanis, and set off west for the final time. I now hoped to make it home within two-and-a-half months, but it still seemed unreal that the journey would come to an end.

We rode through hilly, green pastureland under a blazing sun by day, and camped in fields, forests and dried-up streambeds at night. We spent long hours talking. Over the previous three years I had enjoyed spending time with hitherto unknown people, but it had also been exhausting to be constantly making new friends. It was a joy to catch up with an old friend who knew me from the days before I became a Siberian Cyclist. After ten days, we descended out of the hills to the shores of the Black Sea, and caught a ferry across the Bosporus to Istanbul. Ancient minarets and legendary domes were spread broadside across the skyline. The streets buzzed with mopeds and sizzled with kebab stands. On our day off, a friend from the British consulate invited us for drinks with another British cyclist who happened to be in town.

We sat outside a restaurant on a calm, cobbled backstreet and drank beer. The other cyclist had a young, beard-covered face and introduced himself in a gentle, confident Scottish lilt. His name was Mark Beaumont and he explained that, having begun his journey in Paris three weeks previously, he had already covered over 2,200 miles. Today was his first day off. He was going at such a speed because he was attempting to break the record for 'the fastest man to cycle around the world'. From Istanbul he would proceed, in the opposite direction from me, through Iran, the Indian subcontinent, South-East Asia, Australasia, America and then back through Europe to Paris.

We sipped our beer and plied Mark with questions. Like me, he was used to giving rote answers about his ride. He explained that the *Guinness Book of Records* defines a journey around the world as covering at least 18,000 miles (moving in the same direction) and finishing in the same place that you start. He had spent a year planning and training for the trip and in order to break the existing record of 276 days he would have to ride 100 miles a day, and take only two days off per month.

As we continued talking, it became obvious that, although we were both travelling much of the globe by bicycle, we were on very different types of journey. Mark was putting himself through an incredible physical challenge, with the tangible goal of breaking a record. My voyage had been much more meandering, interspersed with many days off. As I thought about it, I realised that my crazy detours and my time staying with hosts were actually the parts that I had enjoyed the most. I often covered less than half of Mark's daily distance, and found the rare days when I did cover 100 miles both physically exhausting and mentally uneventful. Mark would have to ride these distances almost every day for over six months. I had a deep respect for the focus and determination he would need to pull off the feat. From the drive I could see in his eyes, I was confident that he would succeed.*

*

*On February 15th, 2008, Mark rode into Paris, triumphant, with a spectacular new record of 194 days. In 2009 two separate cyclists plan to challenge Mark's record.

Olly flew home, and three days' fast riding took me into Greece. I was now a mere two months from London and I had expected that crossing into the European Union would be a time of triumph and exhilaration. But, instead, I felt strangely numb. Furthermore, despite having just concluded that I did not like super-strenuous Mark-Beaumont-style cycling, I was now racing to meet another friend, Nate, from America. For five days I dashed across the thickly vegetated mountains of the Greek coast, before reaching the inland town of Trikola. I found Nate at our *rendezvous* outside the train station, standing next to a shiny new bike. He was wearing a clean, grey T-shirt and he grinned when he saw me – I had not showered since Istanbul and was covered in sweat and oil. We set out across the Pindus Mountains and Nate's brilliant American enthusiasm for life shone through straightaway. He yelled with exhausted gusto as we crested hard-fought-for passes, and whooped with deep-felt exhilaration as we soared down the other side. I barely even smiled when I had a fast downhill these days. I was jaded after so many months riding. But my days of wildman living were now numbered, and seeing Nate enjoying himself inspired me to drink it all in and appreciate the thrills of the road while they lasted.

We reached the west coast of Greece, caught a ferry to the heel of Italy's boot, and cut through the Apennines towards Rome. We both enjoyed the zesty charm of the Italian people, though their casual approach to driving felt almost as dangerous as the mad-cap drivers of India and Iran. But it was fun too. Drawing up to a set of red traffic lights on the outskirts of the ancient capital, we were instantly surrounded by a crowd of buzzing, tooting Italians on their mopeds. Everyone edged forwards, as if at the start of a race, and some started to creep beyond the lights, engines revving. The tension rose and then, suddenly, a lone gunner sped off, while the lights were still red. Thus provoked, the rest of us joined in, roaring forwards through an antique archway as if we were in the Grand National.

Nate flew home and I continued north along the hilly, green coast of the Tyrrhenian Sea. I had just passed my three-year anniversary since setting off, and in a matter of weeks my journey would be coming to an end. I was surprised to feel a sense of anticlimax brewing inside me.

I slept in more fields, and because I was now hurrying to meet a final visitor, my young-at-heart, 40-year-old cousin, Richard, I only had time to stop in Pisa to take a quick photo of me with Alanis beneath the Leaning Tower.

The first four days with Richard were spent pressing fast across a sea of foothills that culminated in a huge, daylong climb to the Grand St Bernard's Pass over the Alps. I felt bad making Richard ride so furiously, but I had another deadline to make: lectures at schools in Switzerland. Richard was a fighter, refusing to give up when he was in pain, and keeping a sense of humour at all times. After one especially long day, as we cooked our dinner in a forest, Richard told me wryly that if ever I started a tour company, I should call it 'Non-Stop Agony Tours'.

I enjoyed spending time with friends on this final stage of the journey and I was proud of how well they coped with adapting to my unusual way of life. Yet, at the same time, having companionship after being alone for three years felt strange. I had become accustomed to going at my own speed, choosing my own route and having no one to disagree with apart from myself. Sometimes, when one of my companions was slow packing up in the morning, or tired too quickly during the heat of the day, a terrible impatience began to well up in me. One day, Nate was too tired to make it to a particular city by nightfall, and though it was my fault for being overly ambitious, I was still grumpy with him. I knew that the journey had helped me develop: I had got very fit, become a better problem solver, overcome my shyness at meeting new people and grown slightly braver. However, I had also been hoping that the journey would improve my character. But from the way I sometimes behaved with my companions – my impatience with their weaknesses, my need to prove myself, my overly strong opinions in conversation and my general self-absorbtion – I had reason to be alarmed about what or who I had become. It made me admire Al all the more, for how patient he had been with me in Siberia when he was fast and brave, and I was slow and cautious. It was clearly high time for me to live in one place again, amidst a community of friends, church and family who would help rub the rough edges off me.

We reached Switzerland, from where Richard flew home and I continued alone. It was now early October. A cool sunshine broke through a half-clouded sky and the air was fresh on my face. The dry grasses and arid air of a Mediterranean summer turned into the russet leaves and windy showers of an Alpine autumn. Riding in the cooler temperatures was easier and I made good progress. But one morning, as I cycled up a grey valley beside the Rhône River, Alanis' rear-end suddenly started to shake around. It felt like a puncture. I stopped and squeezed the back tyre. It was still inflated so I started riding again. The shaking continued. I laid Alanis on her side to try to discover what was wrong.

I was shocked by what I saw. One centimetre from where the metal stays connected to the wheel, Alanis's frame had worn through and snapped. After carrying me 30,000 miles, and with only five hundred miles left to go to home, she was finally broken. I took a deep breath, leant her against a wall and stroked my beard as I tried to work out a solution. I recalled that, when I had bought Alanis ten years beforehand, the one piece of advice I had followed was that I should buy a steel-framed bike, because it would be far easier to weld should it break. Maybe I could find a welding shop. I was on the outskirts of a village and I could see a middle-aged woman walking towards me. In my best French, I asked if there was a bicycle shop or welder nearby. She gestured behind me. I turned around. On the other side of the street, 20 metres away, there was a shop with a sign outside saying *cycles-coucet-moto*. I pushed Alanis through the door, and inside there was a mechanic with a welding torch.

Twenty-four hours later Alanis was fixed. I was glad that I would be able to finish the ride with her after all. I reached the western end of Lake Lemon, passed through the serene, tram-rattled streets of Geneva, and ten miles later camped behind a clump of trees in a perfect, green field. The next day I crossed back into France.

If I pedalled fast, I could now be home in just a matter of days. However, I knew that as soon as I arrived in London I would probably be swept up into its fast pace of life. I was already feeling rushed from the previous two months of frantic riding through Europe, and I suddenly wanted to slow down. To do that, I decided to give myself some compulsory stillness. Just beyond the medieval village of Cluny, my route through France was passing a place called Taizé. It was a Christian retreat centre for healing and reconciliation, and an ideal place to be still for a while. I stopped there for a week and, at regular intervals throughout each day, I joined the monks and hundreds of other pilgrims for deep, melodic church services. I also had time to sleep, read, think and pray. I thanked God that I had survived my three years of adventuring, and prayed that he would help me with whatever came next.

I had little idea of what the future held. I wondered if I might go back to teaching geography. It would be the obvious thing to do but something in me knew the ride had changed me, and I might not be satisfied. However, teaching was an invigorating and fulfilling job and I knew that I should be thinking about a career. I was 30, after all. In the stillness of a service at Taizé I reflected that, despite living simply for the last few years, I had become more driven and ambitious than ever before. I had begun to worry about money, status and the lack of time in life to achieve the things I wanted to do. I wanted to keep life in perspective but these feelings were pervasive. I again wondered if my life as a solo-adventurer-nomad had done me more harm than good. But I had learnt a lot about myself, and about the world, and a hunger to learn more had been kindled.

And then I suddenly thought back on what had happened the day before I reached Taizé: for the first time on the entire journey, I had been refused water in a roadside café. In an image reminiscent of Scrooge I walked into the café to find the owner, a late-middle-aged lady, sitting at a table counting money. I politely asked her if I could fill my bottles from the tap. She scowled at me, sniffed and said, '*Au revoir*,' while gesturing that I should leave. In shock, I asked again, but she repeated, '*Au revoir*' without even bothering to look up. Her reaction may have been due to my bedraggled appearance, but even so I could feel the anger rising in me. I wanted to tell her of all the places I had been and the kindness of the many people I had met – from Russia to the Philippines, from Tibet to Afghanistan to Iran, and yet it was here in Europe, where people were so rich, that I was refused water. However, my French was not good enough to explain my annoyance, and I lost my nerve, so I just huffed, walked back outside and pedalled off again.

From Taizé I rode north through France to Belgium. The French drove fast, and the main roads had little space for cyclists. It occurred to me how tragic it would be if, having made it this far, I was killed in a traffic accident. A French road repair man flagged me down and gave me his reflective vest. After that I felt slightly safer.

I reached Brussels and stayed with a friend. As I left the city I knew that I would be home in 48 hours. I had been anticipating the end for so long, but now I felt strangely apprehensive. I wondered what it would be like catching up with old friends. Would we still get on? And what about Christine? What would it be like living in the same city and seeing each other more often? One thing for certain was that I'd had enough of living the life of a nomad. I was suddenly impatient for it to all be over.

On my penultimate night I camped beside a Belgian canal. The following day I pedalled hard for 14 hours to the coast. Despite my week off at Taizé, I was exhausted again. Lost in one town, I asked a man who was parking his car for directions. He kindly ran inside his flat to photocopy a map for me. His mother arrived while I was waiting and we started chatting. She could not believe that I had cycled all the way from eastern Siberia. Neither could I.

Just before midnight, I freewheeled into the ferry terminal at Dunkirk. I had missed the last ferry that evening, so my final night was spent sleeping on the floor of an empty French ferry terminal. At 5 a.m. I rose and boarded the first ferry of the day. Rather than staring at the sea or writing a momentous diary entry about this return to England that I had so often imagined, I fell asleep on the floor. When I awoke it was light outside and, like a troop of well-mannered zombies, my fellow passengers were beginning to file down to the car deck. I joined them, found Alanis and emerged from the warren into a grey English dawn. And there before me were the White Cliffs of Dover.

70
Last day in the life of a Siberian cyclist

Distance to home = 70 miles

28 OCTOBER 2007

I ride out onto English concrete. After weaving past a series of checkpoints, car parks and barriers I roll into Dover itself. It is seven o'clock on a Sunday morning, and the grey streets are still asleep. All the cafés are shut, but lying in the gutter I can see discarded kebab and chip wrappers from last night's revelry. I stop at a petrol station to buy my first breakfast in England – three bars of chocolate and a packet of chewing gum. I smile at the lady behind the till. I want to tell her how significant a meal this is for me, but she is eyeing me suspiciously so I decide not to. Back outside I climb a steep hill, cross a roundabout and follow the signs for London.

A blanket of cloud fills the sky to the horizon in every direction as my wheels spin me through a succession of thick hedgerows, ploughed fields and sporadic villages. I have always enjoyed the first hour of riding through the morning. Fresh air, a clear mind and a sense of freedom and destiny. But this will be the final such morning. My mind flits through memories of the many roads I have battled through to bring me to this one. I also think of my parents' front door, now just 70 miles away. Cars zoom past, their yellow number plates looking both strange and familiar. I notice that I can understand the road signs. I take deep lungfuls of the cold, damp air, and memories of childhood camping holidays come flooding back.

As the morning progresses, a cold headwind picks up. I have told my family I will be home before nightfall, but at this rate I am going to be late. The traffic on the road thickens, and the hard shoulder narrows. I pass Canterbury, and it starts to rain. I try to remember how many days I have had rain during the expedition: our third morning in Siberia; the day that Al and I decided to split up in Japan; a dozen or so crackling thunderstorms in China and Malaysia. I am surprised it has been so few – fewer than 30 days of proper rain during a 35,000-mile journey.

The traffic, hurried and indifferent to my presence, continues to increase. I see the car drivers are looking straight ahead and do not even notice me. This is just a normal day for everyone in England, and yet it is a life-changing one for me. The main road becomes so busy that I take a turnoff onto the B-roads, even though I know I will probably get lost. I enter a series of sprawling towns and catch sight of signposts that look vaguely familiar. I stop at a petrol station to browse their road atlases, and make a plan to reach central London.

By 2 p.m. the gloom of late October is beginning to descend and the drizzle intensifies. Feeling cold and hungry, I stop beneath the Golden Arches for my first lunch back in England – a Big Mac meal. After that, the fields and hedgerows disappear behind me and I am swallowed into a maze of grey houses. The gloom gets worse, and I attach my dim, inadequate bike lights. Car lights flash past in the darkness, and hurrying tyres spray me with cold puddles. These last few hours seem to be summing up the part of the journey that I have enjoyed least – getting lost in a city at night. Encroaching deeper into the London sprawl, I am overtaken by my first black cabs and my first red buses. I see signs to places I know: Brixton, Peckham, Westminster.

The streets are dark now, and I have a sense of unreality as I hug the roadside and the aggressive traffic continues to zip past. My emotions are muted. There are no tears. I just want to get home. And then finally I know where I am – there is the Waterloo roundabout and, beyond it, there is Westminster Bridge, the Houses of Parliament, Big Ben.

I have arranged to meet my parents on the bridge. I see them standing in the downpour looking for me. My mum is wearing her blue fleece, and my dad is in his red raincoat and is holding a camera. They have not spotted me yet but I am close enough to see that my mum's hair is wet. I climb off, push Alanis onto the pavement and start walking towards them. They are talking to each other and scanning the road. And then they see me coming and smile. I do not really know what I am feeling: a mixture of gratitude and surreal disbelief combined with exhaustion, coldness and wet. It feels like a dream.

'Hello,' I say to them, unable to think of anything more epic.

'Welcome back,' says my mum, taking a step towards me. How much worrying has she been through in these past three years; praying, hoping and waiting for her son to arrive home safely?

I reach them, and we hug. I can feel that they are sodden through from waiting in the rain. We talk for a few minutes about my ride from Dover. I apologise for being late and explain that I have been getting lost continuously ever since I reached Gravesend. We all laugh. They take some photos of me riding over the bridge with Big Ben in the background, veiled in rain.

My parents set off ahead of me to drive home and I say I will be along shortly. There are tourists on the bridge, pointing at the famous landmarks, but I am not a sightseer any more. I don't even need to ask directions. I know where I am going and there are only five miles of the journey left. I cross the Thames, pass Buckingham Palace and, a few minutes later, glide beneath the arch at Hyde Park Corner. I skirt around the edge of the park for quarter of an hour and then reach Notting Hill and begin freewheeling down it. Two miles to go.

'Do you want this to end?' I ask myself.

'Yes. It is time for the next thing,' I reply. 'And you will have to get used to not talking to yourself.'

And then just one mile is left. I am riding more slowly now. I suddenly feel frightened of what will happen when I am back. This life has become so easy, so routine to me. How will I cope with the real world again?

*

I reach the penultimate street, and coast through the dark rain. Familiar houses flit past.

'Well,' I think to myself, 'that's the end of that. Lord, thank you.'

I turn into my own street and see a small huddle of people holding umbrellas and smiling: my sister and her new husband, Mark; my mother and father; my cousin Richard; my neighbour John. And there is Christine. She has had a long journey too, from the night we met in the trendy air-conditioned bar in Hong Kong, all the way to standing in the drizzle in the dark on a west London backstreet, waiting for a dishevelled, bearded cyclist boyfriend. She looks so caring and beautiful, as always.

As if in slow motion I ride through a banner proclaiming, 'Welcome Home!' I brake to a halt, turn round and smile. Everyone cheers. There is a pop as my father opens a bottle of champagne. The London rain continues to fall and we take photos and hug. Yet my mind is empty of words. I have nothing to say. But I am home, at long last. Home.

Epilogue

Five days later, after I had unpacked my panniers and washed or thrown away my ragged clothes, I caught a lift with my old friend Dave to a small village in Kent. We parked outside an ancient church and went inside to meet Al and his fiancée, Sarah. Since he had arrived home two years previously, Al had written two books about his ride*; got a good job with the Foreign Office (and then quit because he got bored); got a good job at a nice school (and then quit because he got bored); and he was now planning an expedition to walk to the South Pole. But first, the next day, he was going to marry Sarah. Dave and I shared the task of being his best men.

Their wedding was a fabulous celebration, and I was delighted to have made it back in time. The day after, I went back to London and knew that I had to get on with the rest of my life. I'd heard that some travellers had a sense of fulfilment and completion at the end of their journey, while others struggled with a feeling of anticlimax. My experience was more the latter. I did not feel any sense of achievement, but rather a strange emptiness. Clearly, as Al said to me over pizza a while later, such adventures 'are not the answer to every man's mid-life crisis'. For a while I thought the journey had actually provoked a premature one. Some days my confidence plummetted, my faith felt shaken, and on a couple of frightening occasions I felt despair might overwhelm me.

Perhaps the emptiness was partly due to the relative ease of the last few months of the journey – there was no challenging grand finale. Or maybe it was because I had made the two trips home to see my family in between (though, in fact, these had made the

***Moods of Future Joys* and *Thunder and Sunshine*, both available from www.alastairhumphreys.com

expedition harder, not easier). Or perhaps it was because I had lost my sense of purpose. I had been cycling for over three years with the tangible goal of getting 'home' on my bicycle. Now that I was 'home', I tried to remember the reason why I was trying to get here. When I thought about it, I could hardly work out why I had set out on the journey in the first place. It had certainly helped me to grow up, but it had also stirred a discontent deep inside. But if that discontent motivated me to throw my whole heart into life, maybe that wasn't such a bad result.

I started to make myself busy with giving lectures and applying for jobs. The lectures went well, perhaps because I always tried to make it clear to my audiences that I was no hero. Rather, I was a normal guy who struggled with fear and worry, like everyone else. However, people who heard the lecture sometimes concluded that the main lessons to take away from the trip were: 'anything is possible if you put your mind to it', and 'the world is full of good people'. The more I thought about it, the more I felt uncomfortable with these two conclusions. Although I had been thrilled to discover the world is full of wonder, beauty and good people, I had also seen meanness, misery, conflict, poverty and the cruelty of life. Although I had come to see that more is possible than I had dreamt of, I had come to know my limits and I had become far more aware of my own mortality. I had also come to accept more than ever before that I, for one, was a contorted mixture of good and bad. I needed love and help and forgiveness – from God and from other people. Sometimes people say God is a crutch. I used to disagree. The idea made me feel weak and needy. Now I agree. I do need God to make it through life, and to help me to be the kind of person I want to be. I am no authorised spokesperson for Christianity, but rather a constantly searching, often confused, sometimes bewildered, now and then amazed, occasionally at peace, Christian pilgrim. And I want to keep asking God to help me see what is really important in life, and what 'success' looks like to him.

For the next 18 months, as well as the lecturing, I completed a theology diploma at Oxford, negotiated a television deal for my video footage with National Geographic, and began work on this book. My health was mostly okay, but my stomach felt slightly unsettled. I went to see the doctor and, after some tests, he gave me a prescription for a form of amoebic dysentry that was living in my intestines. I continued to use Alanis to ride around London, though one evening when I left her locked outside the library where I did my writing, somebody stole her front wheel.

I got involved in a small, loving church community, and enjoyed spending time with friends and family. My parents generously let me live at home. It was a joy to spend time with them, though sometimes I was ashamed of how adolescent and stroppy I could still be.

I also spent time with Christine. Just before I arrived home, she had handed in her notice at her law firm and had started working for a charity. We now saw each other several times a week, rather than just a few times a year, though we could never quite agree about how long we had been together. Did the months when we corresponded by email, thousands of miles apart, actually count, or did our relationship only really begin after I returned?

We knew that we had probably put a lot of expectation on ourselves to make it work, and we were apprehensive about what would happen. Sometimes it was tough and there were seasons of painful emotional strain as we learnt to communicate better. But we were getting to know each other in a more settled context and Christine showed me an extraordinary amount of patience as I adjusted to being home. I learnt that she helped me to be a better person and that she was becoming the best friend I'd ever had. I had very strong feelings for her. And yet, like many, I was daunted by thoughts of total commitment.

Over time though, I came to see that 'love' was not just about romantic feelings; it was, even more, a decision to bless and care for someone else. I also started to understand that my 'love' had little meaning if it was not connected to deep, genuine commitment.

Then last weekend, on a sunny April afternoon, Christine and I went for a picnic in Kew Gardens. After lunch, I suggested a game of Scrabble. As she put her hand into the bag of letters, rather than a white plastic tile, she found a small black box. She opened it to find a diamond engagement ring. She cried while I read her a three-page proposal letter. Then I asked her to marry me.

Early in the journey, I had sometimes joked to the Russians that I was only doing the bike ride because I was in search of a good wife. In the end, rather to my surprise, I found one. And so the next adventure begins.

Statistics for Part 7 (India–England)

Dates:	May 2007–October 2007
Total distance covered from start:	35,178 miles
Distance left to reach home:	0 miles
Distance covered by bicycle:	5,187 miles
Distance covered by boat:	235 miles
Age:	30
Number of days since I flew to Siberia:	1138
Alternative modes of transport (Afghanistan):	1 taxi (35 miles)
	1 mini-bus (200 miles)
	2 vans (3 miles & 3 miles)
Number of camels seen:	8
Number of crashes:	1
Times hit by mini-bus-taxi:	1
Bottles of coke drunk:	82 (mostly Iran)

Statistics Overall (Cycling Home From Siberia)

Amount of languages learnt to say hello in:	21
People who had me to stay:	Over 200
Number of lectures given:	Over 70
Emails sent:	Thousands
Money raised for charity:	Over £23,000
Total money spent on journey:	Approx £8,000 (my life savings)
Total punctures on journey:	157

Acknowledgements

A three-year journey is a long time, considerably longer than is described in most travel books, and so for that reason only a small proportion of the people who hosted, talked to, advised, fed, encouraged and smiled at me during the ride are actually mentioned in these pages. I hope you will be happy with the way I have depicted you in these pages. Some of the people who are mentioned have been disguised for their own protection. Furthermore, the majority of the people who helped me will never lay eyes on this book. But, whether you are mentioned or not, my deep thanks go to all of you.

An early inspiration for the journey came from my godmother, Caroline, who paid my subscription to the Royal Geographical Society on my eighteenth birthday. Sadly, she died just before I completed this book. I remember her with gratitude.

Thank you to Olly, Nate and Richard for flying out to cycle with me in Europe. Thanks for helping to resocialise me before I got home and for your patience with my habits of the road.

A number of friends also helped with reading parts of or the entire manuscript, often amidst very busy lives. Your comments have certainly helped improve the book. Thank you to Stephen Backhouse, Tim Brewer, Mike Brodie, Mary Ann Minha, Ian Devilliers, Katherine Devilliers, Paul Moore-Bridger, Emily Seed, Ladonna Hall, Christopher Hope, Heather Sharp, Michael Shaw and my sister, Rosanna.

Huge thanks also to:

All those who prayed for me during my three years away and while I was writing.

Nick Dunse, for designing and running the phenomenal website that opened so many doors both during and after the ride.

Sarah Marshall, for going well beyond the call of duty in her production of the excellent maps.

Tim Steward, for the superb drawings at the start of each section of this book, and John Cairns for photographing them.

Julia Evans, my editor, for skilful editing, timely encouragement and impressive patience (and Joanna Davey for completing the production process).

Al Humphreys, a redoubtable friend and the one on whom I blame the entire escapade. You taught me not only how to survive, but how to thrive on the road. Your honest comments on the draft of the book also made a huge difference. I hope that one day we can go on another adventure together.

My parents: for all that you have taught me, for your patience, selflessness and care, and for letting me choose my own path through life, as well as for your encouragement with this book.

Finally, thank you to Christine. I am so grateful to you and for you. You made going on this whole journey worthwhile.

A note on Viva

At the time of publishing, this expedition has raised over £23,000 for Viva and their work on behalf of extremely vulnerable children around the world. To find out more or support their amazing work, please see:

www.viva.org.uk

Cycling Home From Siberia DVD (produced in association with National Geographic)

As I cycled across Europe, I gave lectures at several international schools along the way. In one of the lectures, a student put up her hand and asked if I had taken any video footage of the ride. I explained that I had done some filming but I did not really know why I was doing it. Most journalists that I met during the ride told me that it was unlikely for a television company to be interested in such amateur recordings. I knew that they were probably right, though I prayed that an opportunity might emerge.

The next morning I packed the bike and prepared to set off again. Just before leaving the flat, I checked my email. I was surprised to see a message from the CEO of National Geographic Television Channels waiting for me in my inbox. The CEO explained that his daughter was a student at the school. She had been very inspired by what I had said, and he was grateful for the work I was doing with young people. He also asked if I had any video footage, and offered to put me in touch with the production people in Washington DC. When I reached London, National Geographic outsourced the project to a UK-based producer and, to my surprise, they went on to make a spectacular six-part series about the journey. To watch clips or order the DVD, please visit: www.cyclinghomefromsiberia.com

Booking the author for a lecture or event

Rob Lilwall has lectured on his experiences in schools, universities and travel clubs and at after-dinner speeches and motivational events around the world.

For references, further information, booking and contact details, please visit: www.cyclinghomefromsiberia.com